How to Repair Automotive

Air-Conditioning & Heating Systems

Jerry Clemons

S-A DESIGN

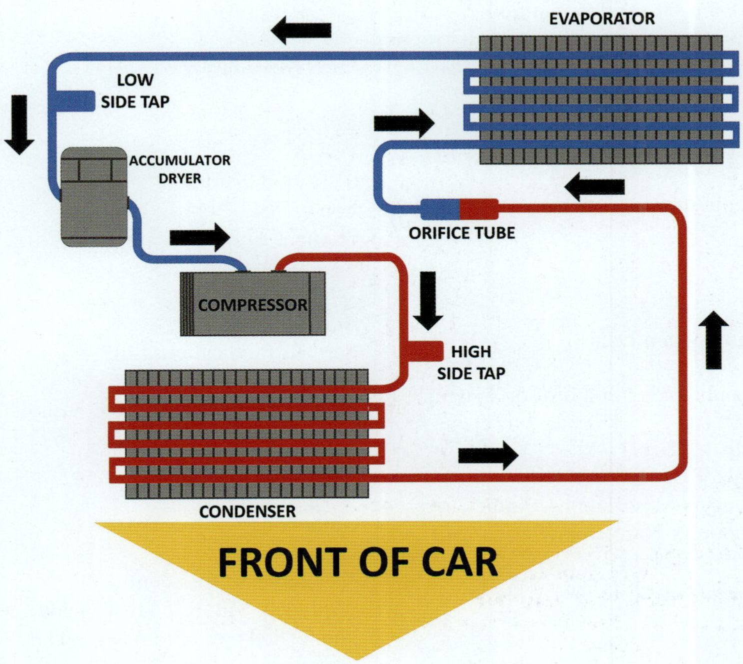

CarTech®

CarTech®

CarTech®, Inc.
6118 Main Street
North Branch, MN 55056
Phone: 651-277-1200 or 800-551-4754
Fax: 651-277-1203
www.cartechbooks.com

Edit by Bob Wilson
Layout by Hailey Samples

Many thanks to Joe Palazzolo for his photo contributions.

ISBN 978-1-61325-500-1
Item No. SA458

Library of Congress Cataloging-in-Publication Data
Names: Clemons, Jerry, author.
Title: How to repair automotive air-conditioning and heating systems / Jerry Clemons.
Description: Forest Lake, MN : CarTech, [2019]
Identifiers: LCCN 2019017593 | ISBN 9781613255001
Subjects: LCSH: Automobiles--Heating and ventilation--Maintenance and repair. | Automobiles--Air conditioning--Maintenance and repair.
Classification: LCC TL271 .C54 2019 | DDC 629.2/7720288--dc23
LC record available at https://lccn.loc.gov/2019017593

Written, edited, and designed in the U.S.A.
Printed in China

10 9 8 7 6 5 4 3

DISTRIBUTION BY:

Europe
PGUK
63 Hatton Garden
London EC1N 8LE, England
Phone: 020 7061 1980 • Fax: 020 7242 3725
www.pguk.co.uk

Australia
Renniks Publications Ltd.
3/37-39 Green Street
Banksmeadow, NSW 2109, Australia
Phone: 2 9695 7055 • Fax: 2 9695 7355
www.renniks.com

Canada
Login Canada
300 Saulteaux Crescent
Winnipeg, MB, R3J 3T2 Canada
Phone: 800 665 1148 • Fax: 800 665 0103
www.lb.ca

CONTENTS

About the Author

Jerry Clemons holds an AAS in Automotive Technology from Southern Illinois University as well as a BS in Technical Education from Western Kentucky University. Jerry also earned an MS degree in Safety, Security, and Emergency Management from Eastern Kentucky University. He has been employed at Elizabethtown Community and Technical College since 1999, where he is a professor and program coordinator for the Automotive and Diesel Technology programs. He is certified by ASE as a master automotive technician as well as a master truck technician. Jerry is an active member of the Mobile Air Conditioning Society (MACS) as well as the North American Council of Automotive Teachers (NACAT).

ACKNOWLEDGMENTS

Before getting started, I would like to give some recognition to some great people who supported me through this project. First of all, I would like to thank my family for their patience and understanding while I worked on this book during some late nights, early mornings, and many weekends and holidays. My son, Austin Clemons, was especially supportive in sharing his expertise with the photography and setting up scenes for the photographs. I would also like to thank Jim Halderman for his expert advice and guidance as I worked through this project. Jim has been an automotive author for many years and his support was very valuable as I completed this book.

I also want to acknowledge the following individuals at Elizabethtown Community and Technical College: Mike Hazzard, dean of the Technical Division; Brent Doty, program coordinator of the Computer Aided Drafting and Design (CADD) program; Thomas Frost, CADD student; Calista Reid, CADD student; and John Chism, automotive professor.

There were also several local businesses that supported this project in various ways and deserve recognition: Swope's Cars of Yesteryear Museum in Elizabethtown, Kentucky; Fisher Auto Parts in Elizabethtown, Kentucky; O'Reilly Auto Parts in Leitchfield, Kentucky; and NAPA in Elizabethtown, Kentucky.

CHAPTER 1

Introduction and History

Automobiles have been around since the late 1800s, and changes have come along to improve them in every imaginable way. The vehicles from the 1800s did not have an enclosed cab to protect the occupants from the elements.

History of Cabin Heating Systems

Closed-body cars first appeared in the early 1900s, and the occupants used gas lamps and gas burners to provide heat. These heating techniques were the same methods that horse-drawn carriages were using. As time passed by, manufacturers used engine exhaust heat as well as hot air off of the engine to produce a little heat for the cabin and its occupants.

Car manufacturers began using heated engine coolant in the 1930s, which was a more effective method to provide comfort. General Motors and the Nash brand were among the first companies to use heater cores to provide heat for the cabin of the vehicle. Another milestone that General Motors was involved in was the heated seats that were available on a few models. Development of heating systems on a wide sector of the market was somewhat slow because it was the late 1950s when most models had heating systems. By the 1960s, heating systems were standard equipment across most major car brands.

The heater hoses route the engine coolant into the heater core of this 1969 Chevrolet Camaro.

The climate control head on this 1969 Camaro has settings for blower speed, air temperature, and defrost. This system uses cables to move the doors on the duct box.

History of Air-Conditioning Systems

Keeping the driver and passengers comfortable in hot weather was also a challenge for car manufacturers. Techniques used in the early history of the car business included canvas covers, vent windows, and crank-style windows.

Providing shade to keep direct sunlight off of the occupants was an improvement over open-air vehicles. In addition, providing windows that could be positioned to provide increased velocity of the air provided more cooling capacity for the cabin.

Air-conditioning systems that used a pressurized refrigerant first appeared in the early 1930s. The Packard Motor Car Company was

The windshield on this 1936 Rolls-Royce folds forward to allow increased airflow into the cabin to help keep the occupants comfortable in hot weather. This vehicle also has side windows and vent windows that operate with a crank.

This two-door 1957 Chevrolet Bel Air has side windows and vent windows that operate with a window crank arm. The vent window was a popular option that caused a strong airflow when it was opened up.

The window crank arms and door handle are within easy reach for the passenger of this two-door 1957 Chevrolet Bel Air.

the first manufacturer to offer air-conditioning as an option around 1939. The system used by Packard was manufactured by Bishop and Babcock and was called the weather conditioner. This air-conditioning system was mounted in the trunk and involved a lot of plumbing and piping, which was a disadvantage because there were many places that could develop a leak. This system used a compressor that ran at all times and did not have any temperature adjustments. The $274 price for this system made it a very expensive option for that time period.

Chrysler and General Motors began offering air-conditioning as an option in the early 1950s. In 1954, the Nash Ambassador used a system called the "weather eye," which was the first fully integrated climate control system with air-conditioning. It included dash controls and an air-conditioning compressor with a clutch that could turn on and off as needed.

By the 1960s, air-conditioning was growing in popularity and market share. In 1969, 54 percent of cars sold in the United States were equipped with air-conditioning. Characteristics of cars from this era were the large compressors and large quantities of refrigerant used to make them work. A good sales pitch for this popular system was that it would increase resale value on the vehicle. As time passed, more and more vehicles were sold with air-conditioning as standard equipment.

Evolution of Heating and Air-Conditioning Systems

Cabin comfort in automobiles has seen many changes in the last 100 years. The industry has gone from not having cabin heat or an air-conditioning system to both becoming standard equipment. Many other advances have become common on cars and trucks as well. Some advancements that are available on modern cars and trucks include dual zone systems, rear heat and air systems, automatic temperature control systems, heated and cooled seats, and remote starting systems.

Dual zone climate control systems allow the driver and the passenger to have different air temperatures delivered to each side of the car. These systems are typically available on upscale vehicles and are made possible by having a more complex duct box system that has separate blend doors for each side of the vehicle. The drawback of these systems is that with more complexity in the system, more potential

This dual zone climate control head allows the driver and the passenger to choose different temperature settings for each side of the vehicle. This control head also has the switches for the heated seats for the driver and the passenger.

The heat and air-conditioning controls are located at the roof area within easy reach of those in the second-row seats on the driver's side. This control allows the blower speed, the temperature, and the mode to be chosen.

This control head features automatic temperature control, dual zone, and rear defogger controls. Most vehicles with automatic temperature control also allow the operator to manually pick the air distribution point, blower speed, and air temperature.

The remote control for the door locks also features a button for the remote start function for this vehicle. Most vehicles with factory remote start require a sequence of buttons to be pressed in order to activate the function, which reduces the chances of accidentally starting the vehicle.

problems can occur when the vehicle begins to get older and in the higher-mileage category.

Many larger vehicles are equipped with rear heat and air systems that provide heat and air-conditioning directly to the rear section of the cabin. Having the added capacity to heat and cool the rear of a larger vehicle provides much improved comfort for the passengers of these vehicles. These systems require hoses and lines for heated coolant as well as pressurized refrigerant to be routed to the back section of the vehicle. This requires increased capacity for both the cooling system as well as the refrigeration system. In addition, these systems have more serviceable parts that must be operational as well as more potential leak locations for the coolant and refrigerant.

Automatic temperature control is another convenient option that is available on many modern vehicles. These advanced systems incorporate many sensors and computers to automatically control the temperature to the desired level. When these systems are in automatic mode, the operator selects the desired cabin temperature and the system works to move the cabin temperature to that level. Many of these systems are also equipped with dual zone capabilities, as mentioned previously.

Heated and cooled seats have become very popular in modern upscale vehicles. This added capacity to keep the occupants comfortable is a great advancement that is popular with consumers. Heated seats have been available for many years, but cooled seats have only been available for a few years.

Remote start systems have become a popular option in recent years. These systems are incorporated into the keyless remote systems and allow the user to start the vehicle by using the remote transmitter. Being able to start the engine with a remote control allows the heater or air-conditioning system to begin working before the driver enters the vehicle. This process allows the operator and passengers to enter a climate-controlled vehicle rather than having to wait for the system to get to the efficient zone after entering the unit.

The rest of this book will provide information on how the air-conditioning and heating systems operate as well as how to diagnose and repair many of the common problems that could occur with these systems.

HVAC System

The heating, ventilation, and air-conditioning (HVAC) system is a fascinating series of components that all work together to help control the temperature and humidity of the cabin in a vehicle. These systems work by adding heat to the air in the duct box when the heat mode is chosen and removing heat from the air in the duct box when the air-conditioning (AC) mode is chosen. The information in this book will help you understand how the system works as well as how to troubleshoot and repair the system when it is not functioning properly.

Working Safely

Many precautions must be taken when working around the HVAC system on cars and trucks. This section provides information and procedures to help prevent injuries, accidents, and unwanted disposal of the fluids and chemicals within the HVAC system.

Always wear personal protection equipment (PPE) when performing repair and maintenance on a vehicle's AC or heating system. Quality Z87-rated safety glasses will provide eye protection. Wearing quality latex or nitrile gloves protects the hands from potential frostbite.

Refrigerant

The substance inside the AC system that is used to flow through the components and remove heat from the cabin is called refrigerant. There are three main types of refrigerant that have been used by original equipment manufacturers (OEMS): R12, R134a, and R1234yf. All of them have some characteristics that need to be understood, and they will all be explained in greater detail later in this chapter.

All three of these refrigerants behave in a similar way. First of all, these substances are pressurized when in an enclosed vessel or when in a closed system, such as the AC system on your car. Care must be taken when working around this pressurized refrigerant because it can cause frostbite if liquid refrigerant gets on your body. A person could also get burned by the refrigerant while the system is in operation due to the high pressures and temperatures within the AC system. When working around refrigerants, do the following:

1. Wear safety glasses to protect from getting refrigerant in your eyes.
2. Wear latex or nitrile gloves to give a layer of protection for your skin.
3. Store refrigerant containers in a cool, dry location away from any heat source, such as a heater or direct sunlight.
4. Work with confident and meaningful actions when connecting or disconnecting service hoses to the service ports on the AC system.

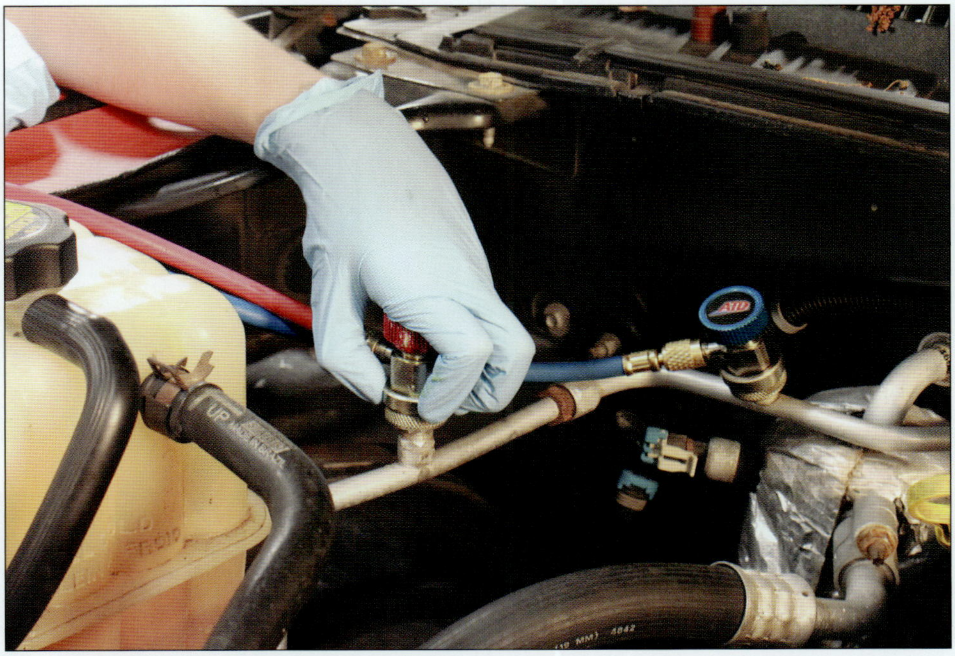

It is vital to use confident actions when connecting and disconnecting service hoses to the service ports on the AC system. The valve should also be in the released position when connecting and disconnecting it from the system.

Cooling System

The cooling system on cars and trucks must be dealt with in a safe manner. The liquid that transfers heat from the engine to the radiator as well as into the cab to the heater core is called coolant, and it is typically a mixture of antifreeze and pure water. Care must be taken to never attempt to repair a cooling system when the engine is at operating temperature or above due to the system operating under a pressure of 14 to 17 pounds per square inch (psi). This means time should always be taken to allow the engine to cool down before removing the cap that holds the coolant in the system.

In addition to hot systems being a safety concern, coolant should always be drained into a suitable container when it is removed from the engine for maintenance or repair. Used coolant should also be disposed of in a proper and legal manner. Many parts stores allow customers to bring in used fluids to be recycled. The store will typically record the names of people who bring in used fluids. Coolant should never be poured out on the ground or into a drain that connects to public sewer systems.

Refrigerant should only be stored in areas that are free from direct sunlight or added heat. The pressurized refrigerant should also be stored away from areas where lots of movement and sharp objects are present to prevent one of the containers from being punctured.

A reliable drain pan should be placed under the drain valve when releasing coolant from the radiator. There is typically an open path for the draining coolant to reach the pan without running down the frame, but care should be taken to catch as much of the draining coolant as possible.

Belts

The drive belts on an engine are an area where caution must be used in order to prevent injuries when working on the AC system. Many drive belts on late-model vehicles are held in place by a spring-loaded tensioner that holds strong pressure on the belt at all times. The belt tensioner must be released with the proper tool to safely remove or install the drive belt.

Drive belts on older vehicles are typically a V-belt type and are adjusted by moving one of the accessories on a pivot to allow the belt to be loosened or tightened. The key point to remember when dealing with adjustable V-belts is to tighten the belt to the correct level but not overtighten it. Overtightening these belts adds stress on the pulley and bearing of the accessories and could lead to early failure. It is also a prudent action to recheck and possibly adjust the belt tension on brand-new V-belts after they have been installed for a few days.

The accessories on most late-model vehicles are driven by a serpentine belt that is much wider than the belts on older vehicles. This belt system typically uses a spring-loaded tensioner that holds constant pressure on the belt during operation.

The belt tensioner on a serpentine belt must be released when removing or installing the drive belt. Some vehicles allow a ratchet or a socket to be used to release the belt tensioner, while other vehicles require a special belt-release tool to be used to service the drive belt.

V-belts are used on older-generation cars and trucks. These belts are adjusted by physically moving one of the driven components within an open groove in the mounting brackets or by installing an adjustment strut that allows the belt tension to be adjusted by shortening or lengthening the bar.

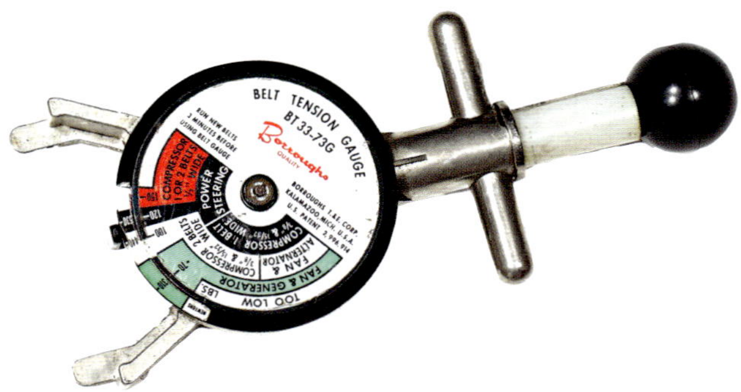

A belt tension gauge is a valuable tool to use when installing a new V-belt or when adjusting the tension on a used V-belt. After this tool is inserted on a section of the belt, it measures the deflection of the belt and lets the user know if the tension is correct. If the tension is too loose, then the belt can be tightened up. If the tension is too tight, then the belt can be loosened.

Electrical System

The vehicle's battery and electrical systems must be respected when working on the air-conditioning system. Disconnect the battery prior to performing work under the dash, such as replacing the heater core or the evaporator core. Repairing the HVAC system often requires electronic components to be disconnected, so this process should be handled carefully.

Airbags

All modern-era vehicles have airbags located on the steering wheel and passenger-side dash panel. In addition, airbag assemblies are also found in the side pillars, seats, and doors of many late-model vehicles. Extreme caution must be used when performing diagnosis and repair inside the vehicle and under the dash area. The first step that should be taken prior to performing extensive disassembly of the instrument panel is to disconnect the battery negative cable and secure it with a shop towel or similar item to prevent the cable from moving back into contact with the battery terminal. After removing an airbag assembly, it should be handled carefully and stored in a safe place facing upward to prevent the unit from being projected in case of an inadvertent deployment.

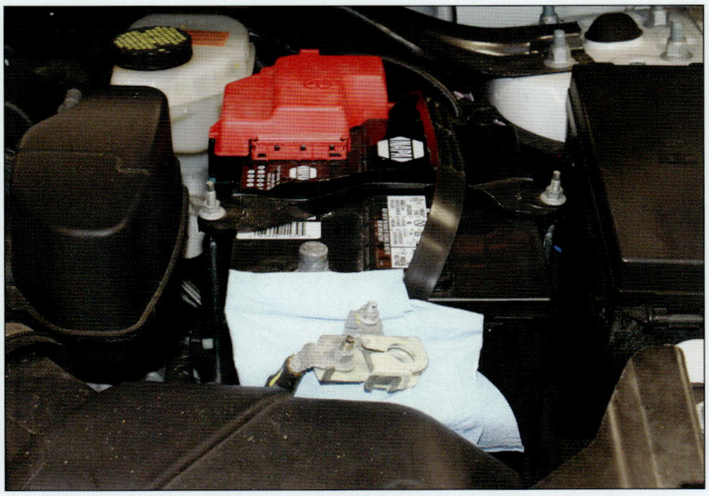

The negative battery cable should be removed and secured prior to performing extensive repairs on the AC or heating system. Having the power removed from the vehicle reduces the chance of shorting out a live circuit when performing repair work.

All modern vehicles are equipped with an airbag assembly that is mounted directly in front of the driver in the steering wheel. Care must be taken when working around the driver-side airbag assembly to prevent accidental deployment during service of the AC and heating system.

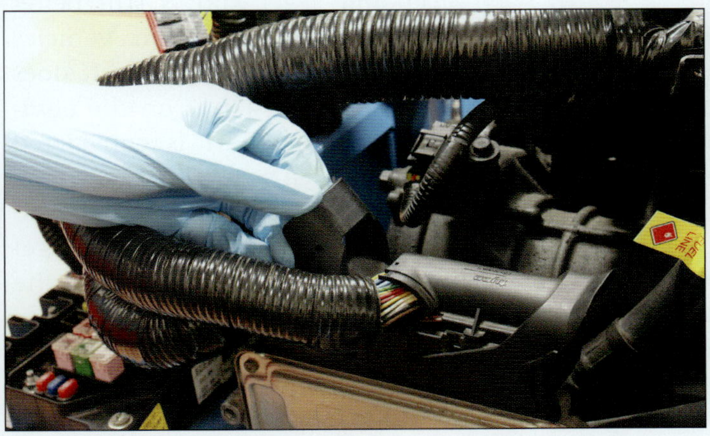

Extra caution should be used when connecting and disconnecting electrical connectors on cars and trucks. Most connectors have locking tangs that must be carefully released when disconnecting the device or module.

Passenger-side airbags are available on most late-model vehicles and must be carefully handled when working around the dash panel assembly. Yellow wire covering is used on most of the circuits that are used in airbag systems.

Airbag assemblies should be handled in a very careful manner by using a secure grip with both hands. The top of the airbag should be facing away from the body to add another layer of protection in case of accidental deployment.

Airbag assemblies being stored during a repair process should be kept in a safe place facing upward. This prevents the airbag from becoming a projectile if the airbag accidentally deploys.

Legal Issues

There are a variety of laws that must be followed when working on the HVAC system on a vehicle. The item that comes to the forefront is allowing refrigerant to be vented into the atmosphere. It is against the law to willfully allow refrigerant to be released from a vehicle's AC system or from a container. Care should be taken to prevent the loss of refrigerant during any process being performed on the vehicle. In addition to not venting refrigerant, the lubricant for the AC system should be collected and stored in a safe container. The oil can be collected by a reputable company and disposed of properly.

Professional technicians who repair mobile AC systems are required to attain a Section 609 certification from a reputable entity such as Mobile Air Conditioning Society (MACS) or Automotive Service Excellence (ASE). These certifications cover how to safely and legally handle and store refrigerants and AC systems. As of January 1, 2018, a person must possess a 609 certification in order to purchase a container of refrigerant larger than 2 pounds. This means that the small cans of refrigerant are still available for the general public to purchase without any restrictions.

The engine coolant is another substance that must be handled in a safe and legal manner. If the coolant is not going to be reinstalled into the vehicle, then it must be recycled according to the laws in your area. Coolant should never be poured onto the ground or into a drain.

Types of Refrigerant

The three types of refrigerant that have been used by OEMs are known as R12, R134a, and R1234yf. Many people describe the refrigerant as Freon, but that is not accurate. Freon is a brand name of a product from the Chemours Company, but many people still use the term Freon to describe the refrigerants used in mobile, fixed, or even refrigeration systems.

R12 was first refrigerant used in mobile AC systems in the early 1930s. R12 was used widely until around 1992, when it began being phased out due to the chlorine in the chemical causing ozone depletion in Earth's atmosphere.

R134a followed R12 as the refrigerant of choice in OEM installation beginning around 1993. This refrigerant performed very similarly to the previous R12. Systems that were built to use R12 can be converted to use R134a with a process called a retrofit. This process will be covered in great detail in chapter 6 of this book. R134a performs at an acceptable level and is still being used in new production vehicles at the time of this writing. It does have a negative effect on the environment because it is considered to be a global warming gas. Much research and funding was put into the development of the replacement refrigerant for R134a, and the result is R1234yf.

Many new model vehicles have already been switched over to R1234yf with more to follow as each year passes. Beginning with model year 2021, all new cars and trucks will have the new refrigerant installed in the AC system.

The vessels of R12 are 30 pounds and white in color. They have a shutoff valve on top as well as a threaded connection point that allows the yellow hose of a manifold set to be connected. R12 has not been manufactured since the mid-1990s, which has caused the supply and cost of the substance to rise greatly.

The 30-pound vessels of R134a are light blue in color and equipped with a shutoff valve as well as a threaded connection point that allows refrigerant to be removed from the container. R134a also comes in smaller containers that can be used to recharge the AC system.

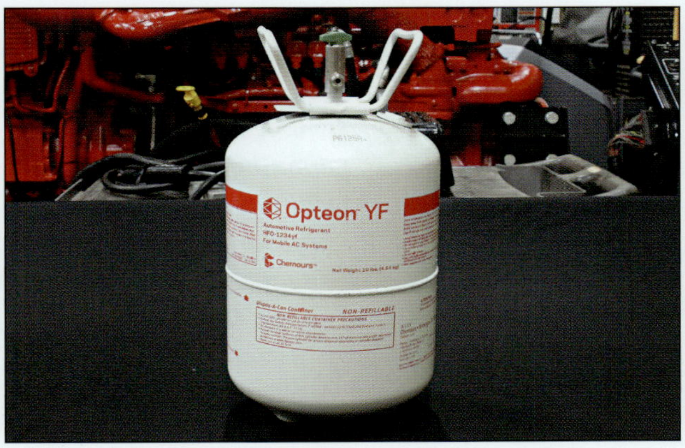

The 10-pound cylinders of R1234yf are white in color and equipped with a shutoff valve as well as a threaded connection point that allows refrigerant to be removed from the container. R1234yf also comes in 2-pound containers that have a connection point and a shutoff valve.

R12 AC systems use a mineral-based refrigerant oil to lubricate the compressor. This oil comes in one viscosity and needs to be kept sealed when not in use. Mineral oil can be added into the system during the repair process; it can be added into the components as they are being replaced.

The lubricant required for the older R12 systems was a mineral-based oil that only came in one viscosity. The lubricant required for R134a and R1234yf systems is a polyalkylene glycol (PAG) type. This lubricant comes in several viscosity levels and extreme attention should be used when installing lubricant into a system. PAG oil is very hygroscopic, so it should be purchased in small quantities and resealed when not in use. PAG oil that has been open for longer than a few days should be discarded due to moisture absorption.

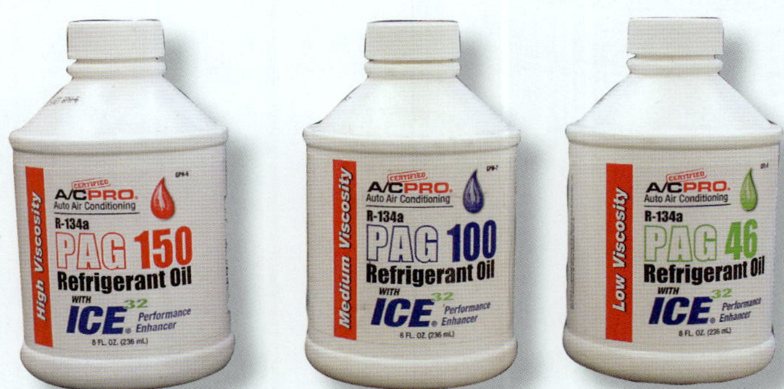

R134a uses a polyalkylene glycol (PAG) lubricant that is available in different viscosities depending on the manufacturer's recommendations. The correct type and amount of PAG oil should be used during the repair of the AC system. Using the wrong type or amount of PAG oil can cause system damage and early failure of the compressor.

In addition to the three refrigerants mentioned, there are other refrigerant options that can be purchased in the marketplace. Examples of these options include Freeze 12, Free Zone, Hot Shot, and FrigC, just to name a few. All of these types of refrigerants are legal to install, but it is recommended to use one of the three types that the OEM engineers recommend.

The problem with these alternative refrigerant options is that they are typically not a pure substance, which means they have blends of more than one type of refrigerant. This causes a problem when it is time to recover the refrigerant into an air-conditioning recovery machine because the refrigerant storage vessel on the machine will be tainted with blended refrigerant. It is recommended that a refrigerant identifier be used on every system to protect against recovering a mixed refrigerant.

Another major consideration when choosing the refrigerant to use in the repair process is whether to use pure refrigerant or a type that has additives in the mixture. Additives that are considered acceptable by most professionals include dye or oil. There are times when it is appropriate to use the small can of refrigerant to add either dye for leak detection or oil for lubrication of the system.

There are many other options for the do-it-yourself (DIY) consumer that need to be addressed. A large section of the small can refrigerant market contains a stop-leak type of substance that sounds like a great choice when the cause of many refrigerant issues is that there is a leak. The chemical in this refrigerant is supposed to change from a liquid into a solid when it is exposed to air. The problem with using this type of product on a DIY-type repair is that there will very likely be moisture in the system that will cause the sealer chemical to turn into a solid on contact. This will cause damage to the compressor as well as block passages in the heat exchangers.

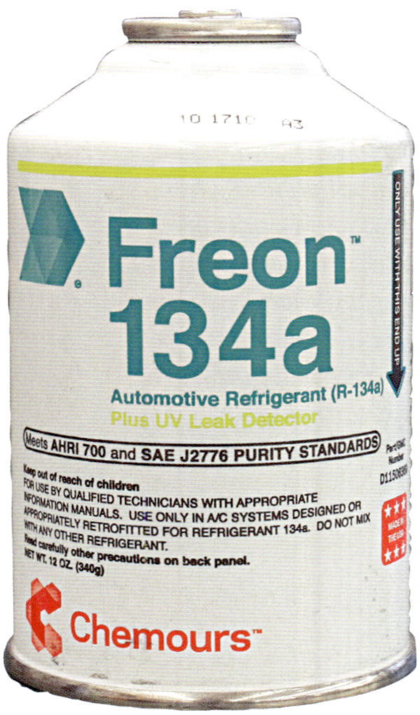

Small cans of R134a are available with dye added to the refrigerant. This is a good product to use when dye needs to be injected into a system that is still under pressure. If the system has a leak, the dye will exit at the leak point and can be detected by shining a black light on it.

Small cans of refrigerant with the PAG oil mixed with it are available as a method for adding oil with the system under pressure. Adding PAG oil directly into the system during the repair process is a more accurate way of keeping the system oil level near optimal levels.

Refrigerant that has unwanted additives, such as sealer, is widely available in the marketplace. Many of these products are equipped with a charging hose as well as a little gauge that gives some feedback on how much refrigerant to add to the system. This is a very inaccurate method of recharging that will be covered in greater detail in chapter 4.

Heat Transfer

The HVAC system uses hot engine coolant to move heat into the passenger compartment when the heat mode is chosen on the control head. The HVAC system uses refrigerant to remove heat from the passenger compartment when the AC mode is chosen on the control head. To understand how this transfer of heat takes place, an explanation of the three main types of heat transfer is needed. The three types of heat transfer include conduction, convection, and radiation.

Conduction is the transfer of heat directly from molecule to molecule. An example of conduction is how the fasteners on the exhaust manifold get hot because they are in direct contact with the exhaust. Another example is a person accidently touching the hot exhaust manifold while the engine is running. The extreme discomfort felt by touching the hot exhaust manifold would be a result of conduction.

Convection is the transfer of heat by using a substance, such as air, water, coolant, or refrigerant. The engine cooling system is a prime example of convection because the coolant absorbs large quantities of heat from the hot engine block and cylinder heads and is then pumped to the radiator where the heat is released into the surrounding air. The AC system is another example of convection because the refrigerant absorbs large quantities of heat from the warm air in the passenger compartment and is then pumped out to the condenser, where the heat is released into the surrounding air.

Radiation is the transfer of heat through rays without heating the air as it passes through. Sunlight is the best example of transferring heat through radiation. This concept can be understood due to the fact that it is possible to have a sunny day during the winter while the outside temperature can still be very cold. Radiant heat also greatly changes the temperature inside of dark-colored vehicles due to how the sunlight is absorbed by the dark color. Light-colored vehicles reflect the sunlight instead of absorbing the radiant heat. This concept can be seen by measuring the cabin temperature of a dark-colored vehicle on a hot day and comparing the findings with that from a light-colored vehicle.

Air Handling System Operation

The air handling system controls the speed, the temperature, and the distribution location of the air being discharged into the cabin of the vehicle. The types of systems include manual control and automatic temperature control (ATC).

Manual Control Systems

In a manual control system, the driver or the front-seat passenger has the option to pick the blower speed, the air temperature, and the distribution location by moving the selectors on the HVAC control head to the desired position. A large portion of the vehicles on the road today, as well as older vehicles, use this type of HVAC control system.

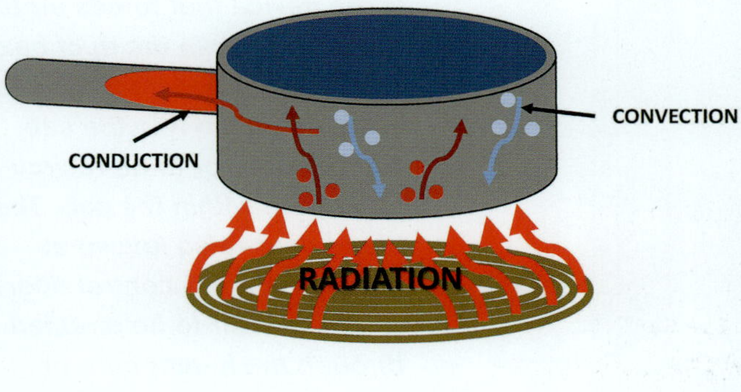

This diagram shows examples of heat transfer. Conduction is the transfer of heat directly through a material. Convection is the transfer of heat through air, fluid, or gas. Radiation is the transfer of heat through heat rays.

Manual climate control heads are found on many vehicles of every era. This type of control head has a knob for blower speed, air temperature, air distribution location, air-conditioning, and recirculated air. This control head will also have a rear defogger switch if the vehicle is equipped with that option.

Manual climate control heads have been a reliable method to control the blower speed, the air temperature, the mode of air distribution, the air source, and the operation of the AC system for many years.

An overhead view is shown of the duct box that was removed from a late-model vehicle. This duct box must be removed and taken apart in order to replace the heater core or evaporator core. The blower motor, door actuators, and blower resistor are typically serviceable without having to remove the duct box.

The duct box is where the action happens when the levers and knobs are moved on the control head. The duct box is typically located under the dash panel and is fairly simple in operation. Items that are located in the duct box include the blower motor, the evaporator core, the heater core, the fresh/recirculated air door, the blend door, and the mode doors. Here is an explanation of how each of the main items inside the duct box functions.

Blower Motor: This device is a multispeed electric motor that has a round impeller that forces the air to flow through the duct box and be directed to the desired location by the mode doors.

Evaporator Core: This device is the heat exchanger for the AC system that the air in the duct box always passes through. When the AC system is turned on, the evaporator core surface is cold and causes the heat and moisture to be removed from the air that passes through it, resulting in cool and dry air.

Heater Core: This device is the heat exchanger for the heating system. Once the engine is warmed up, the heater core has hot engine coolant flowing through its passages. Heated engine coolant is routed to the heater core through hoses or pipes. The duct box air only passes through the heater core when the blend air door is set to a position that allows this to happen. As the air

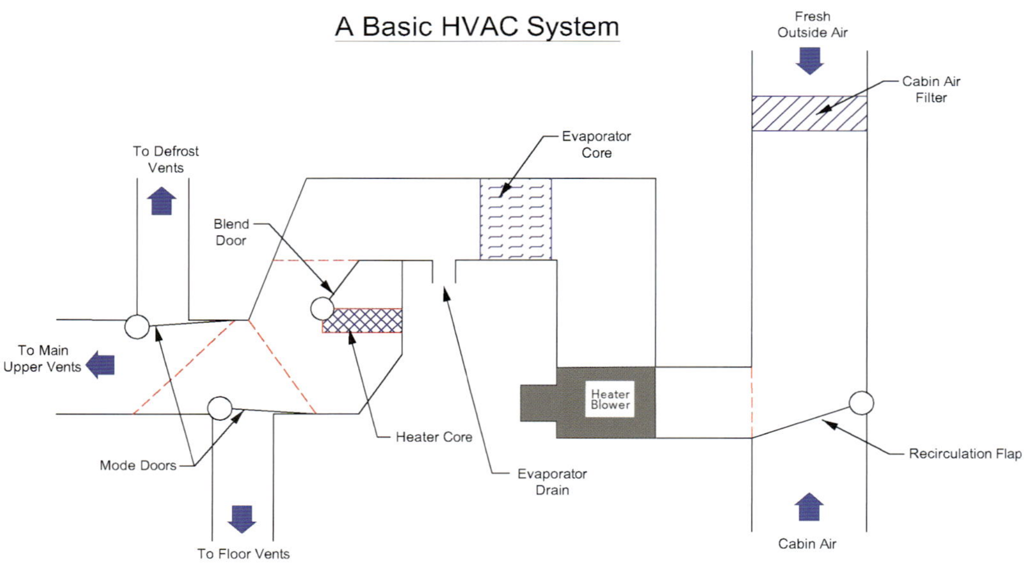

Air is routed through the duct box with a blower motor and a series of doors and heat exchangers. The blower motor is the device that forces air to be moved within the duct box. The recirculation door causes air to be pulled into the cab from outside or to be recirculated from within the cab. The blend door (also known as the temperature control door) causes the air to be directed through the heater core or around the heater core, which controls the temperature of the air. The mode doors cause the air to be directed at either defrost, vent, or floor ducts.

passes through the heater core, heat is released from the hot coolant and absorbed by the air, which results in warm air.

Fresh/Recirculated Air Door: This door controls where the air is pulled from by the blower motor. The two sources for air in the duct box are fresh air from outside the cab and recirculated air from inside the cab.

Blend Door: This door is located between the evaporator core and the heater core. This door controls the amount of air directed to the heater core that controls the temperature of the air that will be distributed by the mode doors. This door is sometimes called the temperature control door. When the door is in full heat mode, all of the air is directed to the heater core, which results in maximum heating in the cab. When the door is in full cool mode, it blocks air from passing through the heater core, which results in maximum cooling in the cab. Many times, the blend door is positioned somewhere between the maximum points, which causes a blending action to occur and results in the desired air temperature being sent into the cab. This door is controlled by the position of the temperature lever on the control head.

Mode Doors: These doors control where the duct box air is distributed in the cab. The different available modes include defrost, vent, and heat modes that are all controlled by the mode doors. Many systems have bi-level options that allow air to be distributed at two locations simultaneously, such as defrost and heat or vent and heat.

The doors in the duct box can be moved using cables, vacuum actuators, or electric motors. Cables and vacuum were the methods used on all early AC-equipped vehicles, and electric actuators are always used on late-model vehicles. Vehicles with cable-operated mechanisms to move the duct box doors typically had a method to adjust the cable length in case the door needed an adjustment. Vacuum-operated systems used either engine vacuum or some type of vacuum pump to create the negative pressure needed to move the doors. The electric actuators used on all late-model and current vehicles receive a command from the control head or logic device when movement is needed. The electric actuators seem to fail more often than the other devices used to move the doors.

A cable is used to move this blend door as the temperature lever is moved. Cables were used on many older-model vehicles and provided reliable operation of these systems.

Vacuum actuators are widely used on vehicles as a method to move the duct doors. These devices can be used on all of the duct box doors except the blend air/temperature door. Vacuum is directed to these actuators from the control head as the different options are requested. Vacuum is supplied to these systems by the engine or by a vacuum pump.

Electric actuators are used to move the duct box doors to the correct location when the controls are activated in the control head. These actuators are usually serviceable without having to remove the complete duct box assembly. These actuators may need to be recalibrated when they are replaced or at times when the battery has lost power or has been disconnected.

Electric actuators are widely used on late-model vehicles to move the duct box doors. These actuators are used to move the blend door, the mode doors, and the fresh/recirculated air door. These actuators are typically mounted with very small fasteners in a location that allows them to be replaced without having to remove the whole duct box.

Automatic Temperature Control and Dual Zone Systems

Many late-model cars, trucks, and sport utility vehicles (SUVs) have more complex HVAC systems that require less input from the occupants of the vehicle. With an increase in computing power, high-tech systems can now control the blower speed, air temperature, and air distribution point automatically by using electronic control heads or smart interfaces with touch screen capabilities along with many sensors and logic devices.

These automatic temperature control (ATC) systems operate in automatic mode by letting the operator set the desired temperature in the cab, and then the sensors, computers, and actuators operate to deliver the correct results. These systems most often have dual zone capabilities that allow the driver and the passenger to choose different temperature settings. The duct box is more complex with these dual zone systems because it is able to deliver air at different temperatures to each side of the vehicle. These systems also have some diagnostic capabilities built into the logic that will often display messages or codes when a problem is present in the system. The codes need to be researched in a technical database to determine the action needed to correct the problem.

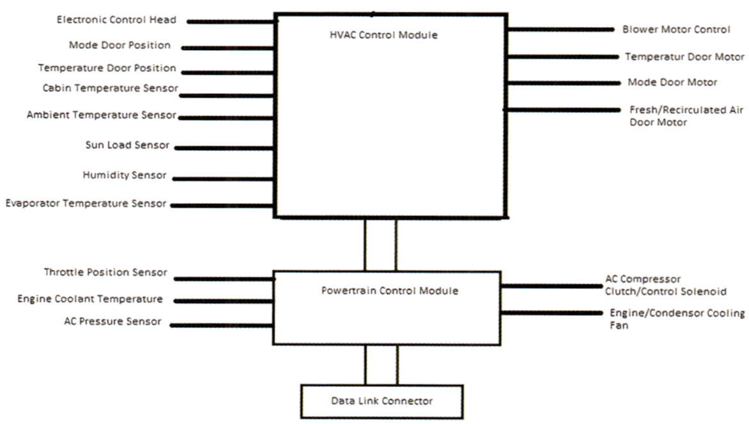

ATC systems use modules, sensors, and actuators to control the temperature and humidity in the cab. The HVAC control module receives inputs from several sensors while communicating with the powertrain control module (PCM) over a data network. Both of these modules have control over the output devices that determine the temperature and humidity in the cab. The data link connector allows a scan tool to be connected to the vehicle to retrieve trouble codes and live data from the electronic systems on the vehicle.

Vehicles with ATC are equipped with electronic control heads that allow the driver or the passenger to choose the desired temperature, and then the system automatically functions to achieve that temperature. Many of these ATC control heads also incorporate other functions into the platform, such as the audio system and the mobile phone connectivity.

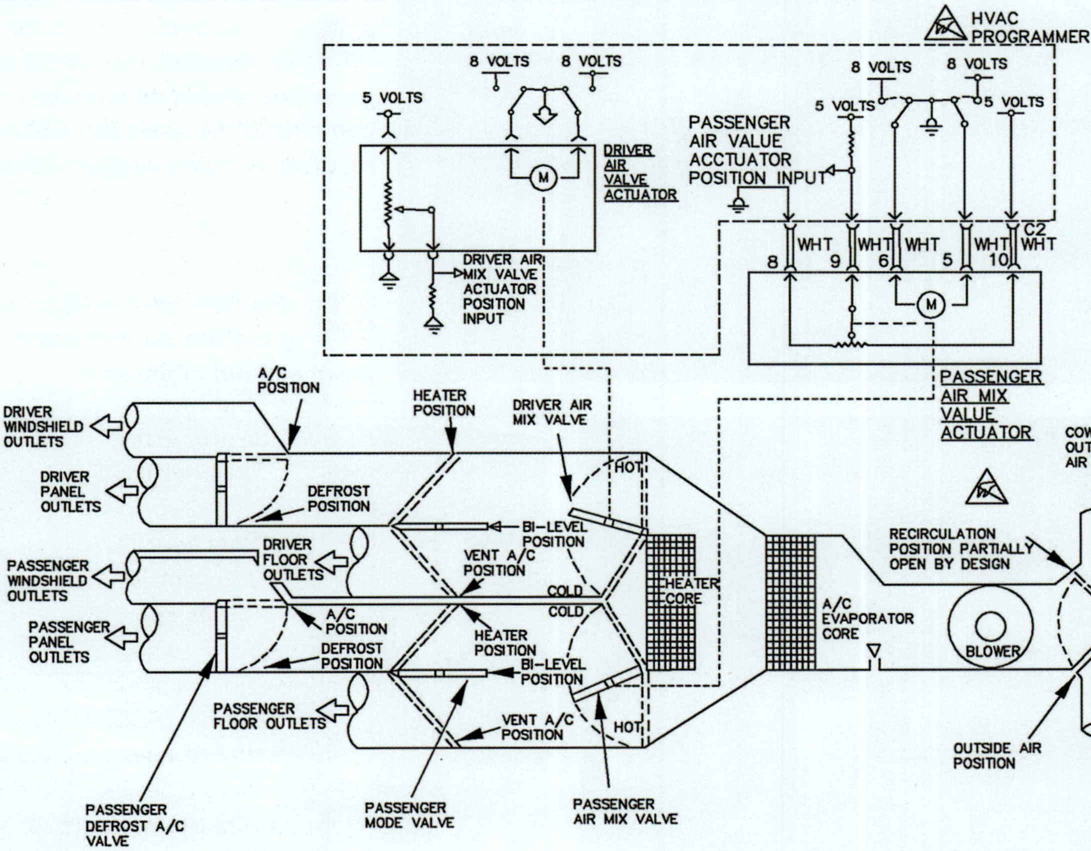

The duct box on vehicles with dual zone climate control is more complex because it can be configured to distribute cold air on one side and warm air on the other side of the vehicle. These duct boxes must have two air mix doors (temperature control doors) to accomplish this task. The doors on dual zone climate control systems are moved with electric actuators.

Cabin Filter Replacement

Many modern vehicles use a cabin air filter that is mounted in the HVAC duct box to clean the air that is distributed to the passenger compartment. The steps to replace the cabin air filter are listed below.

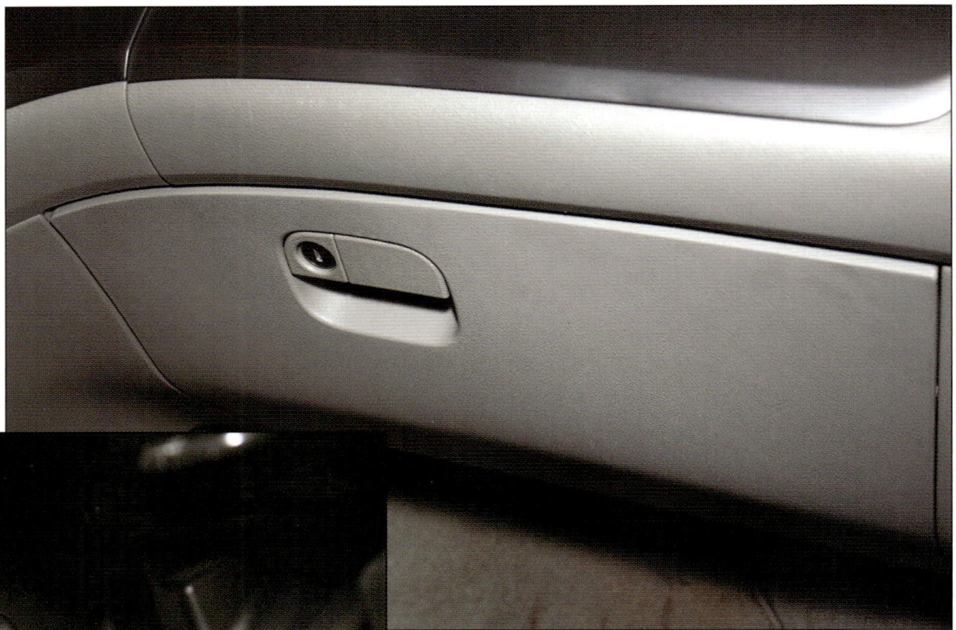

1 *The cabin air filter is typically located on the back side of the glove box. The glove box should be opened and then the contents of the glove box will need to be carefully removed and stored in a safe place.*

2 *Find the release clip that allows the glove box door to completely fold down and out of the way.*

3 *Once the glove box door is moved out of the way, find the cover for the cabin air filter.*

4 *Release the clips on the cabin filter cover and then pull on the cover to remove the filter from the duct box housing.*

5 *Gently pull the cabin filter from the duct box housing,* ***paying attention to the orientation of the filter*** *so that the new filter will be correctly installed.*

6 *Once the old cabin filter is removed from the vehicle, remove it from the cabin filter carrier.*

7 *Install the new cabin filter onto the cabin filter carrier while making sure that the arrow on the filter is pointing the same way as the old cabin filter. Typically, there is an arrow on the filter that should point in the direction of airflow through the duct box.*

8 *Carefully reinstall the new cabin filter back into the duct box housing.*

9 *Continue pushing the new cabin filter into the duct box housing until it snaps into place. Reconnect the linkage for the glove box door and then repack the glove box with its contents and close the door.*

AC Refrigeration Systems

To understand the physics of how the temperature and humidity is controlled in the cabin of cars and trucks, it is important to expand on the discussion about heat transfer from chapter 2. The heat transfer process of convection is used to move heat into and out of the cabin depending on how the control head is set. The AC system will be explained in this chapter and the heat system will be covered in more detail in chapter 8.

Heat Transfer

In the AC system, refrigerant is the substance that is used to move the heat out of the cabin. In a similar way, coolant is the substance that is used to move heat away from the engine. A main difference between these two systems is that the refrigerant changes from a liquid to a gas during the process of moving the heat, but the engine coolant maintains its liquid state when the system is operating normally.

To understand how the heat is moved and how these state changes take place, more explanation is needed in the area of sensible heat and latent heat.

Sensible Heat

Sensible heat is the measure of heat that can be felt and measured on a thermometer. When a thermometer gives a reading of 75°F, sensible heat is being measured.

Latent Heat

Latent heat is different from sensible heat because it is not able to be measured on a thermometer. Latent heat is a hidden heat that causes a substance to change states. For example, when water changes from a liquid to a gas, the latent heat of evaporation takes place. When water vapor or steam is cooled down and changes from a gas back to a liquid, the latent heat of condensation takes place.

These two processes are continually happening with the refrigerant in a functioning AC system. The last type of latent heat is when water turns into a solid and this is called the latent heat of fusion. This is not supposed to happen in a normally functioning AC system. However, if the AC system malfunctions, then ice may be seen forming on some of the low side components while in operation.

Heat quantity is a unit of measure for heat and there are two terms that are commonly used to measure this: the British thermal unit (BTU) and the calorie. The BTU is the amount of heat it takes to change 1 pound of water 1 degree Fahrenheit. The calorie is the amount of heat it takes to change 1 gram of water 1 degree Celsius.

As stated above, the refrigerant is continually moving between the liquid and vaporous states when the AC system is functioning. A key point to remember is that large quantities of heat are transferred during the changes of state of the refrigerant. It takes 180 BTU of heat to change 1 pound of water from 32°F to 212°F. It then takes 970 BTU to change the 212°F water into a vapor. On the contrary, 970 BTU of heat must be released from the water vapor to change it back to a liquid. The processes of great heat absorption during evaporation and great heat released during condensation is why the AC system is so efficient at moving heat out of the cabin.

Orifice Tube Systems

One design for automotive AC systems uses an orifice tube as the metering device. This system has been used for a long time by many manufacturers and is still being

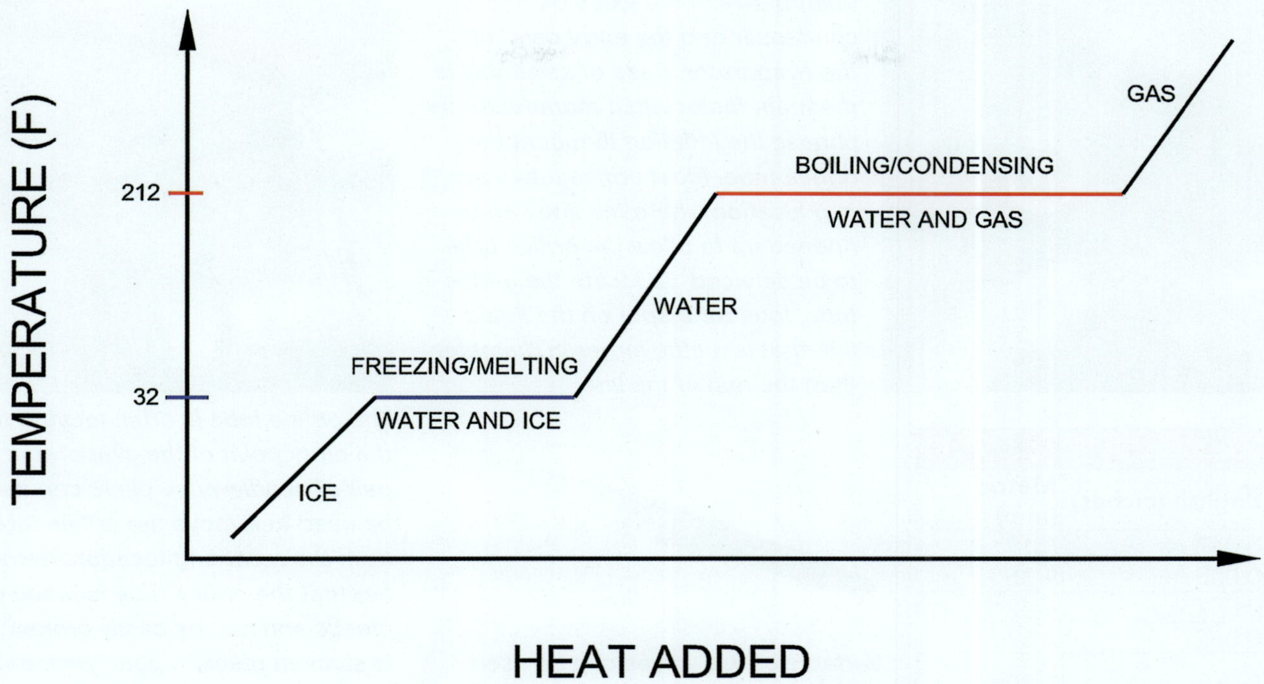

It takes 180 BTU to raise a pound of water from 32 to 212°F, but it takes 970 BTU to change 212°F water into a gas because of the large amount of heat absorbed during the latent heat of evaporation. This concept is why the warm air that is pushed through the evaporator core loses its heat and the result is very cool and dry air that is then directed to the passenger compartment through the mode doors.

used on modern cars and trucks. As stated previously, the main purpose of the AC system is to remove heat from the cabin, which leaves cool and dry air that cools the cabin and passengers.

Orifice tubes are devices that are used to meter a fixed amount of refrigerant into the evaporator core. They can be located in the liquid line at some point after the condenser and before the evaporator core. These devices are available in several different sizes, which is why they are made to be different colors. The color of the orifice tube assists the individual who is servicing the system in choosing the correct size for replacing the original device. It is not advisable to change the color/size of the original orifice tube when replacing it during service procedures.

The following chart gives the size of the opening for each color of orifice tube.

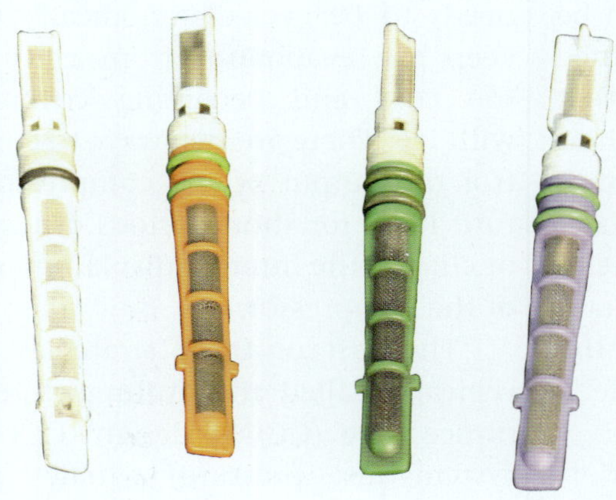

Orifice tubes are available in a variety of sizes that are designed by engineers to meter the correct amount of refrigerant into the evaporator core. The different colors represent the different sizes of the internal passage that the refrigerant must pass through during the operation of the AC system. Orifice tubes also have a screen that prevents contaminants from passing into the evaporator core. If the orifice tube screen is covered by a large number of foreign particles, then the system needs to be closely checked to determine where it came from.

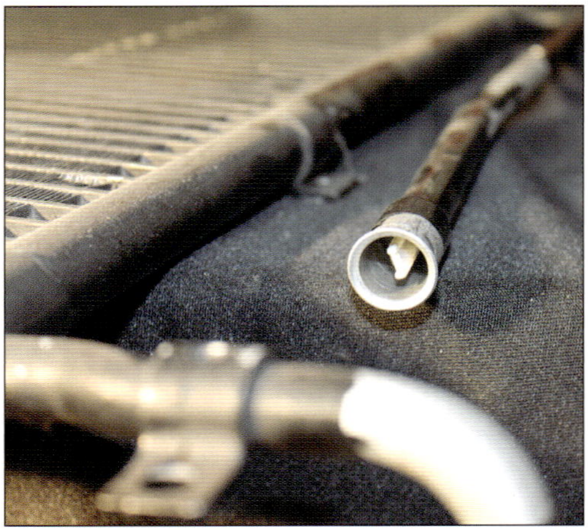

Orifice tubes can be located at any point between the exit side of the condenser and the entry point of the evaporator. Ease of assembly is the main factor when manufacturers choose the location to mount the orifice tube. Most orifice tubes are in a location where the line can be opened up to allow the orifice tube to be serviced. To locate the orifice tube, look for a spot on the liquid line that is a little larger in diameter than the rest of the line.

The orifice tube is often located near the entry point of the evaporator. A pair of needle-nose pliers can usually be used to remove the orifice tube from the mounting location. Remember that the orifice tube is made of plastic and can be easily broken if it is stuck in place. A good penetrant or lubricant can be sprayed into the area to free up a stuck orifice tube.

Orifice Tube Sizes		
Color	English (inches)	Metric (mm)
Green	0.047	1.19
Brown	0.053	1.35
Orange	0.057	1.45
Red	0.062	1.57
Black/ Blue	0.067	1.70

Variable orifice valves can be used in place of standard fixed orifice tubes because they are the same size and will fit in the same space. These devices vary the flow rate of refrigerant as the heat load changes in a similar way that a thermal expansion valve operates.

While most of the vehicles that use orifice tubes are like the ones described above, there are a couple of variations that need to be discussed. The variable orifice valve and the electronic orifice tube have been used in certain applications. Both of these types allow for some variable operation.

The variable orifice valve can be used in place of a standard orifice tube and is recommended for vehicles that idle for long periods of time, such as police cars and taxis. Electric orifice tubes are used on a few late-model vehicles, and they have the capacity to increase the flow rate under certain conditions when commanded by the vehicle's electronic control module.

Normal Operating Characteristics

Orifice tube AC systems are very effective designs that have been used for many years. The one drawback of this system design is that the orifice tube does not change the flow rate of refrigerant into the evaporator core, so the compressor needs to be cycled periodically to keep the evaporator from getting too cold and becoming covered with ice. There are two ways to control the output of the compressor: turn it off for short periods of time or change the internal displacement of the compressor.

The first of these strategies is typically called the cycling clutch orifice tube (CCOT) design. CCOT systems use pressure switches or temperature switches to monitor the conditions of the AC system, which then causes the AC compressor to be turned off to prevent evaporator freeze up. The cycle rate of these systems will vary depending on the ambient temperature and the humidity level. It is common to notice the compressor turning on and off during operation. A clicking sound will be heard in the engine area as the compressor is cycled, which is often accompanied by a slight change in engine RPM.

In recent years, vehicles that use orifice tubes have used compressors that are a variable-displacement style. Many variable-displacement compressors use mechanical operation to change the internal capacity of the compressor. This action was accomplished by using a valve that sensed the temperature of the suction side of the compressor and changing the angle of the wobble plate, which caused the internal pistons to change the length of the stroke.

Flow of Refrigerant Through the AC System

It is helpful to understand the refrigerant flow through an operable AC system. The refrigerant is continuously moving and changing pressures and states while the system is running. Here is a step-by-step description of what is happening to the refrigerant as it moves through the components of the AC system.

1. The compressor pulls in low-pressure refrigerant gas from the suction line and then compresses it to raise the pressure and temperature. The refrigerant exits the compressor as a high-pressure gas.
2. The refrigerant is routed to the condenser through the discharge line. The refrigerant enters the condenser as a heated high-pressure gas. Airflow through the condenser fins causes the refrigerant to cool down, which causes the gas to condense into a liquid. The refrigerant exits the condenser as a hot, high-pressure liquid. The temperature of the liquid is typically 20 to 50 degrees cooler at the exit than it was on entry of the condenser. The temperatures at the condenser inlet will vary greatly because of the wide variance of pressures that can exist at the condenser. On very hot days, the pressures can be as high as 300 psi, which would create inlet temperatures in the 275 to 300°F range. On a 70°F day, the pressure would be approximately 150 to 175 psi, which would create inlet temperatures in the 150 to 175°F range.
3. The refrigerant is routed to the orifice tube through the liquid line. The orifice tube acts as a restriction device since the passage pipe is much smaller than the liquid line. High-pressure liquid enters the orifice tube and low-pressure atomized liquid exits the orifice tube and then is routed into the evaporator core. Atomized liquid will have small droplets of bubbles due to the pressure drop as it exits the orifice tube.
4. The refrigerant enters the evaporator core as a cool low-pressure atomized liquid. Duct box air is routed through the fins of the evaporator core, which causes the liquid refrigerant to begin to vaporize into a gas. This process of latent heat of evaporation absorbs the heat from the duct box air, which causes the air to be cool and dry as it exits the evaporator fins. The refrigerant exits the evaporator core as a low-pressure gas and is then routed to the accumulator dryer.
5. The refrigerant enters the accumulator dryer as a cold low-pressure gas. The accumulator dryer stores and dries the refrigerant and prevents any liquid refrigerant from being routed to the compressor. The exit point is near the top of the accumulator to prevent any liquid from being sent to the compressor through the suction line.

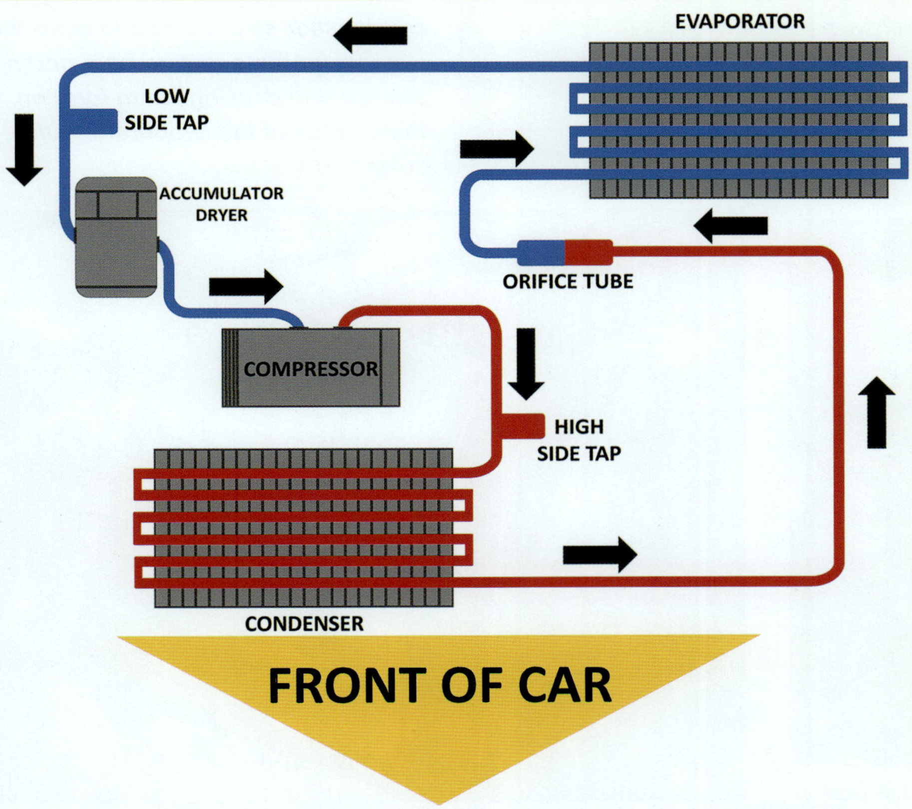

It is helpful to understand the flow of refrigerant as it passes through each section of the AC system. The low side of the AC system runs from the exit of the orifice tube up to the entry point of the compressor. The high side of the AC system runs from the exit point of the compressor to the entry point of the orifice tube.

On late-model vehicles, the mechanical valve that adjusted the output of the compressor has been changed to a solenoid, which works much better. The engine computer monitors the conditions of the pressure and the temperature and adjusts the command to the solenoid, which adjusts the output of the compressor. Both of these variable-style compressors did not need to be cycled on and off to control the temperature in the evaporator core.

Variable-displacement compressors mechanically adjust their output by monitoring the temperature of the suction gasses that are drawn in from the suction line. When low temperatures are sensed by the internal valve, the angle of the swash plate is changed, which reduces the stroke of the pistons inside the compressor. Many manufacturers used this type of compressor as a method to keep the evaporator temperature from getting too low and causing ice to form on the surface of the evaporator core.

Normal Operating Characteristics

The key characteristics to look for under the hood while an orifice tube system is running are:

- The suction line will be cold and likely have water droplets on the line.
- The accumulator dryer will be cold to the touch and likely have water droplets on the device.
- The discharge line, condenser, and liquid line will be hot and should be checked with a laser thermometer/pyrometer.
- There will be water draining from the duct box drain tube after the system has run for several minutes.

The compressor is driven by the engine drive belt and is energized when power is sent to a stationary coil that creates a magnetic field to pull the front clutch plate into the drive pulley. This action causes the internal parts of the compressor to begin compressing the refrigerant.

It is common to hear a clicking sound when the compressor cycles on and off during the normal operation of a cycling AC system. The clutch coil creates a magnetic field that pulls the front plate into the rotating pulley. This causes the internal compressor components to begin operating.

The suction line will be cold and have water droplets on the surface when the AC system is operating as designed. This line contains cold refrigerant gas that is being routed into the compressor. The cold surface of this line collects moisture from the surrounding air.

It is common for the suction line to be cool or cold when the AC system is operating as designed. It is a good practice to check the temperature of the suction line to see if it is cold as a diagnostic step.

The accumulator dryer will be cold and wet on an AC system that is operating in an efficient manner. One point to keep in mind is that there should not be any ice or frost on any of the lines or components during operation. Visible ice or frost is a sign that the deicing systems are not working correctly.

The accumulator dryer will be cold and wet when the AC system is working well. The accumulator is located between the exit of the evaporator core and the entry point of the AC compressor in orifice tube systems. If the accumulator is not cold while the system is operating, then the system is not functioning properly.

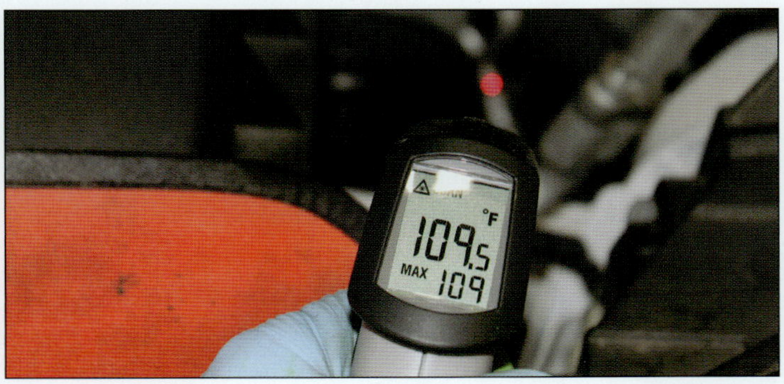

The high side components of the AC system will be warm or hot when the system is operating correctly. The compressor raises the pressure and temperature of the refrigerant gas, which is then routed to the discharge line that connects to the condenser. The liquid line connects the exit of the condenser to the inlet of the evaporator core. All of the components in the high side of the system will be at a high temperature while the system is operating.

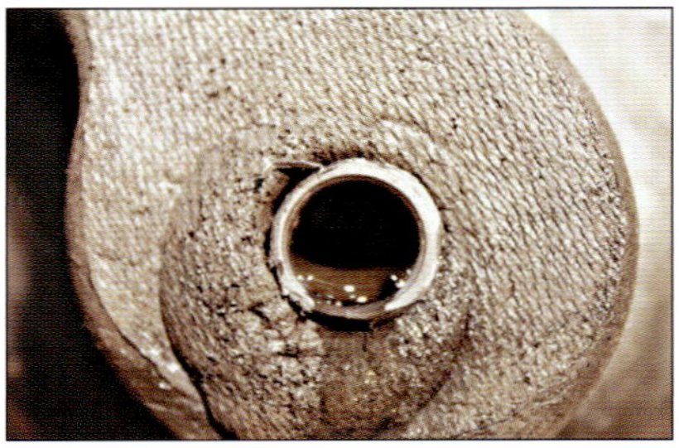

The evaporator drain tube will have water droplets dripping when the AC is used on hot days. The water originates from the hot, humid air that is pushed through the evaporator core. As the heat is absorbed into the boiling refrigerant, the water that was in the hot air sticks to the surface of the evaporator and then runs down the bottom of the duct box where it drains out of the drain tube. Refrigerant boils at very low pressures/temperatures. The refrigerant is turning from a liquid to a gas in the evaporator while taking on the latent heat of evaporation, which is why the duct air turns cool and dry after it passes through the evaporator core.

It is common to see a puddle of water under the area below the evaporator drain tube when a vehicle is parked after running the AC on a hot and humid day. This water is a sign that the system is working to remove the heat and humidity from the cabin air, which results in cool and dry air being directed into the passenger compartment through the mode doors.

Operation of Each Major AC Component

The following list explains what each component of the AC system is and what it does.

Compressor: The AC compressor serves as the pumping device that causes the refrigerant to move through the system when the AC is commanded to run. The different compressor types include the piston, scroll, and vane pump styles. The compressor is needed to pull in cold, low-pressure gaseous refrigerant into hot, high-pressure gaseous refrigerant. The temperature of the gaseous refrigerant needs to be increased in order to use the ambient air flowing past the condenser to create a cooling effect that causes the refrigerant to condense into a liquid.

Condenser: The condenser is a large heat exchanger located in front of the radiator. It is used to cool the hot gaseous refrigerant, which causes it to condense back into a liquid. Airflow across the condenser is very important and is accomplished by the ram air effect when the vehicle is traveling at highway speeds and by the fan assembly when the vehicle is traveling slowly or stopped.

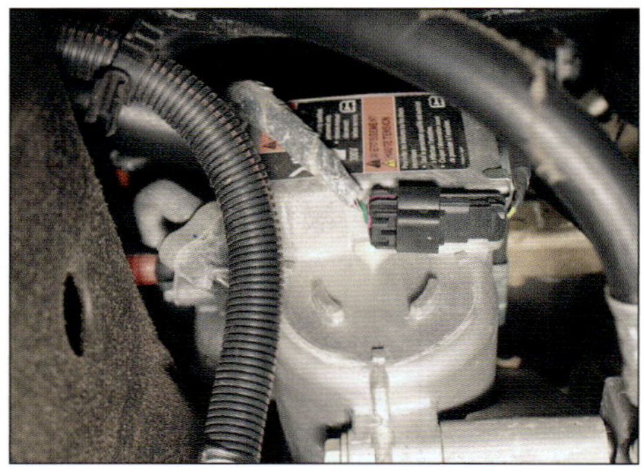

Many electric and hybrid vehicles use compressors that are driven by a high-voltage battery instead of the engine drive belt. This design increases fuel economy by reducing the need to have the internal combustion engine run. Caution must be followed when performing service and repair on vehicles with electric compressors because these compressors operate on three-phase AC high voltage.

The compressor has a pulley that spins at all times when the engine is operating. The front plate only turns when the AC is commanded to be turned on. Power is sent to the AC clutch coil when the AC compressor needs to run.

The compressor should be carefully tightened with equal torque at all of the mounting bolts to minimize the chance of the body getting in a bind, which could cause a leak. Some compressors use a pigtail connector that connects to the vehicle harness connector.

The condenser is the heat exchanger located in front of the engine radiator and allows for generous airflow to pass through the fins. The condenser is connected to the discharge line on the inlet and the liquid line on the exit side.

Many condensers used on vehicles with a thermal expansion valve (TXV) have a condenser that combines with the receiver dryer. This design is very effective and it reduces the potential leak points by welding the dryer to the condenser.

Orifice Tube: The orifice tube is used as a metering device that causes the pressure to be reduced in the AC system. The refrigerant pressure needs to be lowered in order for it to be able to absorb heat from the duct box air and begin to boil and take on the latent heat of evaporation. Orifice tubes also have a screen that serves as a filter to prevent contaminants from passing into the evaporator core.

Evaporator Core: The evaporator core is a heat exchanger located inside the duct box that is used to provide a place for the low-pressure atomized liquid refrigerant to begin to boil. This change of state of the refrigerant causes it to take on the latent heat of evaporation, which absorbs large amounts of heat from the duct box air. The result is that the duct box air is much cooler and drier after moving past the evaporator core. The cool air is distributed to the passenger compartment, and the moisture drops to the bottom of the duct box and drains outside the vehicle.

Accumulator Dryer: The accumulator dryer container is located between the evaporator core and the compressor and is used to store and dry the refrigerant. The dryer

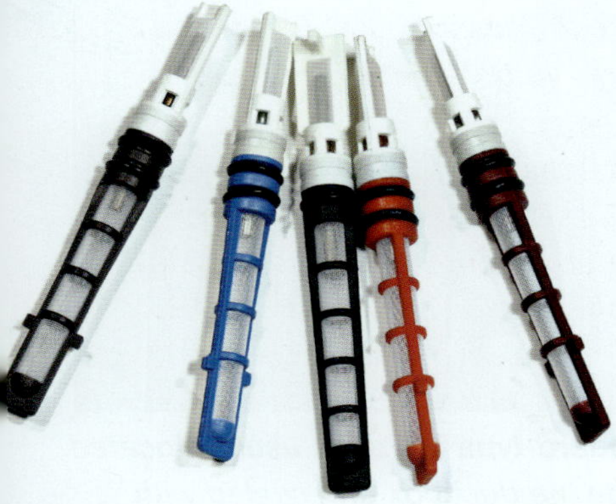

Orifice tubes are made in different colors that align with the various sizes, and care should be taken to use the one that is designed for the vehicle being repaired. It is important to remember to use the correct orifice tube during a service procedure.

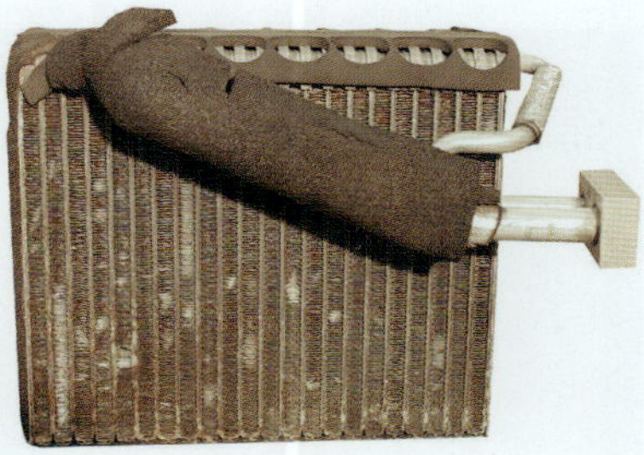

The evaporator core is the heat exchanger on the low side of the AC system and is located in the duct box. It is important to transfer the insulation from the old evaporator core to the new unit when replacing it. A block-type TXV would be mounted on the flat surface of this evaporator core.

Evaporator cores often collect dirt and debris in the fins. This problem is usually reduced on vehicles that use a cabin air filter that gets replaced on a regular basis. This evaporator core has one threaded connecting point as well as a quick-connect coupling.

contains a desiccant that is used to absorb any moisture that could be present inside the AC system. The location of the accumulator is important on orifice tube systems because it prevents any liquid refrigerant from being supplied to the compressor. The compressor would be damaged if liquid refrigerant was pulled in. The exit point of the accumulator dryer is near the top, which only allows gaseous refrigerant to be sent to the compressor. There typically is a small feed hole at the bottom of the dryer that feeds refrigerant oil to the compressor.

Basic Cycle for TXV Systems

A second style of metering device that is used in many AC systems is the thermal expansion valve (TXV). The TXV metering device has been used for many years and is increasing in use in recent years because it varies the flow rate based on operating conditions. There are two styles of TXVs in use: the standard type and the block type. The standard type TXV is almost always located inside the duct box, while the block style is almost always located on the firewall.

As stated, the TXV metering device varies the flow rate through the valve based on operating conditions. This variable operation occurs by the valve sensing the temperature of the exit line of the evaporator and changing the internal opening as the temperature changes. When the sensing element is exposed to warm temperatures, the valve opens, and when the sensing element is exposed to cold temperatures, the valve closes. The continual opening and closing helps control the temperature in the evaporator core, which helps prevent the temperature from reaching freezing levels, which would cause the core to form ice on the surface.

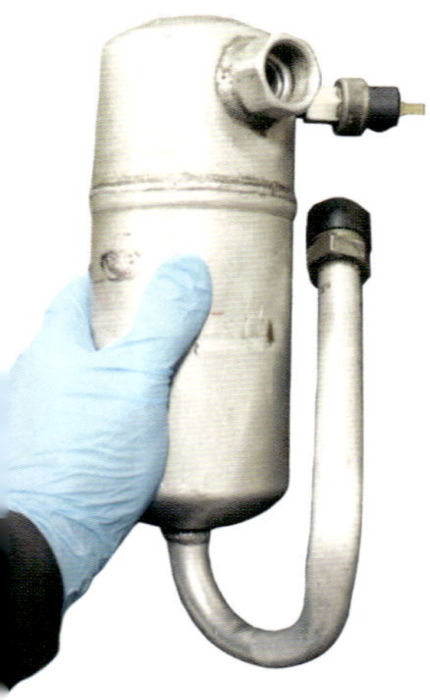

Accumulator dryers can be connected to the lines and hoses with bolted connections that use O-rings to seal the joint from potential leaks. Low side pressure switches are often mounted to the accumulator dryer as well.

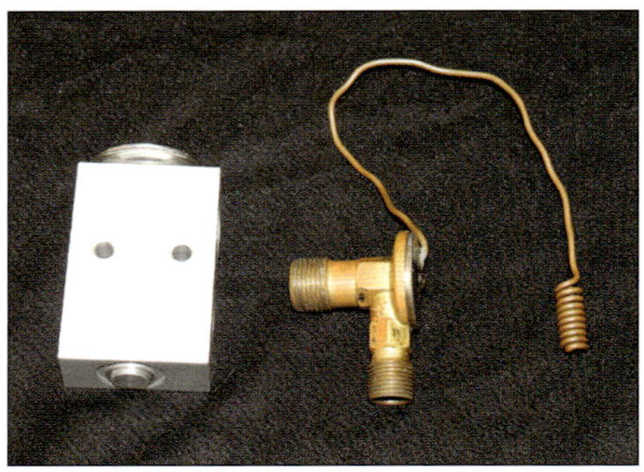

Thermal expansion valves (TXVs) are a popular choice to use as a metering device to feed low-pressure atomized liquid into the evaporator core. The two types of TXVs include the block type (left) and standard type (right). Both styles operate by varying the opening inside the valve to feed refrigerant into the evaporator core.

Many accumulator dryers are connected to the lines and hoses with quick-connect couplings. The low side service port is often mounted on the accumulator dryer as well as a fitting to mount a low side pressure switch.

Block type TXVs are located near the firewall and are visible from under the hood. O-rings and metal gaskets are used to seal the lines to the body of the valve.

Standard-type TXVs are usually located inside the duct box and sealed with O-rings. It is important to make sure that the sensing element is securely attached to the exit line of the evaporator core so that it can accurately sense the temperature of this line. The valve opens up when the sensing element is warm and the valve closes when the sensing element is cold.

Flow of Refrigerant Through the TXV System

The flow of refrigerant through the TXV system is very similar to the flow through the orifice tube system. The refrigerant is the substance that flows through the components, which is used to absorb heat from the passenger compartment and carry it outside the cab and release it at the condenser to the outside air. Here is a step-by-step description of the refrigerant flow through a TXV system:

1. The compressor pulls in low-pressure refrigerant gas from the suction line and compresses it to raise the pressure and temperature. The refrigerant exits the compressor as a high-pressure gas.
2. The refrigerant is routed to the condenser through the discharge line. The refrigerant enters the condenser as a heated high-pressure gas. Airflow through the condenser fins causes the refrigerant to cool down, which causes the gas to condense into a liquid. The refrigerant exits the condenser as a hot high-pressure liquid. The temperature of the liquid is typically 20 to 50 degrees cooler at the exit than it was on entry of the condenser.
3. The refrigerant enters the receiver dryer as a warm high-pressure liquid. The receiver dryer stores and dries the refrigerant and prevents any gaseous refrigerant from being sent to the TXV. The exit point is at the bottom of the receiver dryer to ensure that only liquid is able to leave the receiver dryer. There should not be any temperature drop across the receiver dryer.
4. The refrigerant is routed to the TXV through the liquid line as a high-pressure liquid. The TXV acts as a restriction, which causes the pressure and temperature to drop and the refrigerant exits the TXV as a low-pressure, atomized liquid.
5. The refrigerant enters the evaporator core as a cool low-pressure atomized liquid. Duct box air is routed through the fins of the evaporator core, which causes the liquid refrigerant to begin to vaporize into a gas. This process of latent heat of evaporation absorbs the heat from the duct box air, which causes the air to be cool and dry as it exits the evaporator fins. The refrigerant exits the evaporator core as a low-pressure gas and is directed to the compressor as a cold low-pressure gas.

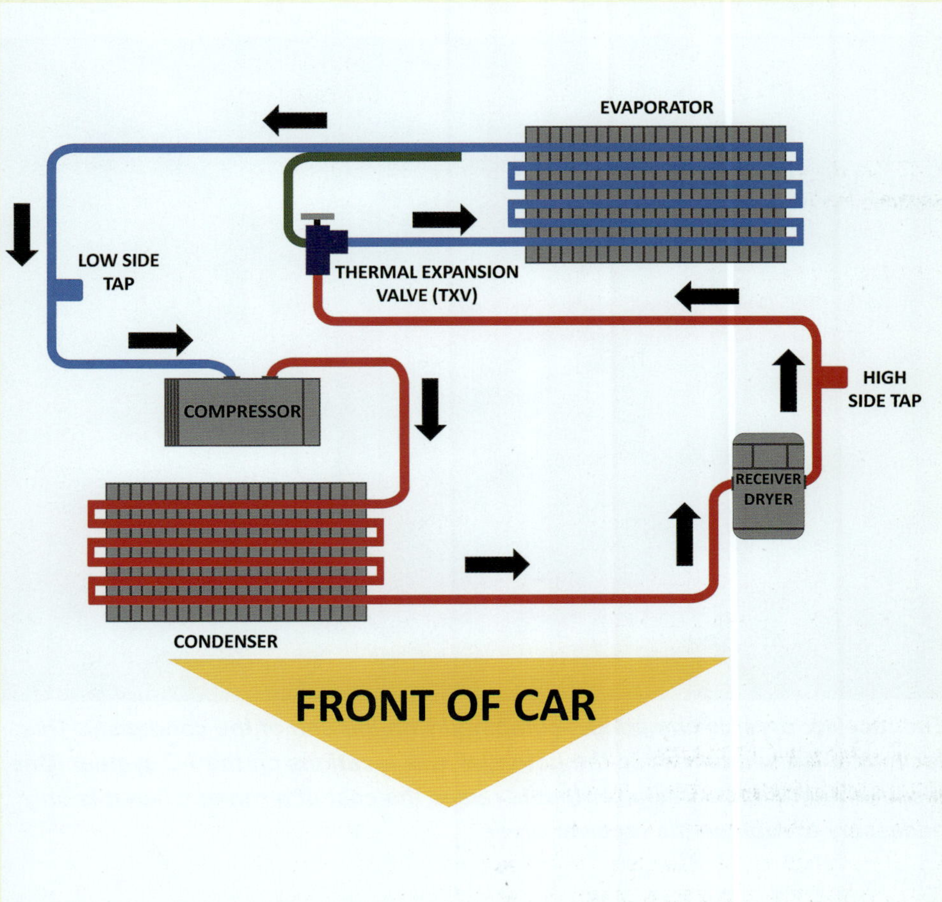

It is helpful to learn to understand the flow of refrigerant as it passes through each section of the AC system. The low side of the AC system runs from the exit of the TXV up to the entry point of the compressor. The high side of the AC system runs from the compressor exit up to the entry point of the TXV.

Normal Operating Characteristics

TXV AC systems have been used for many years and continue to be a good choice for modern cars and trucks. Even though the TXV is a variable device that assists with preventing the evaporator core from getting too cold, it is necessary to vary the output of the AC compressor during certain operating conditions. This is accomplished the same way as orifice tube systems that cycle the compressor off and on using switches and sensors to monitor system pressures and temperatures. It is also common to see TXV systems with variable-displacement compressors.

Many of the characteristics of an orifice tube system will be the same on a TXV system with the exception of the location of the receiver dryer being in the high side of the AC system between the output of the condenser and the TXV. Since the receiver dryer is located on the high side of the system, it will be hot and not have any water droplets on it.

Receiver dryers often have high side switches mounted onto the body. Some receiver dryers incorporate a sight glass in the top side to allow for a visible view of the refrigerant flowing in the unit. R134a systems will appear cloudy when functioning properly due to the PAG oil moving with the refrigerant.

Operation of Each Major Component

1. The compressor, condenser, and evaporator core function the same on TXV systems as they do on orifice tube systems. See the explanation in the orifice tube section.
2. The TXV is used as the metering device that causes the pressure to be reduced in the AC system. After the refrigerant passes through the TXV, it's in a low-pressure, atomized liquid state and is routed into the evaporator core, where it begins to boil and absorb heat from the duct box air.
3. The receiver dryer is a container located between the exit of the condenser and the TXV and is used to store and dry the refrigerant. The receiver dryer contains a desiccant that is used to absorb moisture that could be present in the AC system. The location of the receiver dryer is in the part of the AC system where high-pressure liquid is present. The refrigerant exits the receiver dryer at the bottom of the vessel to prevent any gaseous refrigerant from being routed to the TXV.

The receiver dryer is sometimes combined with the end of the condenser. This technique is used to reduce the potential leak locations on the AC system. One disadvantage of this design is that is raises the cost of a repair when it is only necessary to replace the receiver dryer.

CHAPTER 4

Diagnosis of the AC System

Of all of the convenience features that have been invented and become common on cars and trucks, an operable AC system remains one that is among the most popular. Having cool and dehumidified air being forced out of the duct vents on a hot day is a refreshing experience, one that promotes a more enjoyable and comfortable ride to your destination. Chances are that if a vehicle is capable of quickly lowering the cabin temperature and humidity levels, there will be no need to diagnose or troubleshoot any problems within the system. However, if the AC system does not perform up to the expected level, the operator or passengers will eagerly want to know what is wrong with the AC system on their vehicle.

As of 2018, it is still legal for any person to purchase small cans of R134a at any auto parts store or any other big-box store that has an auto parts department. It has become very common to run to the store and purchase refrigerant any time the AC system is not cooling as well as the owner would prefer. Adding more refrigerant is not always the solution to improve the performance of an AC system. This chapter will provide the correct steps to follow when an accurate diagnosis is desired.

Visual Inspection

Before learning how to diagnose an AC system that is not performing at optimal levels, it is advisable to understand what a normally operating AC system looks like. The AC control head needs to be set at maximum cold with the blower turned to the highest setting.

Most auto parts stores and big-box stores sell refrigerant along with simple hose connectors that allow vehicle owners to add refrigerant to their vehicles. Most of the refrigerant sold to the do-it-yourself customer has additives that are supposed to cover up bigger problems in your AC system.

Testing AC Operation

Here are some characteristics to look for under the hood with the system turned to high.

- ❑ The lines, hoses, and components in the low side of the system should be cold and likely will have water droplets dripping from them.

It is very common to see water droplets dripping off of components in the low side, such as the suction line and the accumulator dryer, and for them to be cold when the AC is operated on a hot day.

- ❑ The lines, hoses, and components in the high side of the system should be hot, which is best to be tested with a laser thermometer since the surface temperature of these components will range from 100 to 220°F.

The components on the high side of the system are usually at a high temperature while the system is operating. This is a result of the high pressure that is present in the high side components.

- ❑ The compressor should be operating without much audible noise and it may be cycling off and on in order to control the temperature of the evaporator.
- ❑ The cooling fan will likely be operating if the ambient temperature is high enough to cause the high side pressure to reach moderate levels. The cooling fan often runs with the AC when the vehicle is stopped in order to cool the condenser, but the fan typically shuts off when the vehicle is being driven at highway speeds, which provides plenty of ram air to cool the condenser.

The cooling fans are vital to the operation of the AC system. These fans run to pull air through the radiator and condenser, which removes heat from these heat exchangers and allows the engine to be cooled as well as the AC system to operate correctly.

- ❑ The duct air is directed from the passenger vents and is moving at a high velocity since the blower is set to high speed.

The temperature of the air coming out of the air ducts should be in the range of 40 to 50°F when the AC system is set to maximum and the blower is set to high speed.

Leak Testing

The AC system operates by using pressurized refrigerant that is routed to the major components both inside the cab as well as under the hood through metal lines and layered rubber hoses. The AC system works very well for long periods of time, but eventually the refrigerant will leak out of the system. These leaks can be very small at times, but they can also be very large. Obviously, the large leaks are easier to locate than the small leaks. The next section of this text will cover the various methods that can be used to locate refrigerant leaks.

Presence of Oil Residue

The pressurized refrigerant has oil mixed with it at all times to provide lubrication for the AC compressor. When the refrigerant leaks out of the AC system, a small amount of oil will also leak out. Whenever the presence of oily residue is observed, it is definitely a location where some refrigerant has leaked out too.

Refrigerant oil circulates with the refrigerant throughout the whole AC system in order to supply a continuous flow of oil to the compressor as

The compressor should always be closely checked for signs of oily residue. Leaks can occur at the compressor front seal, body, and at the connections with the suction and discharge lines.

The condenser is positioned in front of the radiator and is subject to rocks and debris hitting the surface, which will often cause a leak. There will be an obvious oily area on condensers that have been pierced with an object. There could also be leaks where the discharge line and liquid line connect to the condenser.

The refrigerant in the AC system is under constant pressure, so it can leak out in many different locations. Oily residue on the components of the AC system is a sign of a leak. However, caution needs to be used to make sure that the oily residue did not come from another leak that is nearby, such as engine oil or power steering fluid.

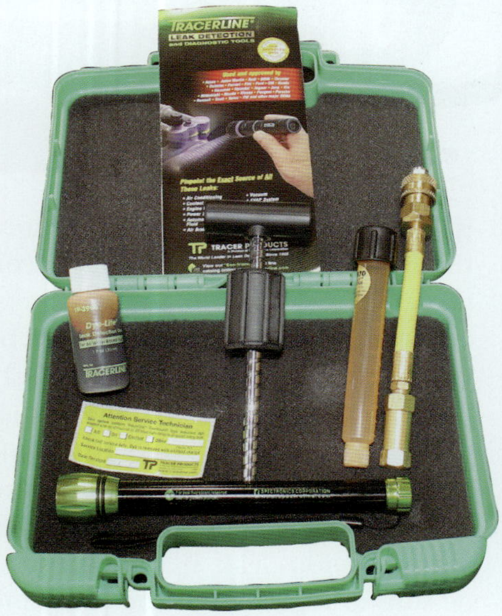

Leak detection kits are a popular choice to use when performing repair and maintenance on a vehicle. This kit comes with a small dye injector, a black light, oil-based dye, and a dye decal.

This dye injector is used to inject a small amount of refrigerant oil with dye mixed with it into a charged AC system. The tool uses a small screw press mechanism to force the dye into the system.

This dye injector uses a screw press mechanism to force dye into a charged AC system. The advantage of this style of injector is that it has a large capacity and enough substance to charge approximately 40 vehicles.

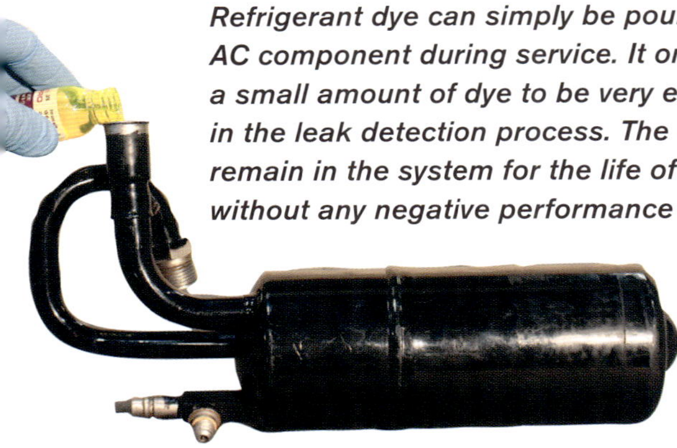

Refrigerant dye can simply be poured into an AC component during service. It only requires a small amount of dye to be very effective in the leak detection process. The dye can remain in the system for the life of the vehicle without any negative performance issues.

it operates. Some typical locations that oily residue can be seen are on the compressor, hoses, lines, dryers, and condensers. It is advisable to be thorough when performing a leak inspection of the AC system because there can often be more than one leak present in a system. If time and money is going to be spent on repairing an obvious leak, it is advisable to be sure to repair all of the leaks and problems with the AC system.

Dye and Black Light

The use of a tracer dye that mixes with the refrigerant oil is often used as a leak detection method. Some

The dye decal needs to be installed in a visible location to alert anyone who works on the vehicle in the future that refrigerant dye has already been added to the system.

A flashlight type of black light along with the yellow-tinted safety glasses is a very affordable option to use when using dye leak detection methods. These glasses can be used on any system that has had dye installed into it.

Kent Moore Tools makes a good corded style of black light that connects to the vehicle battery for a power source. This black light, along with the yellow-tinted glasses, makes finding leaks very easy on systems with dye added.

The black light should be used with the yellow-tinted glasses to locate refrigerant leaks. The flashlight-style tool is very easy to use and should be aimed at the AC components slowly and carefully in order to locate all of the leak points.

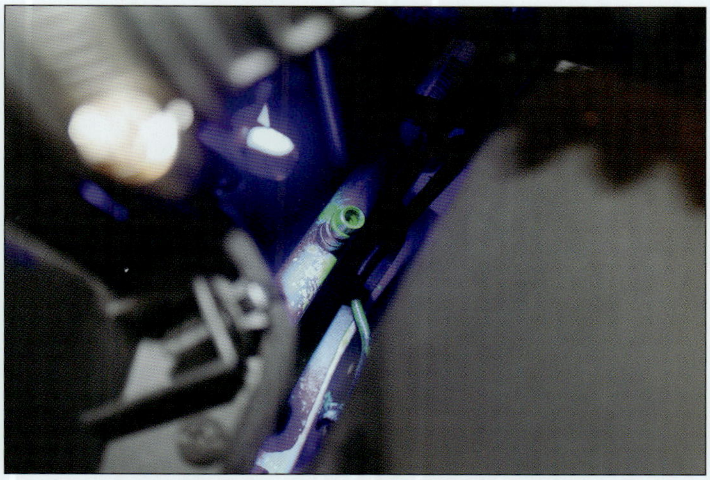

A system leak that has dye installed will show up as bright color when the black light is aimed at the leak. Service ports are a common location of refrigerant leaks and should always be closely checked when using the black light.

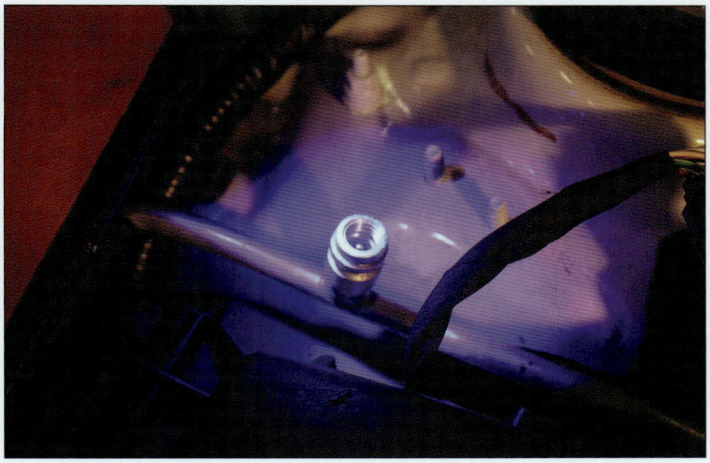

A service port that is not leaking will not show any bright residue when shining the black light at it.

A common leak point is at a joint connection where an AC line is joined with a rubber hose. Leaking lines need to be repaired or replaced to correct the problem.

The AC compressor should be closely inspected with the black light. It is not uncommon for vehicles with high mileage to have compressors with leaks at some point of the body or front seal.

manufacturers install tracer dye into the AC system when the vehicle is built. If the dye needs to be added to the AC system, it can be injected at the service ports or poured into one of the AC components during a repair process. It is advisable to install a decal in a conspicuous location after the dye is added to an AC system in order to notify anyone who may work on the vehicle in the future that dye has been added.

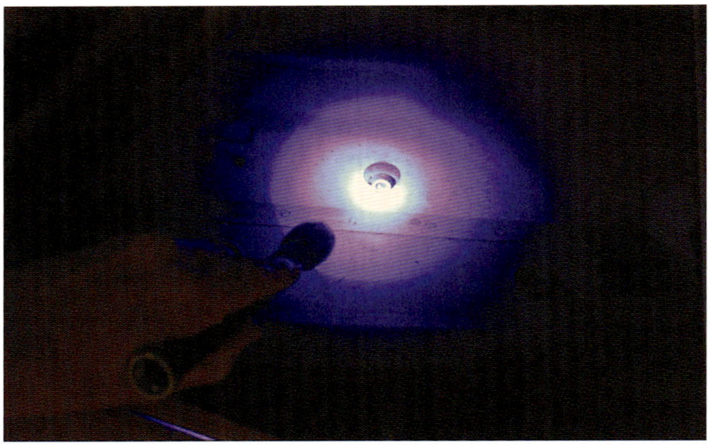

The duct box drain tube should be closely checked with the black light to determine if the evaporator core is leaking. The drain tube and water will have a bright color if the evaporator core is leaking.

A system with a leaking evaporator core will deposit water that has dye mixed with it onto the ground. This water should always be checked when searching for leaks in the AC system.

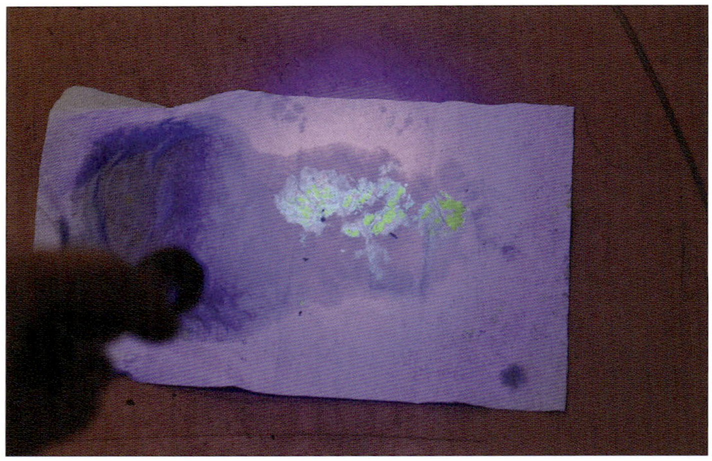

A shop towel that is used to soak up the water that has drained from the AC system can expose refrigerant dye in a vivid way when the black light is directed toward it. A leaking evaporator core would cause this condition.

A black light of some type will need to be used to make the tracer dye very visible. These devices can be corded or flashlight style. The black light should be aimed at as many sections of the AC system as possible in order to be thorough in finding the location of the refrigerant leak. The location of the leak will show up as a bright color. It is important to look at the complete system when leak testing because some systems may have more than one leak.

It is important to remember to look at the duct box drain tube with the black light. A leaking evaporator core will cause the drain tube to turn color and the water that drains out of the tube to have a bright tint.

Electronic Leak Detector

Electronic leak detectors are very useful tools for locating refrigerant leaks. These very sensitive devices should be used when available to pick up traces of refrigerant on and around the AC components. These

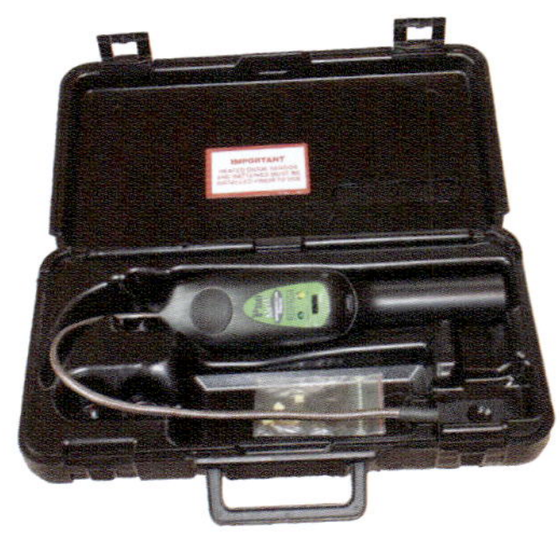

Electronic leak detectors are useful tools to find refrigerant leaks in the AC system. These tools have improved a great deal from the early days of electronic leak detectors.

The electronic leak detector tip should be slowly moved along the components of the AC system. The detector has an audible tone that will sharply increase when the tip picks up refrigerant vapors.

The electronic leak detector can be an effective tool to find leaks on AC system components that are in an area and can be reached with the tip of the tool. The disadvantage to this leak detection method is that some parts of the AC system are not able to be reached with this tool.

An electronic leak detector can often be used to find small leaks in the condenser assembly. It may be necessary to remove covers and shields to access challenging condenser locations.

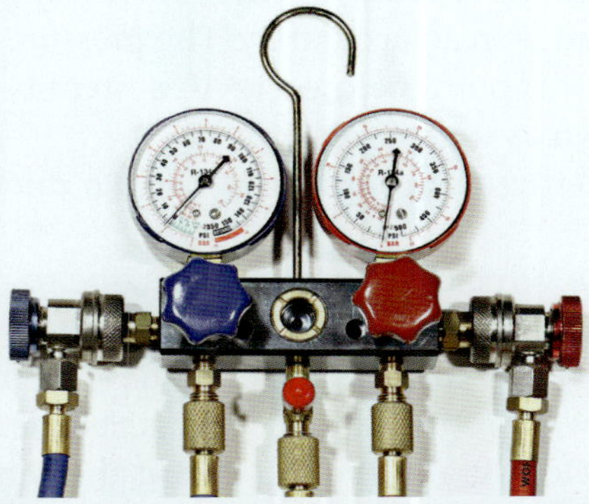

The manifold set is a tool that is used to connect to the AC system to measure pressures. The left side of this tool has a quick-connect coupling attached to the blue hose, which is used to attach to the low side of the AC system. The right side of this tool has a quick-connect coupling attached to the red hose, which is used to attach to the high side of the AC system.

tools should be used in an area with low airflow and with the engine and the AC system turned off. The key to using these tools is to allow the tip to pick up vapors of refrigerant, and if the shop had lots of airflow or if the engine and AC system were running, the leak would likely be hidden from the tool.

The operator of these electronic leak detectors should be very careful to keep from exposing the tip to dirt and grease. Foreign materials near the tip would cause the device to give false and inaccurate readings. It should also be noted that the operator of these devices should move very slowly throughout the AC system in order to not overlook very small leaks.

Another key strategy for using electronic leak detectors is to check each connection and component that was opened or worked with after each repair is made. This is an example of checking the quality of each repair that is performed. This is an important concept to remember because the AC system is always under pressure and the repair techniques need to be finished with high levels of accuracy and expertise.

Performance Testing

An excellent way to determine if the AC system is operating correctly is to conduct a performance test. This provides useful data that can be used to diagnose problems in the system. This section provides detailed instructions on how to perform the test and what expected outcomes should be.

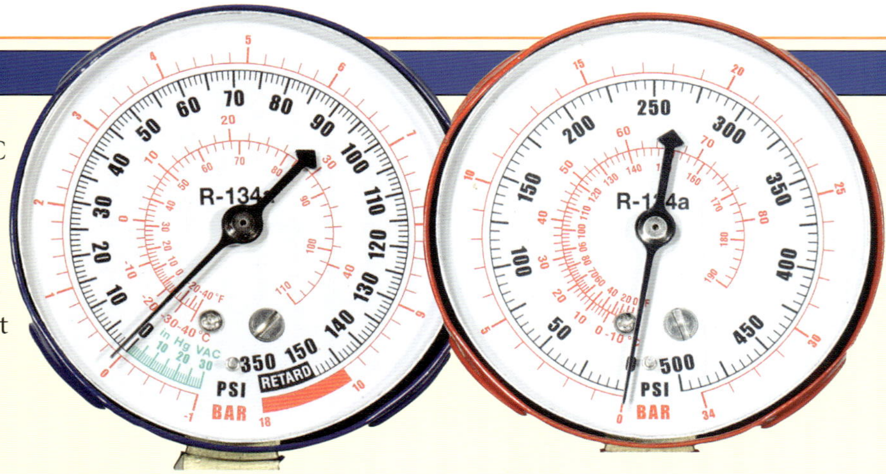

The blue gauge is used to measure the pressure on the low side of the AC system. This gauge has a range from a vacuum up to about 140 psi.

The red gauge is used to measure the pressure on the high side of the AC system. This gauge has a range from 0 to 500 psi.

Setting Up for Performance Testing

1. Connect a manifold set to the service ports of the AC system. The valves at the end of the service hoses should be turned clockwise after connecting them in order to open the check valves on the service ports.
2. Turn the blue knob and red knob on the manifold set clockwise to close off these valves so the pressure can be read accurately. The pressure that is present at this point before the AC system is turned on is known as static pressure.
3. Install a thermometer into the center duct of the vent.
4. Start the vehicle and allow the engine to rise to normal operating temperature.
5. Set the HVAC controls to the coldest setting with the blower on the highest setting. Set the control to recirculated air and the location at the vent.

The red manifold service hose and fitting is connected to the high side service port of the AC system. The round valve needs to be turned clockwise to push the Schrader valve down, which allows refrigerant to pass into the red hose and the high side gauge.

The blue manifold service hose and fitting is connected to the low side service port of the AC system. These fittings use a quick-connect coupling that is similar to an air coupling used on air-powered tools. The round valve needs to be turned clockwise to push the Schrader valve, which allows refrigerant to pass into the blue hose and low side gauge.

The blue valve at the manifold set should be turned clockwise to block any refrigerant from entering the low side connection when the pressures are being observed.

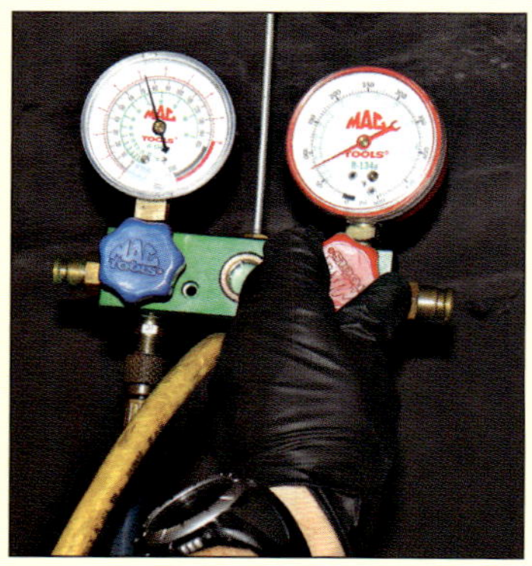

The red valve at the manifold set should be turned clockwise to keep any refrigerant from entering the high side connection when the pressures are being observed.

6 Increase the engine to about 1,200 rpm for a couple of minutes.

7 Inspect the system pressures on the low side as well as on the high side.

8 Inspect the duct air temperature near the end of the test period.

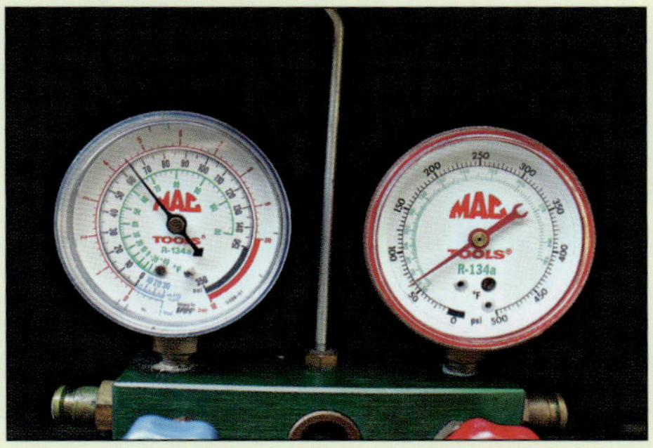

Static pressures should be equal and very close to the same as the ambient temperature since pressure will rise and fall as the temperature changes because of the pressure/temperature relationship of refrigerant.

The engine should be brought to normal operating temperature prior to running a performance test on the AC system.

The engine speed needs to be brought to about 1,200 rpm during the test in order to attain maximum performance and temperatures.

A reliable thermometer needs to be installed into the center duct to measure the duct temperature during the performance test. The ambient air temperature was approximately 80°F on the day of this performance test.

The HVAC controls need to be set on coldest setting with the recirculated air coming out at the vent location. The blower motor needs to be set on high speed.

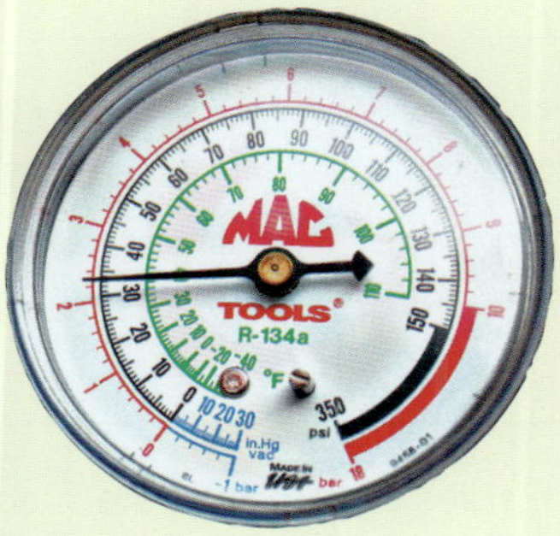

The low side pressure should be checked during the performance test. Keep in mind that the pressure should be noted just before the compressor cycles off when doing this test on a cycling system.

The high side system pressure should be checked during the performance test. Keep in mind that the pressure should be noted just before the compressor cycles off when doing this test on a cycling system.

Performance Testing

Expected Results

1. The duct temperature should be 40 to 50°F.

2. The low side refrigerant pressure should be in the 20 to 40 psi range.

3. The high side refrigerant pressure should be two to three times the ambient temperature, depending on the humidity level. With low to moderate humidity, the high side pressure will be around twice the ambient temperature. With higher humidity levels, the high side pressure will be up to three times the ambient temperature.

4. The suction line will be cold and have water droplets dripping from it.

The duct temperature at the center duct location should be checked to see if the expected temperature was achieved during the test.

See the following chart for diagnostic hints.

Diagnosing Performance Testing

Condition	Potential Causes
Low pressures on both sides of the AC system and a short cycling compressor and poor cooling at the ducts	• Metering device restriction • Low refrigerant charge
Mildly elevated pressures on the low side of AC system and extremely elevated pressures on the high side of the AC system and poor cooling at the ducts	• Airflow problem at the condenser • Refrigerant overcharge
Low pressures in both sides of the AC system found with a cool spot at a location in the high side of the system and poor cooling at the ducts	• Restriction at the point of the cool spot
Elevated low side pressure and reduced high side pressure and poor cooling at the ducts	• Faulty compressor
Mildly elevated pressures on both sides of the AC system and reduced performance of the system during very hot conditions	• Excessive air in the refrigerant system
Normal pressures and duct temperatures for the first few minutes of operation followed by reduced airflow at the ducts and the low side components freezing up	• Variable-displacement compressor stuck at high output • Deicing system malfunction
Low pressures on both sides of the AC system and poor cooling at the ducts	• Variable-displacement compressor stuck at low output

Heat Load Testing

Performing a heat load test on an AC system is an effective method of measuring the system's performance. It is important to remember that this test in only valid when the ambient temperature is above 75°F. Performing the test at cooler temperatures will produce faulty results.

Setup for the Heat Load Test

1. Start the vehicle and let the engine reach normal operating temperature.
2. Turn the AC to maximum and the blower to high speed.
3. Open the doors and windows on the vehicle and let it be exposed to the sunlight if possible.

The engine temperature needs to be raised to normal operating range to prepare for running the heat load test.

The HVAC controls need to be set to the coldest setting with the blower speed set to the highest setting during the heat load test.

The heat load test is the most accurate when the vehicle is exposed to sunlight and the windows and doors are open on the vehicle.

The temperature of the line entering the condenser needs to be checked with some type of temperature-sensing device.

The temperature of the line exiting the condenser needs to be measured. The temperature needs to be measured at approximately the same distance away from the condenser as the previous step.

Heat Load Testing *(Continued)*

4 Let the engine run at idle speed.

5 Measure the inlet line and the exit line at the condenser.

6 Measure the ambient temperature as well as the duct temperature.

The ambient temperature needs to be measured and documented. This test is only valid with ambient temperatures above 75°F.

Expected Results

1 The duct temperature should be at least 30 degrees cooler than the ambient temperature.

2 The condenser outlet temperature should be between 20 and 50 degrees cooler than the inlet temperature.

The duct temperature at the center duct needs to be measured and documented during the heat load test. The temperature at the center duct will usually not be as cold as it is during a performance test because this test is done at idle and with the doors open.

See the following charts for diagnostic hints.

Diagnosing Heat Load Testing

Test Results	Potential Causes
Temperature drop across condenser between 20 and 50°F	Normal
Temperature drop across condenser less than 20°F	• Bent condenser fins • Debris blocking condenser • Fan problem • Fan shroud problem
Temperature drop across condenser more than 50°F	• Internal restriction in condenser • Low refrigerant charge • Refrigerant contaminated
Temperature drop of ambient to duct temperature more than 30°F	Normal
Temperature drop of ambient to duct less than 30°F	• Blend door not working properly • Heater valve not closing off properly • Recirculated air door not working properly • Low refrigerant charge

Recovery, Evacuation, and Recharging the AC System

As stated in previous chapters, the refrigerant in the AC system is under constant pressure and it is illegal to intentionally perform an action that causes the refrigerant to be vented into the atmosphere.

Refrigerant Identifiers

Due to the fact that there are many cars and trucks operating in this country with AC systems that have had impure refrigerants installed, it is advisable to test each system with a refrigerant identifier prior to connecting your equipment to them. Refrigerant identifiers take a sample of the refrigerant and test for purity of the substance.

Most identifiers on the market will give a percentage of the following substances: R134a, R12, R22, and air. These identifiers will also test for flammable substances and will alert the operator if the system does have a flammable substance.

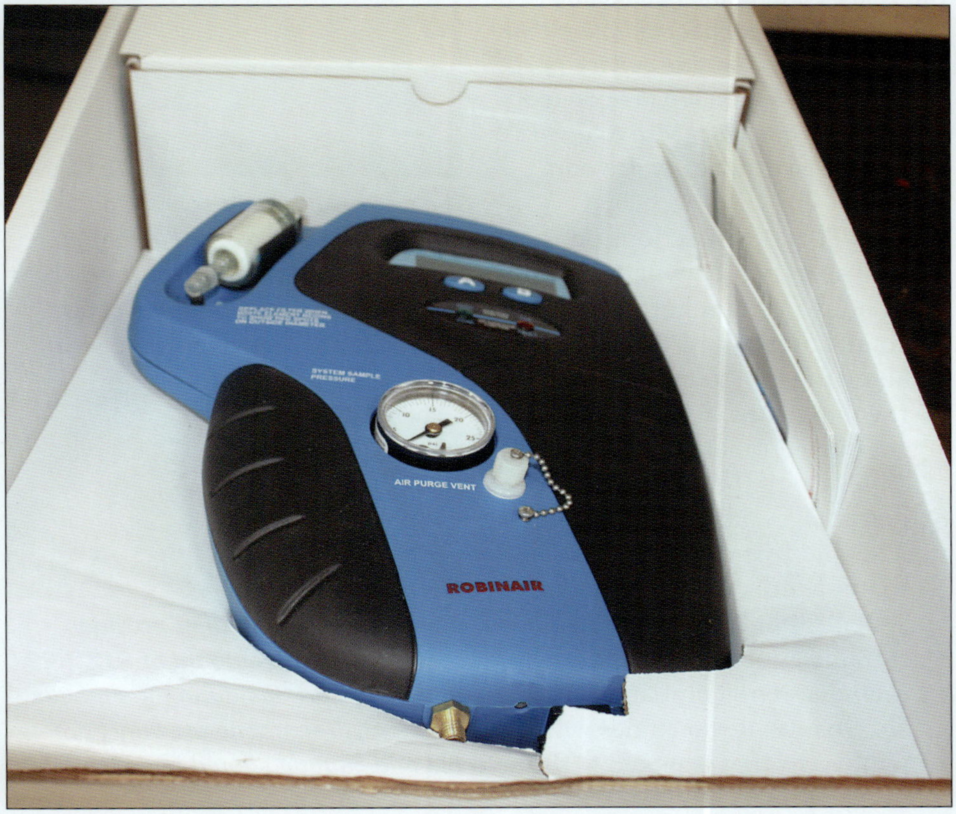

It is important to use a refrigerant identifier prior to connecting expensive AC equipment to a vehicle's refrigerant system.

Testing the Purity of the Refrigerant

Below are the steps for using the refrigerant identifier.

1 Connect the identifier to a power source and let the unit warm up. Some identifiers power up from the vehicle battery and some power up from a 110-volt power cord.

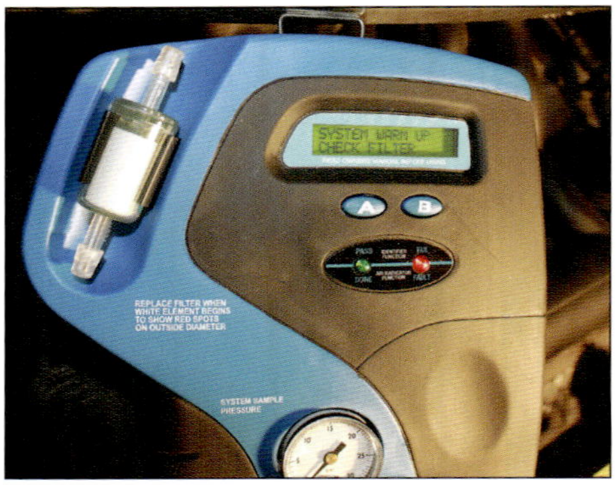

The refrigerant identifier is a very precise electronic tool that needs to go through a warm-up cycle when it is turned on. The user should wait for this process to finish before connecting it to the vehicle.

2 Connect the AC hose to the identifier. Be gentle with this hose because it is typically made from a lightweight plastic.

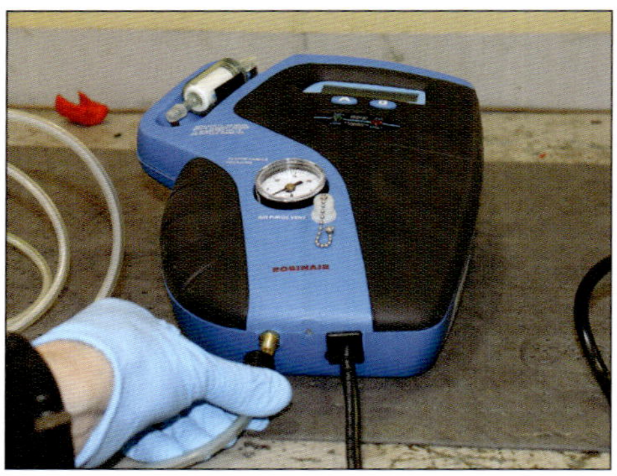

The plastic hose that is used to connect the identifier to the vehicle AC system screws on at the bottom of the tool to a threaded connection. This hose should be handled with care because it is lightweight and fairly fragile.

3 After the identifier warms up, it will direct you to connect it to the vehicle's AC system at the service port. Be sure to turn the valve clockwise to depress the check valve, which will allow refrigerant to pass into the connection.

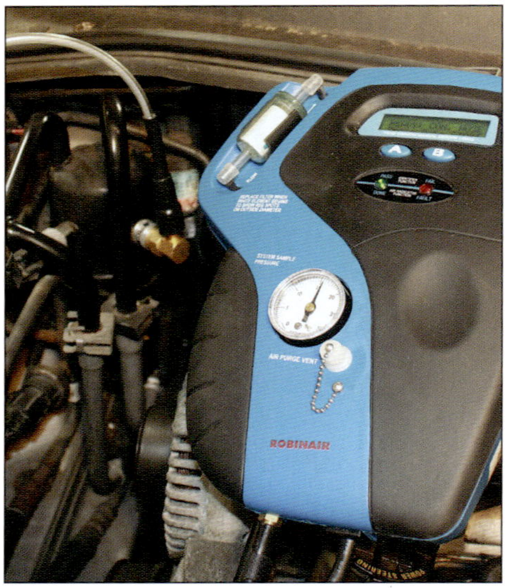

The vehicle end of the connecting hose is a quick-connect coupling that connects to the low side service port. Some identifiers require the connection to be turned clockwise to open the check valve in the service port.

4 Follow the directions on the display, which will direct you to press a certain button for a couple of seconds. This will allow the tool to take a sample of the refrigerant.

5 The identifier will display the results of the test with the percentages of R134a, air, R12, R22, and hydrocarbons. It is vital to not connect AC equipment to systems that have any mixed substances other than the intended refrigerant and some air. Quality AC machines will remove air that is mixed with the refrigerant.

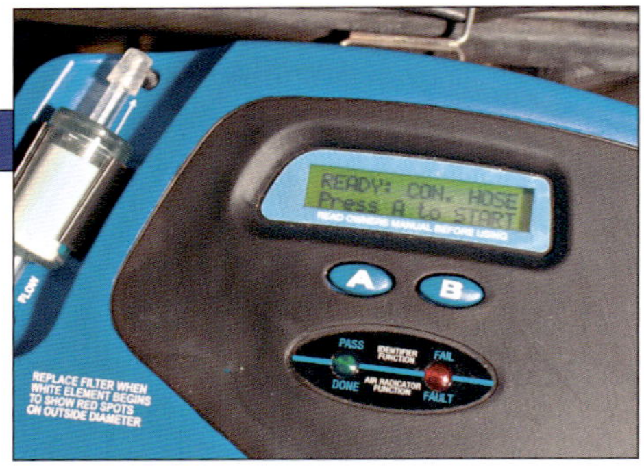

The refrigerant identifier will let the operator know when to begin the test with instructions on the display.

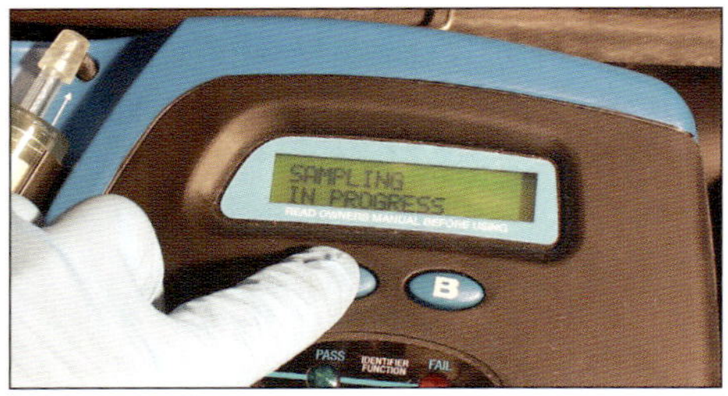

To begin the sampling process, the A button needs to be pressed for a couple of seconds. After pressing the button, the operator waits for the process to finish to see the results.

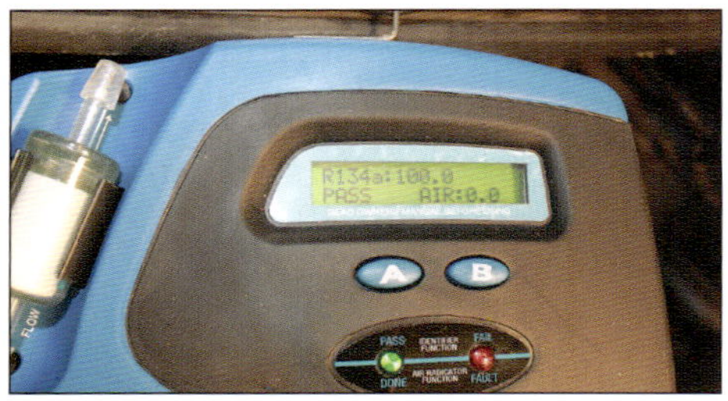

The test results are displayed on the screen and with colored lights. This vehicle passed because the green light is illuminated and the screen shows 100 percent R134a and 0 percent air.

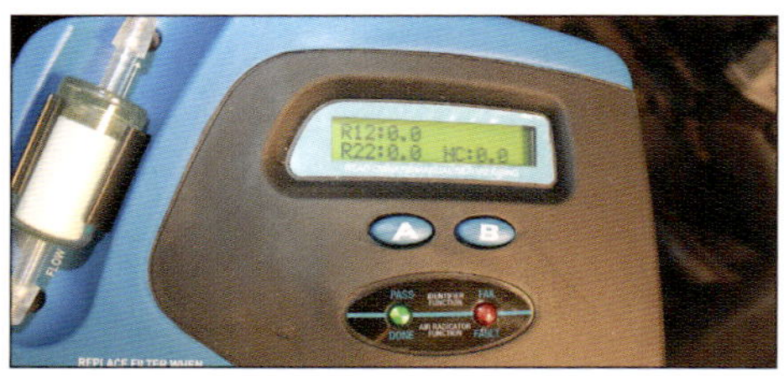

The refrigerant identifier provides feedback on the amount of R12, R22, and hydrocarbons during the results stage. Hydrocarbons are very flammable and caution should be followed if the identifier detects them.

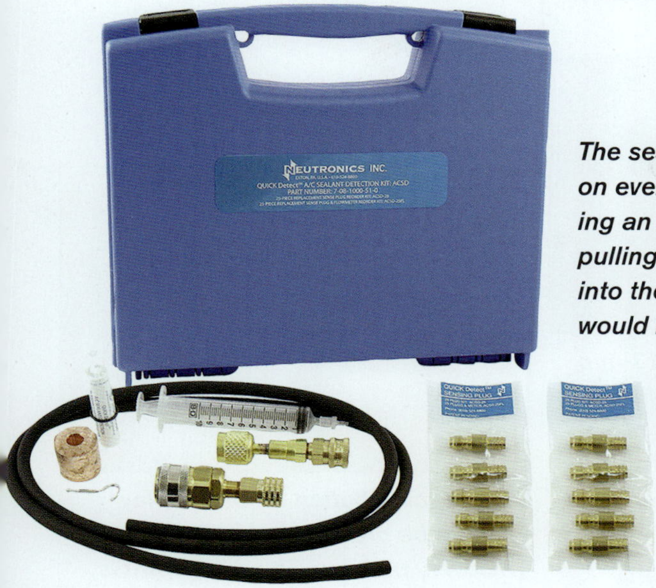

The sealer test kit should be used on every vehicle prior to connecting an AC machine to prevent pulling the stop-leak substance into the machine. The AC machine would become stopped up if the stop-leak substance was pulled in. (Photo Courtesy Neutronics)

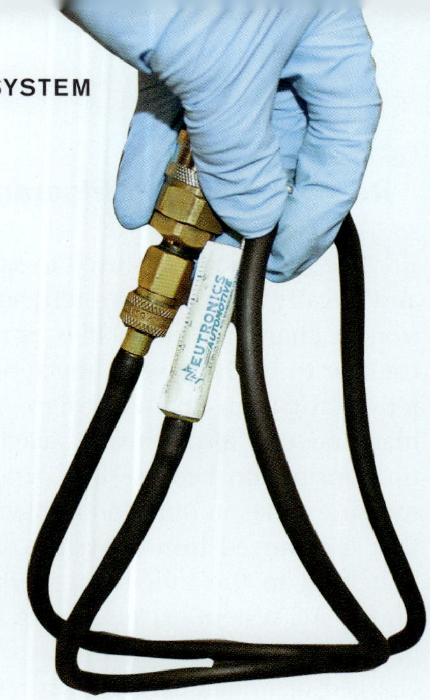

The quick-connect coupling, test plug, hose, and flow gauge are assembled prior to connecting the apparatus to the vehicle.

Sealer Test Kits

Another very common additive that many over-the-counter cans of refrigerant contain is a stop-leak substance. This sealer will cause the internal parts of an AC recovery/recharging machine to become stopped up. It highly recommended to test each vehicle to see if it has refrigerant that contains the sealer before connecting AC equipment. Neutronics makes a reliable test kit that is recommended to be used to test for sealer. Below are the steps to follow when using this kit.

Testing for Sealer

1. Run the vehicle with the AC turned on for more than 2 minutes. Turn off the vehicle and wait 3 minutes before connecting the test fixture to the vehicle.
2. Add a couple drops of water to a test plug.
3. Assemble the hose, test plug, and quick-connect fitting.
4. Connect the quick-connect coupling to the high side service port.
5. Monitor the flow rate on the tool and note the level of the floating ball after about 20 seconds.
6. Wait 2 minutes and monitor the flow rate on the tool.
7. If the rate does not drop, then the refrigerant does not have sealer. If the rate does drop, then the refrigerant is tainted with sealer and an AC machine should not be connected to the system unless it has a special filter that safely removes the sealer.

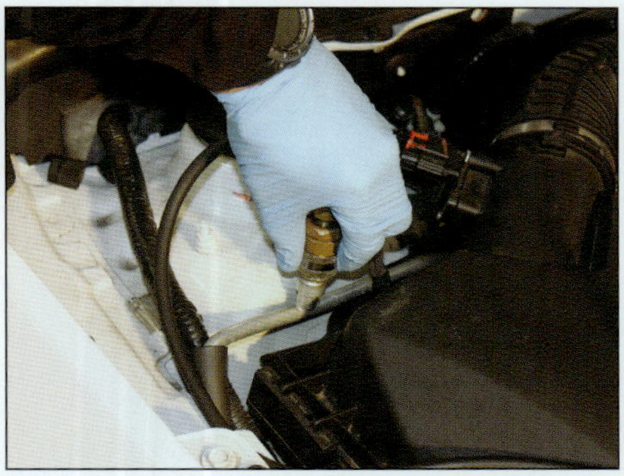

The quick-connect coupling snaps onto the high side service port in the same way as the service hoses do. This process is tedious because the test plug is near the quick connect and could easily snap out while connecting to the vehicle.

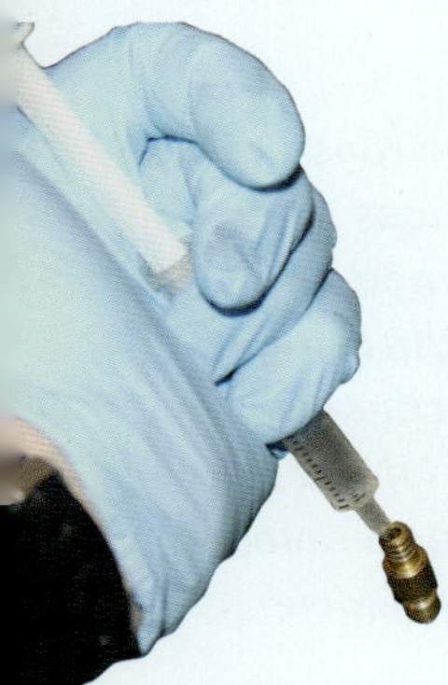

A drop of water should be added to both sides of the small test plug prior to connecting it to the rest of the tester. The water will cause the stop-leak substance to become a solid during the sealer test procedure.

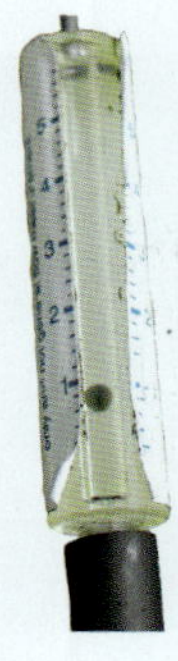

The flow for this test is simply measured with a small ball in a plastic cylinder. The ball moves vertically when the refrigerant is passing through the test plug and up the rubber hose.

The flow of refrigerant is checked after 2 minutes to see if the flow rate has dropped. A drop in flow would indicate that sealer is present in the AC system. The drop in flow would be caused by the sealer mixing with the water that was added in the test plug.

Recovering the Refrigerant

The AC machine is used to safely and legally remove the refrigerant from a charged system. It is against the law to willfully vent any type of refrigerant from an AC system. This machine can also provide diagnostic information because it accurately measures the amount of refrigerant that is removed from a system. This is helpful to the individual working on the AC system because it lets him or her know if the system was overcharged or undercharged with refrigerant. The following are the steps for recovering the refrigerant.

Steps to Recover Refrigerant

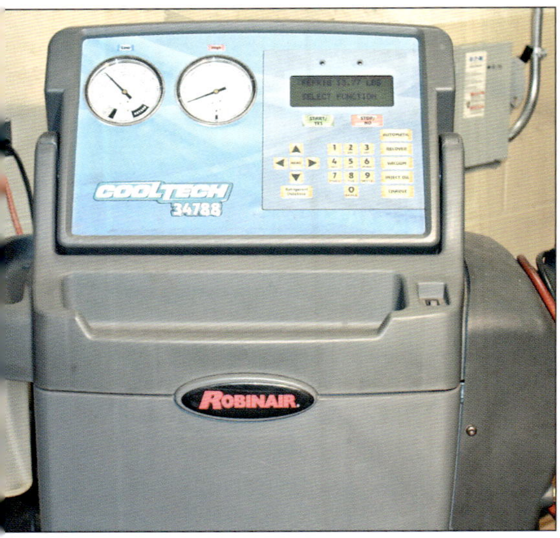

A typical AC machine is critical to have when safely and legally repairing the AC system on cars and trucks. This tool recovers, filters, evacuates, charges, adds oil, and leak tests the AC system.

1 Connect the blue service hose to the low side service port and turn the blue knob clockwise to depress the check valve to allow refrigerant to flow.

The low side service port is a 13-mm quick-connect coupling. The blue hose on the AC machine snaps into place like a pneumatic connection. The knob is then turned clockwise to open the check valve in the service port.

2 Connect the red service hose to the high service port and turn the red knob clockwise to depress the check valve to allow refrigerant to flow.

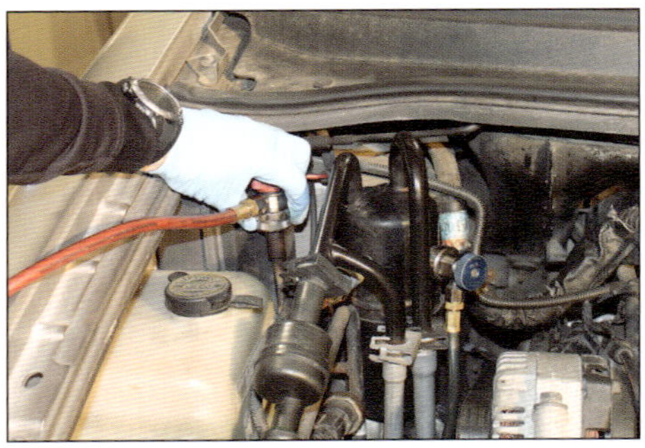

The high side service port is a 16-mm quick-connect coupling. The red hose on the AC machine also snaps into place like a pneumatic connection. The knob is then turned clockwise to open the check valve in the service port.

3 Turn the power button on and let the machine warm up.

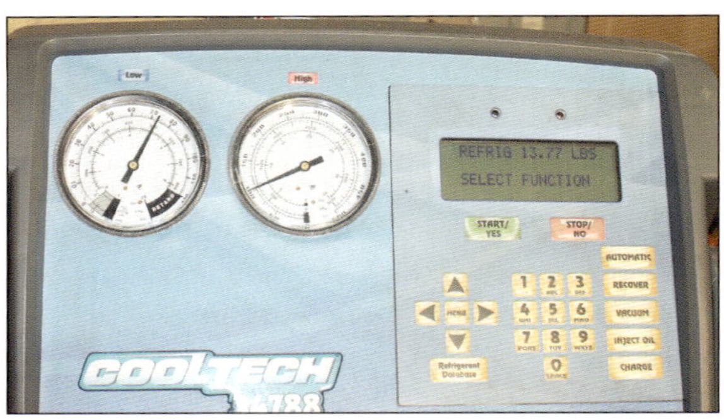

The AC machine runs through a warm-up process when the power is turned on. The display shows the refrigerant amount that is contained in the machine to let the operator know the level before connecting to a vehicle.

4 Start the recovery process by pressing the recover button.

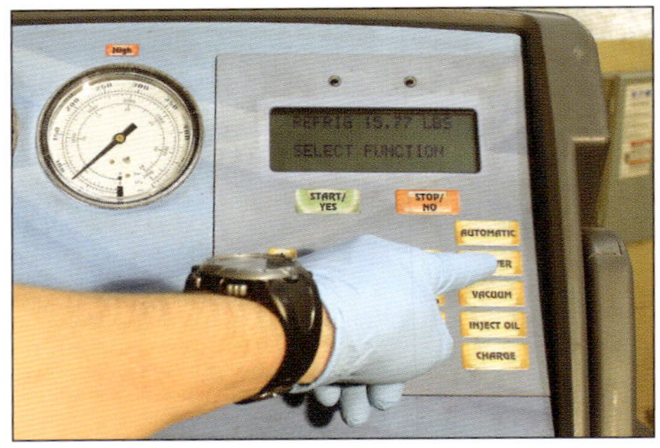

The recover button on the display should be pressed to begin the recovery process. The refrigerant is removed, filtered, and weighed during the recovery process.

5 After the machine goes through a clearing process, it begins to remove the refrigerant from the AC system, and it will show how much refrigerant is being removed from the system.

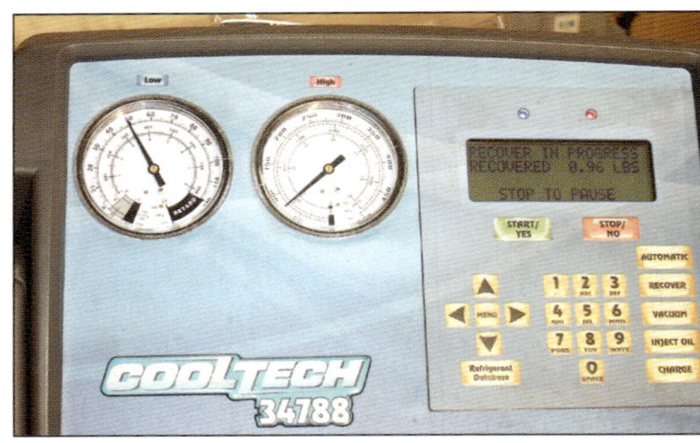

The recovery process removes, filters, and weighs the refrigerant from the vehicle. The display shows a constant readout of the amount of refrigerant that is being removed.

The pressure gauges will begin to drop as the refrigerant is being drawn from the vehicle.

6 The machine will continue the recovery process until the pressure drops into a vacuum and then the display will say "complete" and it will show how much refrigerant has been removed.

The machine will display that the recovery process is complete as well as the total amount of refrigerant that was removed from the vehicle. The machine will also remind the operator to check the oil bottle to determine how much refrigerant oil was removed during the process. Typically, very little oil is pulled out during the recovery process.

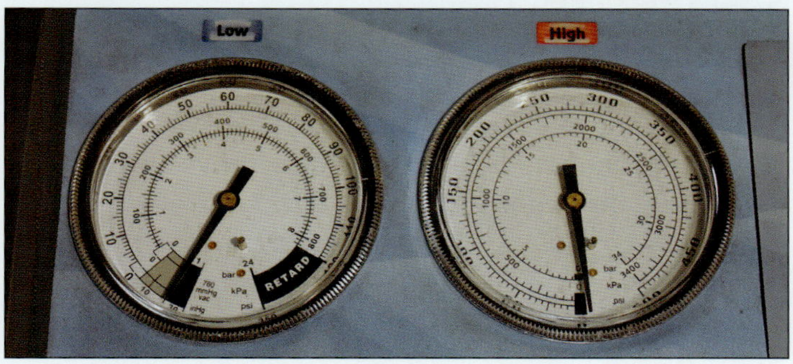

7 The display will check the oil bottle to see if any refrigerant oil was removed during the process. Very little oil is removed during this process on most vehicles. Any measurable oil that is removed during recovery needs to be added back to the system before completing the repair.

The oil bottle shows that very little refrigerant oil was removed during the recovery process. This bottle should be checked after each system is recovered to monitor the amount of oil that was removed during recovery.

8 The power can be turned off and the service hoses can be removed while making repairs to the AC system. Many of the most common repairs that can be made to the AC system will be covered in chapter 6.

The low side gauge will read in the vacuum range and the high side gauge will read 0 after the AC system has been recovered.

Evacuating the System

The AC recovery/recharging machine has a built-in electric vacuum pump that pulls an excellent vacuum on the system without having to connect external hoses or manifolds. Pulling a vacuum on the AC system prior to recharging it with refrigerant is necessary to remove all of the moisture from the system.

The boiling point of water is lowered to 70 or 80°F when a good vacuum is applied to an AC system. If any moisture is left in the AC system, it can mix with the refrigerant and acid will form and cause damage in the system. Below are the steps for vacuuming the system with the AC machine.

Each AC system that has been opened for repair or that has had a leak should be vacuumed for at least 30 minutes to remove all of the air and moisture from the system.

Evacuating the AC System with Robinair AC Machine

1 Connect the blue service hose of the machine to the low side service port and turn the blue knob clockwise to depress the check valve.

2 Connect the red service hose of the machine to the high side service port and turn the red knob clockwise to depress the check valve.

3 Turn the power button on and let the machine warm up.

4 Start the vacuum process by pressing the vacuum button.

5 Program the length of time for the vacuum process to last. The system should be vacuumed for at least 30 minutes to ensure a quality repair.

6 Hit start to allow the machine to begin the process. The low side gauge should immediately start to drop into the vacuum range.

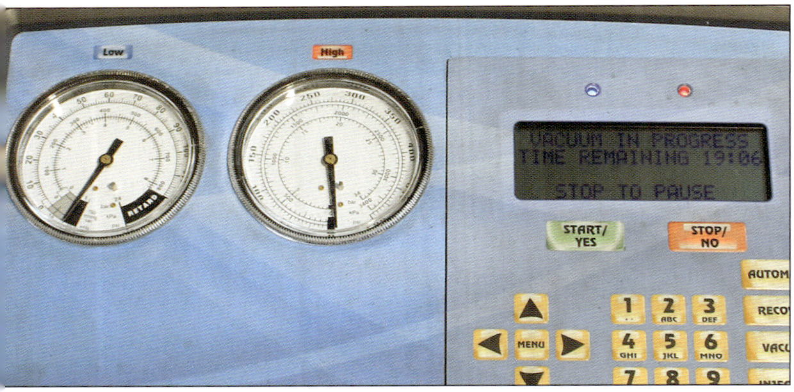

Once the vacuum process begins, the low side gauge is pulled into the vacuum range and the high side gauge is pulled to the lowest setting. The display shows how much time remains in the vacuum process.

7 The machine will continue pulling a vacuum on the system until the timer stops the process.

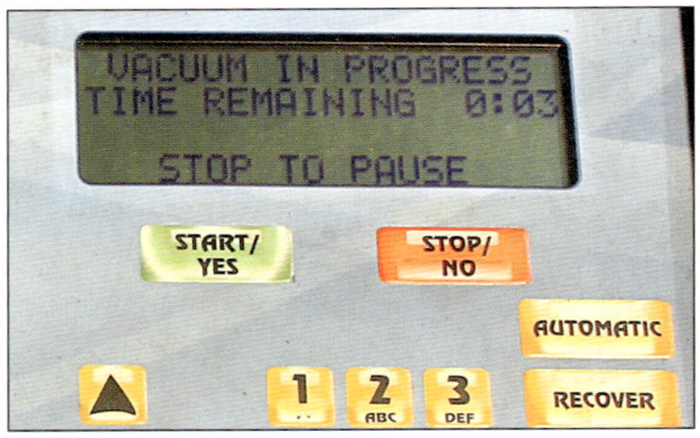

The timer on the machine continuously displays the amount of time remaining in the recovery process.

8 The machine will hold the system in the vacuumed state to test the system for leaks. If the vacuum leaks off during the leak test period, then the display will give a notification that there is a leak. After the leak test has timed out, the system can be recharged with the correct amount of refrigerant.

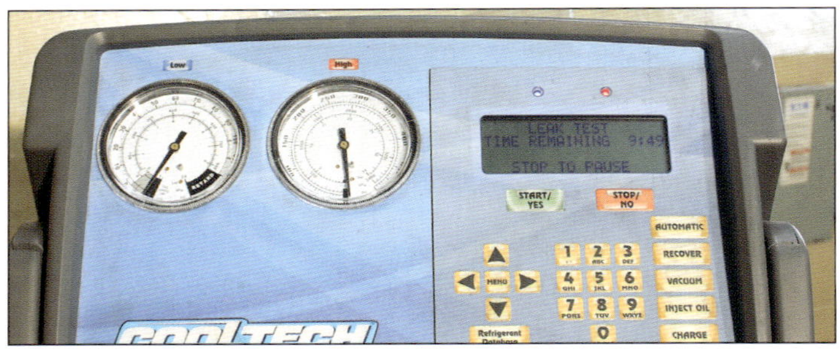

The AC machine can run a leak test after the vacuum pump shuts off by monitoring the vacuum level for several minutes. If the vacuum drops off, the machine will alert the operator that a system leak is present, which should be located and repaired prior to adding the refrigerant to the system.

External Electric Vacuum Pump

Using a high-quality electric vacuum pump along with a manifold set is another good method for evacuating the AC system. This method of pulling a vacuum on an AC system requires a little bit more technical skill than using the recovery/recharging machine because it is important to have all of the valves in the correct position while the process is going on as well as when it is time to stop the vacuum process. Follow these steps to vacuum a system with an electric vacuum pump.

A quality electric vacuum pump is needed to pull a good vacuum on the AC system each time it has been opened for service or each time that the refrigerant has leaked out. Pulling a vacuum on the AC system removes air and moisture prior to adding the refrigerant back into the system.

Evacuating the AC System with an Electric Vacuum Pump

1 Connect the blue hose of the manifold set to the low side service port and turn the blue knob clockwise to depress the check valve.

The blue hose on the manifold set is for connecting to the low side service port. The low side service port is a 13-mm quick-connect coupling.

2 Connect the red hose of the manifold set to the high side service port and turn the red knob clockwise to depress the check valve.

The red hose on the manifold set is for connecting to the high side service port. The high side service port is a 16-mm quick-connect coupling.

3 Connect the yellow hose of the manifold set to the port on the vacuum pump by threading the connection in a clockwise rotation.

The yellow hose from the manifold set connects to the electric vacuum pump threaded connector. This connection should be tightened to a snug level using a firm grip.

4 Open the valves at the manifold by turning the blue and red knobs counterclockwise. This lets the blue and red hoses be open to the yellow hose that is connected to the vacuum pump.

The blue valve on the manifold set should be turned counterclockwise, which opens the valve to allow the yellow hose to pull a vacuum through the blue hose.

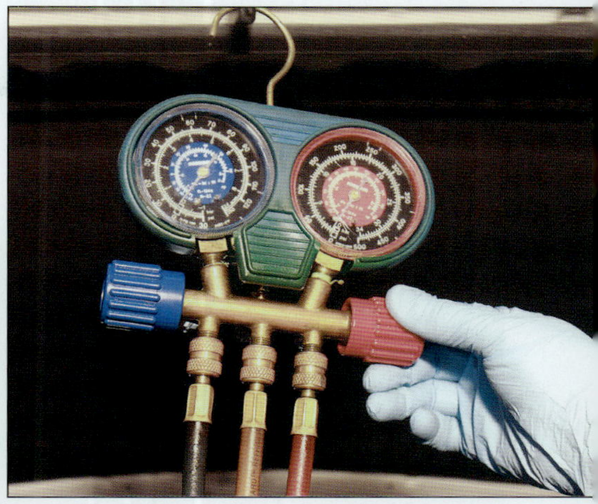

The red valve on the manifold set should be turned counterclockwise, which opens the valve to allow the yellow hose to pull a vacuum through the red hose.

5 Turn the vacuum pump on and make sure the check valve is set to open to allow the pump to pull a vacuum on the service port.

6 Watch the gauges on the manifold set drop. The red gauge will drop down to 0 psi and the blue gauge will drop to below 0 psi, which will be in the vacuum part of the gauge that is in inches of mercury. The blue gauge should reach 20 inches of mercury within 10 minutes of operation.

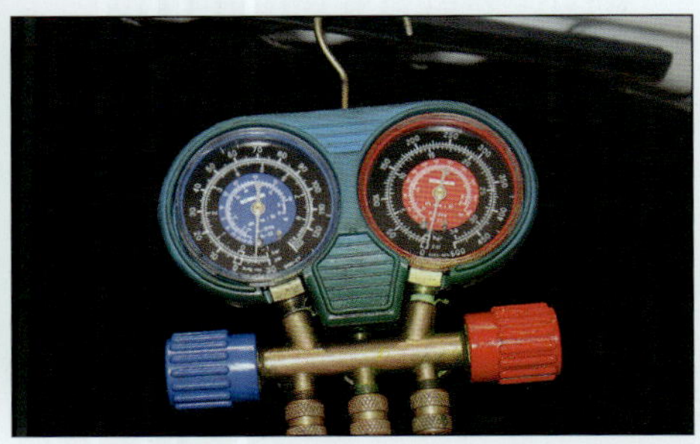

The low side gauge should drop into the vacuum portion of the scale within few a minutes of running the vacuum pump.

7 This process should pull the low side gauge to 29 inches of mercury, which will remove any moisture from the AC system. The vacuum time should be at least 30 minutes if the system has been open to the atmosphere.

The low side gauge should read a deep vacuum and the high side gauge should be pulled to the lowest setting after the vacuum pump has run for at least 30 minutes.

8 To stop the vacuum process, turn the blue and the red knobs on the manifold set clockwise to block the vacuum process. The vacuum pump can now be turned off and the yellow hose can be removed. The vacuum should stay constant on the blue gauge, which shows that the system does not have any leaks. The system is now ready to be charged with refrigerant.

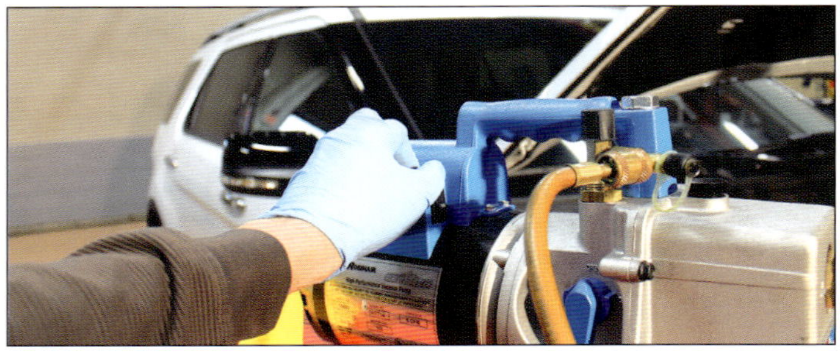

The manifold valves should be turned clockwise, which closes the valve and traps the vacuum in the AC system. The vacuum can be turned off and the yellow hose can be removed from the vacuum pump.

External Pneumatic Vacuum Pump

A pneumatic vacuum pump is a very economical choice for pulling a vacuum on an AC system. This type of pump uses shop air pressure to create a vacuum device that is connected to the yellow hose on the manifold set. These tools require at least 75 psi of air pressure to operate effectively. Follow these steps to use this tool.

A pneumatic vacuum pump is a low-cost method of pulling a vacuum on the AC system. This tool uses compressed air to spin a pumping device that creates enough vacuum to be used on an AC system.

Evacuating the AC System with a Pneumatic Pump

1 Connect the blue hose of the manifold set to the low side service port and turn the blue knob clockwise to depress the check valve.

2 Connect the red hose of the manifold set to the high side service port and turn the red knob clockwise to depress the check valve.

3 Connect the yellow hose of the manifold set to the port on the vacuum pump by threading the connection in a clockwise rotation.

The yellow hose from the manifold set connects to the pneumatic vacuum pump threaded connector. This connection should be tightened to a snug level using a firm grip.

4 Open the valves at the manifold by turning the blue and red knobs counterclockwise. This lets the blue and red hoses be open to the yellow hose, which is connected to the vacuum pump.

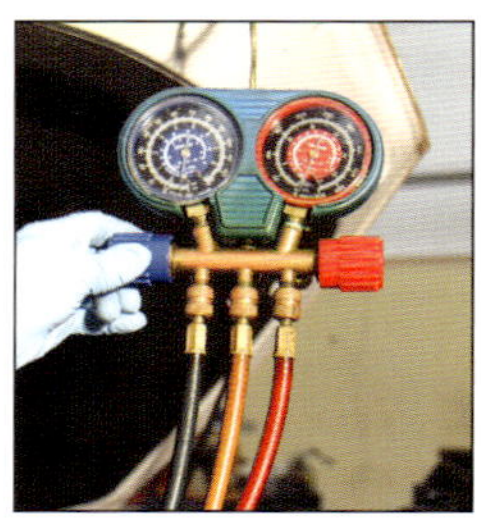

The blue knob on the manifold set must be opened to allow the low side of the AC system to be pulled into a vacuum with the electric vacuum pump.

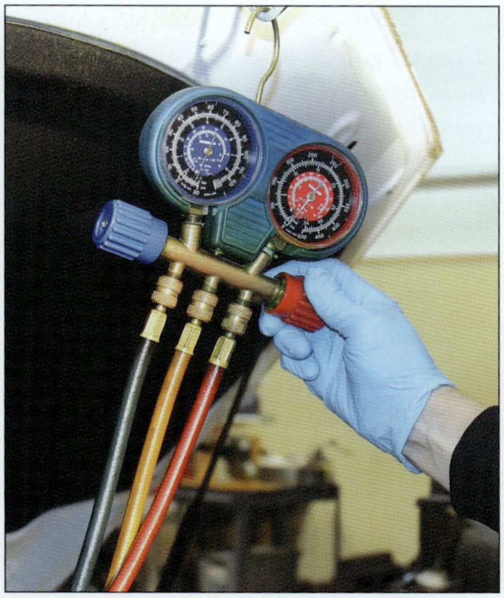

The red knob on the manifold set must be opened to allow the high side of the AC system to be pulled into a vacuum with the electric vacuum pump.

5 Connect an air hose from a good shop air source to the pneumatic vacuum pump and turn on the air supply to start the vacuum operation. Make sure the check valve is open on the vacuum pump.

The pneumatic vacuum pump must be connected to a compressed air source to power the device. When the air hose is connected to the pneumatic pump, an audible sound will begin that indicates that the pump is operating.

6 Watch the gauges on the manifold set drop. The red gauge will drop down to 0 psi and the blue gauge will drop to below 0 psi, which will be in the vacuum part of the gauge in inches of mercury. The blue gauge should reach 20 inches of mercury within 10 minutes of operation.

7 This process should pull the low side gauge to 29 inches of mercury, which will remove any moisture from the AC system. The vacuum time should be at least 30 minutes if the system has been open to the atmosphere.

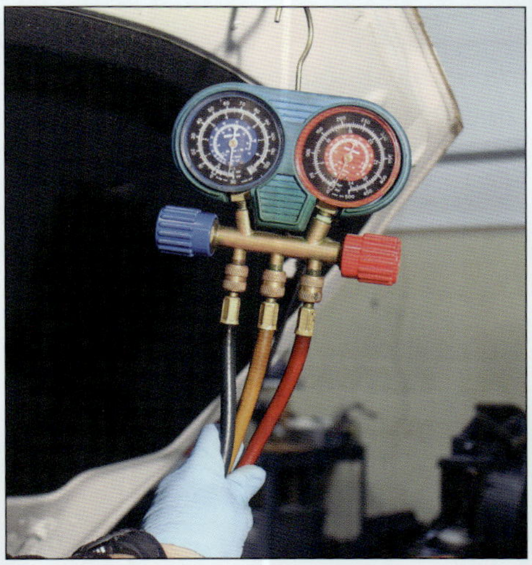

The pneumatic vacuum pump will pull the low side gauge into a tight vacuum and the high side gauge down to zero. Reducing the system pressure to this level removes the air and moisture from the AC system.

8 To stop the vacuum process, turn the blue and red knobs on the manifold set clockwise to block the vacuum process. The vacuum pump can now be turned off and the yellow hose can be removed. The vacuum should stay constant on the blue gauge, which shows that the system does not have any leaks. The system is now ready to be charged with refrigerant.

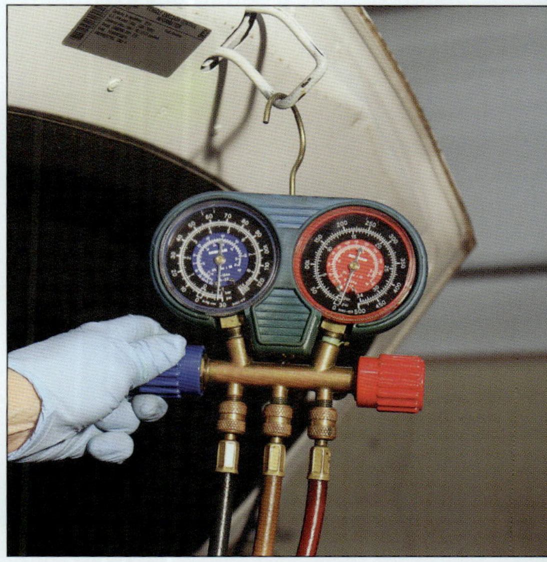

The blue knob on the manifold set must be closed in order to seal the vacuum in the AC system.

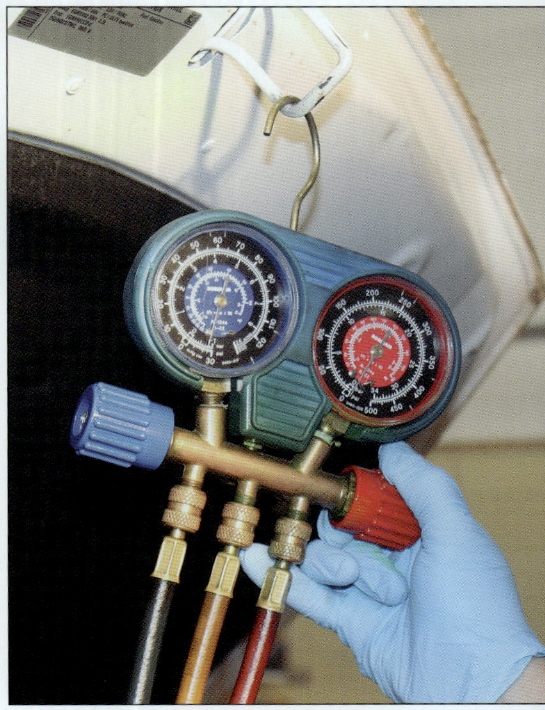

The red knob on the manifold set must be closed in order to seal the vacuum in the AC system.

Charging the AC System

Charging the AC system is a reasonably easy task when using an AC machine. The key to making a quality repair that will provide lasting reliable performance is to pull a long vacuum on the system and then add the exact amount of refrigerant back to the system. The charge amount is usually located on a decal that is under the hood in a conspicuous location. If the decal is missing, then a reliable source of service literature should be used. Once the exact charge amount is known, then the charging process can begin. See the steps to charge the AC system with an AC machine below.

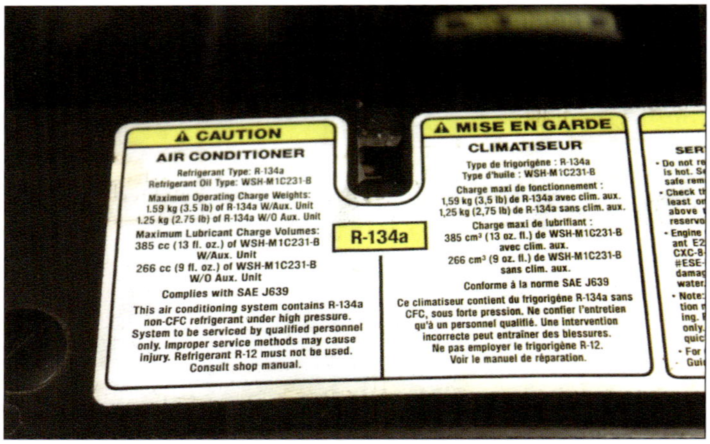

A decal located under the hood will provide details about the refrigerant used, the charge amount, and the lubrication type.

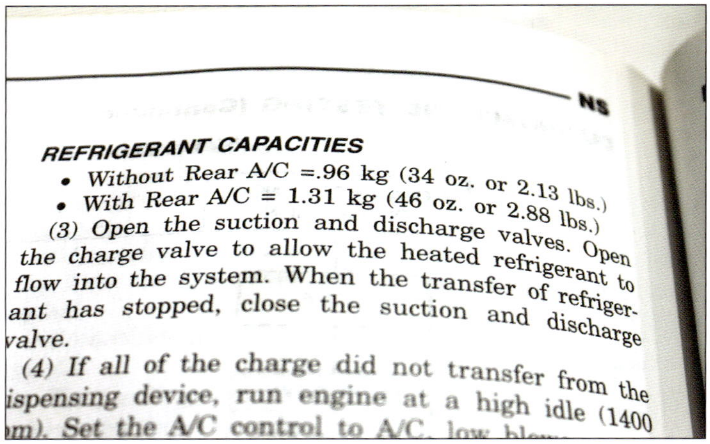

A reliable service manual or electronic database can be used to locate the amount of refrigerant to use when recharging the AC system for your specific application.

Charging the AC System with an Robinair AC Machine

1 See the previous steps on pulling a vacuum with an AC machine. These steps should be followed prior to charging the system with refrigerant.

2 Press the charge button on the control panel.

3 Press the appropriate buttons to program the correct charge amount into the control panel.

4 Press the start button and the machine will add the correct amount of refrigerant to the vehicle and then show "complete" on the display.

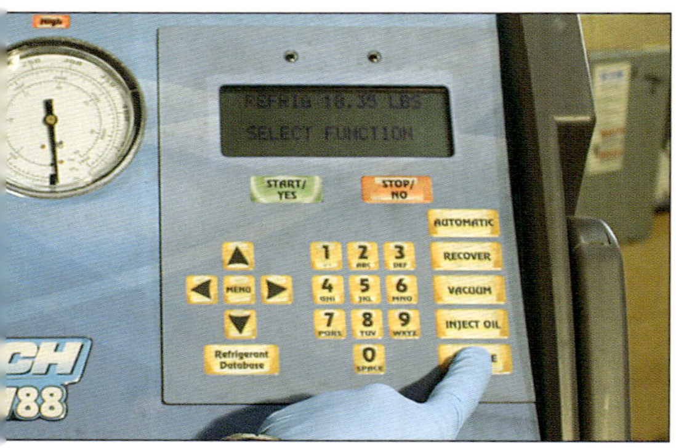

To begin the charge process on the AC machine, the operator presses the charge button on the panel. The display will show "consult database" on the screen, which can be used if the charge amount is not known.

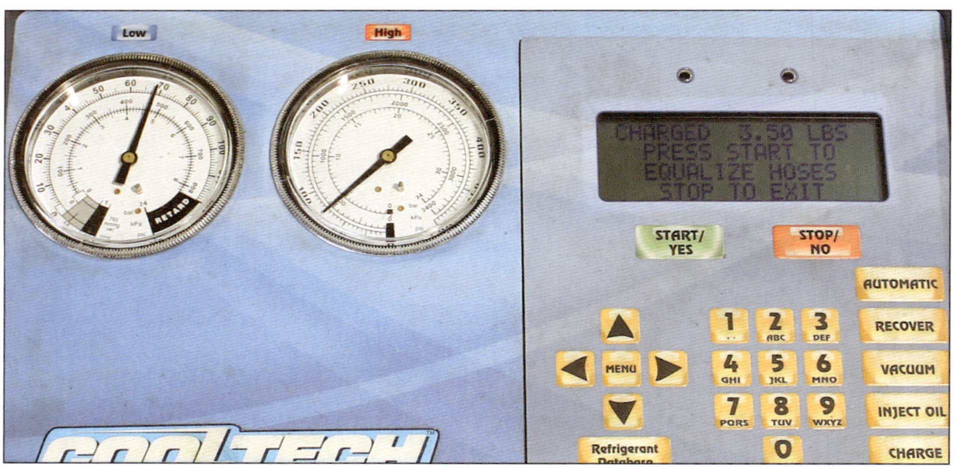

The charge amount is programmed in on the machine using the number keys on the control panel. The AC machine is a very accurate tool that adds the exact amount of refrigerant to the system.

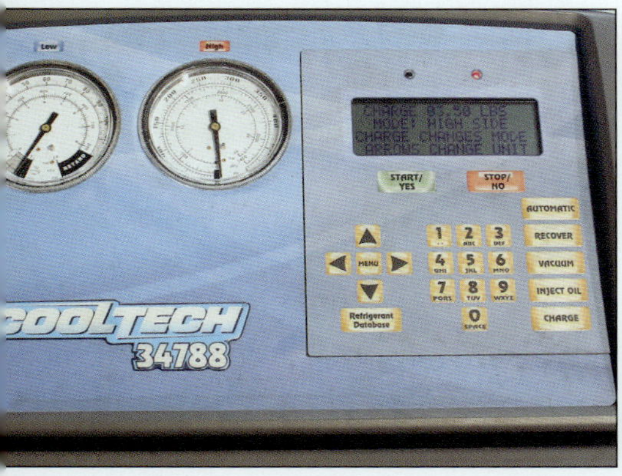

The start/yes button is pressed to begin the charge process, which adds the exact amount that was programmed into the control panel.

5 The machine will display instructions on how to equalize the hoses, which should be followed to get as much of the refrigerant from the hoses and into the vehicle as possible.

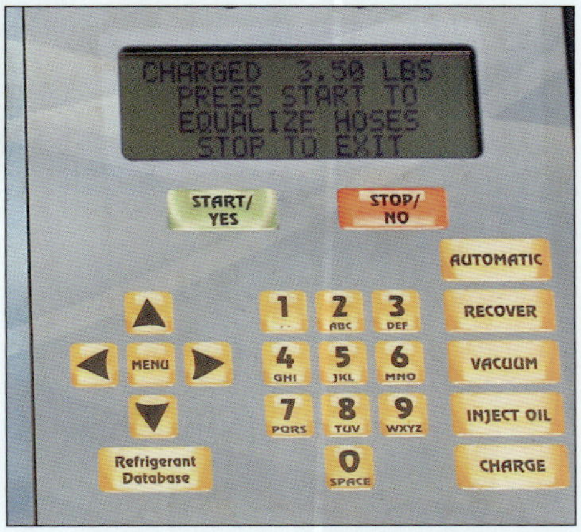

When the correct amount of refrigerant has been added, the display will ask if the hoses need to be equalized. This process should be followed to ensure the most accurate charge process because it removes the small amount of refrigerant from the hoses before disconnecting it from the vehicle.

6 Remove the hoses from the vehicle and put the caps back on the service ports. The AC system can then be turned on and tested.

Charging with Manifold, Scale, and Large Container

Charging the AC system with a large container of refrigerant along with an accurate weight scale and manifold set is a reliable technique. This method of charging the AC system requires more technical knowledge than using the AC machine because of the process of opening and closing valves as well as allowing the vehicle's AC system to operate during the operation. However, a skilled person can charge the AC system with high levels of quality and accuracy if the proper steps are followed. The correct charge amount must be known before beginning the process and can be found on the AC decal or from a reliable database source. Follow these steps to charge the AC system.

Charging the AC System with a Large Container

1 See the previous steps on pulling a vacuum with the electric pump or with the pneumatic pump. These steps must be followed prior to charging the AC system with this method.

2 Place the container of refrigerant on the electric scale.

3 Remove the cap from the container and connect the yellow hose from the manifold set to the port on the container.

4 Open the valve on the container and carefully loosen the yellow hose connection to purge the air from the hose. Quickly tighten the hose connection as soon as any hissing sound is present.

The manual valve on the refrigerant container is opened by turning counterclockwise. The yellow hose should be slightly loosened at the manifold to purge the air from the hose.

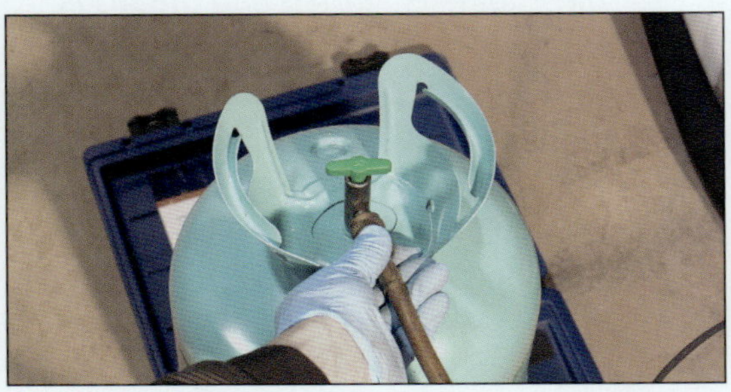

The yellow hose from the manifold set is connected to the threaded fitting on the refrigerant container. This connection should be tightened to a secure torque using a firm grip.

5 Press the power button on the scale and wait for the warm-up process to finish. The scale used in this process moves to a zero setting after warming up and will begin displaying the amount being charged when the valves are opened.

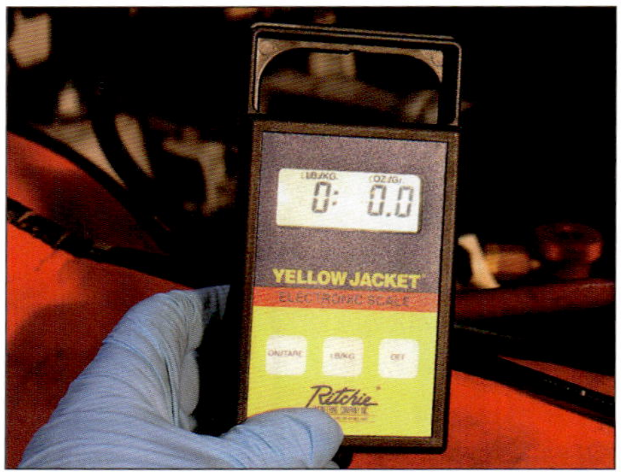

The refrigerant scale is turned on by pressing the on/off button. After warming up, the display shows a 0 amount and will begin displaying the amount that exits the container when the valves are opened. This makes it easy to see how much refrigerant has been added to the AC system.

6 Open the blue and red valves on the manifold to allow the refrigerant to move from the container into the vehicle's AC system. The scale will begin to show the charge amount immediately when this process begins.

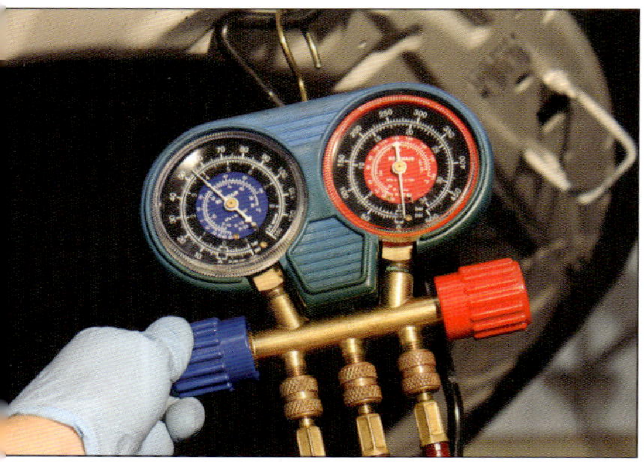

The blue manifold knob needs to be turned counterclockwise to allow the yellow hose to feed refrigerant into the blue hose and the low side of the AC system.

The red manifold knob needs to be turned counter-clockwise to allow the yellow hose to feed refrigerant into the red hose and the high side of the AC system.

7 Once the process slows down, the red valve on the manifold needs to be closed (turned clockwise), the vehicle can be started, and the AC system is turned on.

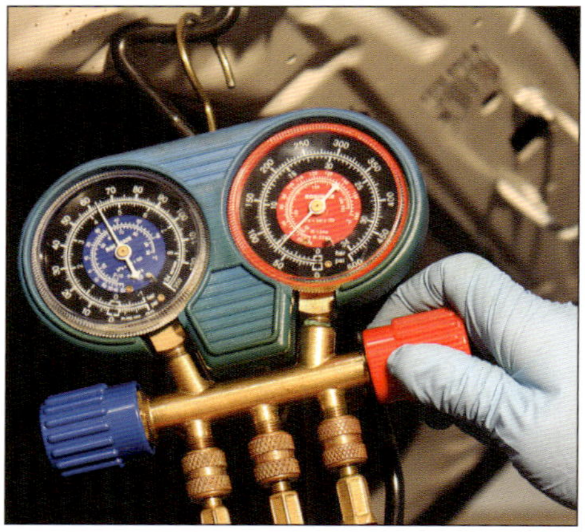

The red manifold valve knob must be closed off to prevent high side system pressure to be directed into the container of refrigerant when the vehicle is started and the AC is turned on.

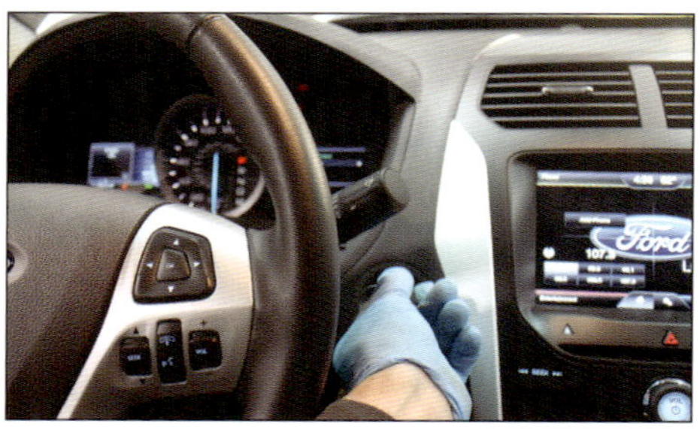

The engine is started and the AC is turned on to assist in the manual charging process by lowering the pressure in the low side of the AC system. This low pressure in the low side of the AC system will cause refrigerant to move from the container to the AC system on the vehicle.

8 The charging process will continue due to the low side pressure being lower than the pressure in the container. Allow this process to continue until the correct amount of refrigerant has been added to the vehicle.

The electronic scale provides a digital readout of the amount of refrigerant that is being added to the vehicle. Using this tool allows an individual to charge an AC system to the exact desired level.

9 Once the correct amount of refrigerant has been added to the vehicle, close the valve on the container and then close the blue valve on the manifold (turn clockwise).

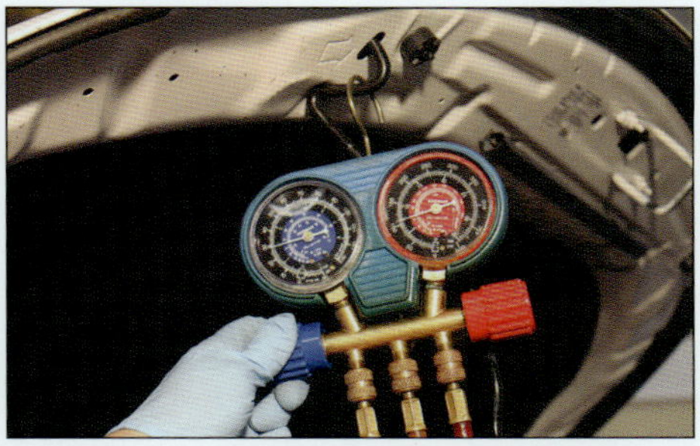

When the vehicle AC system reaches the correct level, the valve on the refrigerant container needs to be closed and the blue manifold valve should be turned clockwise to close off the valve.

10 The AC system is now charged and the pressures can be evaluated along with the duct temperatures to determine if it is operating as designed. See chapter 4 on performance testing the AC system for more information on the expected pressures and temperatures.

Charging with Manifold and Small Cans

Charging the AC system with small cans using a manifold set and a can tapping tool is sometimes used. This method is not an accurate way to ensure the exact amount of refrigerant is added to the AC system, but it is widely used because of the popularity of the small containers of refrigerant in the marketplace. There are a couple of different styles of can tap tools on the market that are used in conjunction with the manifold set. The reason this method is not accurate is because there is no way to measure how much refrigerant is being added to the system. Follow the steps below to charge the AC system.

Two common small can tap devices include the type that screws onto the threaded fitting on top of the can as well as the type that pierces the side of the can. Both of these tap devices are used in conjunction with a manifold set.

Charging the AC System with Small Cans

1 See the previous steps on pulling a vacuum with the electric pump or with the pneumatic pump. These steps must be followed prior to charging the AC system with this method.

2 Connect the yellow hose from the manifold set to the can tapping tool.

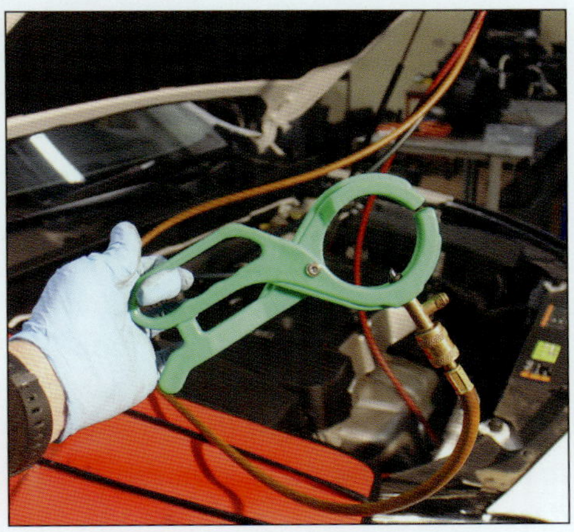

The can tap tool connects to the manifold set's yellow hose through a threaded connection. The yellow hose should be firmly tightened by hand to ensure a tight connection that will not leak.

3 Carefully connect the can tap tool to the small can using a firm grip while being sure that the can tap tool snaps into a locked position.

The can tap tool is opened and the small can is fitted into the opening. The tool is then closed, which pierces an opening in the side of the can that is sealed with a square-cut O-ring. The operator should use a firm grip and make sure that the locks catch on the handle to prevent the can from escaping and leaking refrigerant rapidly.

4 Carefully loosen the yellow hose connection to purge the air from the hose. Quickly tighten the hose connection as soon as any hissing sound is present.

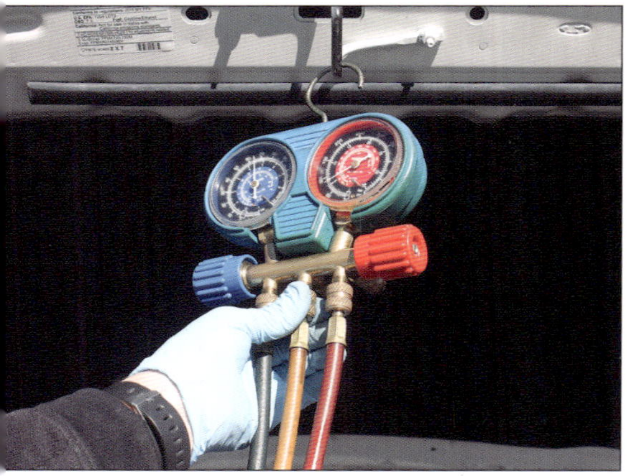

The yellow hose on the manifold should be loosened slightly in order to bleed the air from the hose. As soon as a hissing noise is heard, the hose should be tightened back up.

5 Open the blue and red valves on the manifold to allow the refrigerant to move from the small container into the vehicle's AC system.

The blue knob on the manifold is turned counterclockwise to open up the valve, which lets refrigerant flow from the yellow hose to the blue hose and low side of the AC system.

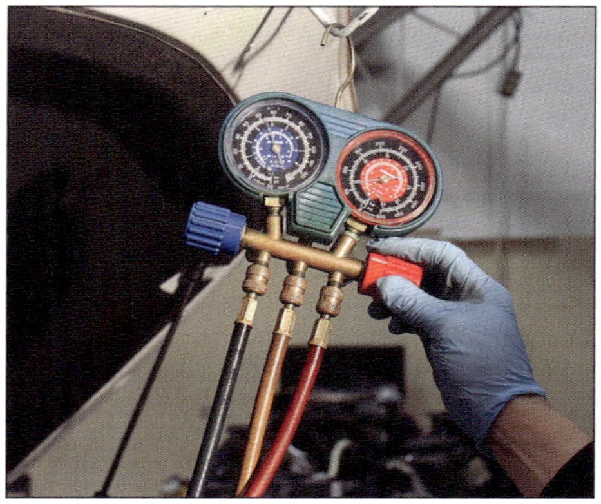

The red knob on the manifold is turned counterclockwise to open up the valve, which lets refrigerant flow from the yellow hose to the red hose and the high side of the system.

6 Once the process slows down, the red valve on the manifold needs to be closed (turned clockwise), the vehicle can be started, and the AC system turned on.

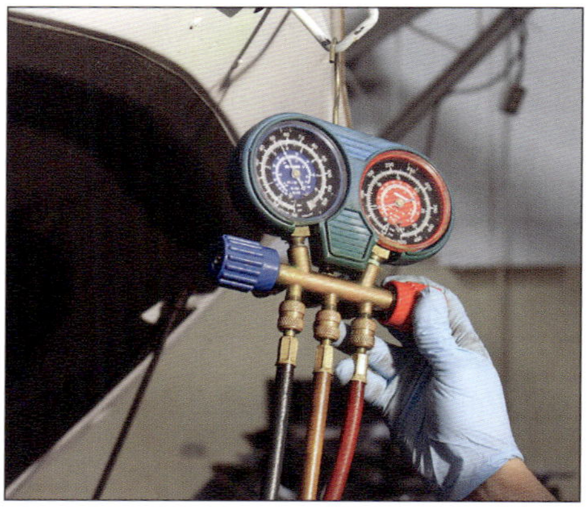

Once the pressures equalize, the red valve on the manifold is closed, the vehicle is started, and the AC is turned on. This action allows the pressure in the low side of the AC system to be reduced so that the charging process can continue.

7 The charging process will continue due to the low side pressure being lower than the pressure in the container. Holding the container in your hands while shaking it will assist in transferring the refrigerant into the vehicle.

Shaking the small can of refrigerant assists in getting as much of the refrigerant out of the can and into the vehicle as possible. This is necessary because the opening that the refrigerant has to pass through is very small and it helps to move the can around while warming up the can in your hands.

8 It will likely be necessary to add another container of

Removing the empty small can of refrigerant from the tap tool is a process that should be done with caution due to a small amount of refrigerant likely still in the can. Hold the tap tool and can away from the body, then unsnap the lock on the tool to release the small can. The empty can is safe to discard in the trash after removing it from the tap tool.

refrigerant into the AC system. Hold the small container away from you when unclipping the lock on the can tap tool. There will typically be a small amount of liquid refrigerant still left in the can, so it should be held at a safe distance to prevent it from being directed at your skin.

9 This process is continued until the AC pressures move into normal ranges and the duct temperature cools to normal ranges too. Once the system is performing in a reasonable manner, the blue manifold knob is closed (turned clockwise) and the manifold set is removed from the vehicle.

Charging with a Small Can and DIY Gauge

Charging the AC system with a small can and a DIY hose connection is the least accurate method available. There are a few different styles of DIY connections on the market today to allow the general consumer to add refrigerant to his or her vehicle. Typically, these kits are used to top off AC systems when the AC is not working well. Follow the steps below to charge the AC system.

The small can of refrigerant has a threaded connecting point at the top of the can and this is where the charging hose is connected. The charging hose should be connected tightly to prevent a leak.

Charging the AC System with DIY-Type Container

1 Connect the charge hose to the small can of refrigerant.

2 Connect the service end of the charge hose to the low side port of the AC system.

The charging hose has a quick-connect coupling that connects to the low side service port. Once this connection is made, the check valve in the service port is opened.

3 Open the valve on the charge hose to allow refrigerant to move from the can into the vehicle.

The valve in the charging hose is turned counterclockwise to open the connection to allow the refrigerant to pass through the connection and into the vehicle AC system.

4 Start the engine and turn on the AC system.

5 Continue adding refrigerant into the AC system until the duct temperatures cool to a normal range.

Refrigerant will continue to be added to the vehicle's AC system until it is necessary to close the valve on the charging hose. The operator should monitor the duct temperature as well as the temperature of the suction hose. When the duct temperature falls to the 40 to 50°F range and the suction line is cold to the touch, the process should be stopped.

6 Close the valve on the charge tool and remove it from the low side service port.

The charging process is stopped by closing the valve on the charging hose. The valve should be turned clockwise to close the valve. The quick-connect coupling can now be removed from the low side service port.

7 Put the cap back onto the service port. If there is any refrigerant left in the small can, it can be used on another vehicle's AC system. However, the refrigerant will typically leak out before being connected to the next vehicle.

Oil for the AC System

The AC system needs to have the correct type and amount of lubricant in order to allow the compressor to operate in a reliable and efficient manner. There are different types of oil used on AC systems depending on the type of refrigerant that is used as well as whether the system uses a standard compressor or an electric compressor. See chapter 2 for more details about refrigerant oil.

The AC machine has an "Inject Oil" function that adds oil into the vehicle's AC system. This process is available after the AC machine has vacuumed the system. The machine will allow the operator to add oil by pressing yes when the screen displays the option. The oil is pulled from a clean bottle located on the side of the machine when the oil inject button on the panel is pressed.

Methods of Adding Oil

Refrigerant oil can be added to the AC in a number of ways. It is common to add the oil directly to the AC components if the system is open for service. The AC machine has a function to add oil to the system following the vacuum process. This process is handy because the oil is pulled from a clean bottle on the side of the machine using the vacuum from the AC system.

Oil can be added during the charging process by using an inline vessel that connects to the manifold set at the low side port. Up to 2 ounces of oil can be added using this method during the charge process. Refrigerant oil is also available in pressurized small containers that can be added in the same manner as using the small cans to add refrigerant to the AC system.

An option to add refrigerant oil during the charging process is to use an oil vessel that connects in series with the low side hose. Up to 2 ounces of oil can be added during the charging process using this method.

Refrigerant oil can be directly added to AC system components during the repair process. Caution should be used to keep from adding too much refrigerant oil to an AC system at any time, which could cause reduced performance. A reliable service database should be used to determine how much oil can be added during AC service.

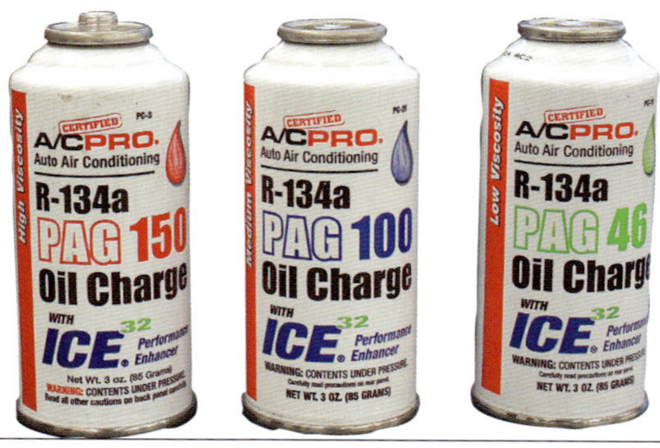

Refrigerant oil can be added by using products that are available in small pressurized cans. A can tap device or a do-it-yourself charge hose is required to connect these small cans to the AC system.

CHAPTER 6

Repairing the AC System

Keeping the occupants of cars and trucks comfortable is a high priority. Accurate and effective repair techniques must be followed in order to perform high-quality repairs on the AC system. This chapter will cover many of the repair procedures that are performed on cars and trucks to keep them working well. It is important to remember that all federal, state, and local laws should be followed when repairing AC systems on cars and trucks.

Repairing and Replacing Parts

As stated in previous chapters, the AC system is under constant pressure, which requires anyone performing replacement or repair to use effective repair techniques. One interesting way to think about this system is to consider the AC system a high-pressure plumbing system; to repair it for long-lasting performance, much attention must be put forth to using excellent sealing techniques and strategies.

This chapter will continuously stress how important it is to always replace seals and O-rings when performing service. In addition, it is very important to pay attention to tightening components to the correct torque as well as paying close attention to quick-connect coupling components.

Lines and Hoses

Lines and hoses are used to connect the main components of the AC system together. The lines are typically made from aluminum and the hoses are made from multilayered flexible rubber that is reinforced with nylon. The hoses used on newer-model cars and trucks are much higher quality than those used in the early days of AC-equipped cars and trucks.

Many lines and hoses are held in place with brackets and clips that prevent them from rubbing against another component. It is important to reinstall these items when replacing the lines or hoses to ensure that the repair will be of high quality. Below are some key points to follow when replacing lines and hoses.

Use the following steps when servicing bolted connection–style lines and hoses.

Bolted Connections

1 Inspect the connection to determine the correct size wrench or socket to use when loosening the connection. It is preferable to use the exact size wrenches when loosening and tightening these connections to prevent damaging the hex corners of the fasteners. If a socket is the tool of choice, then use a six point–style socket.

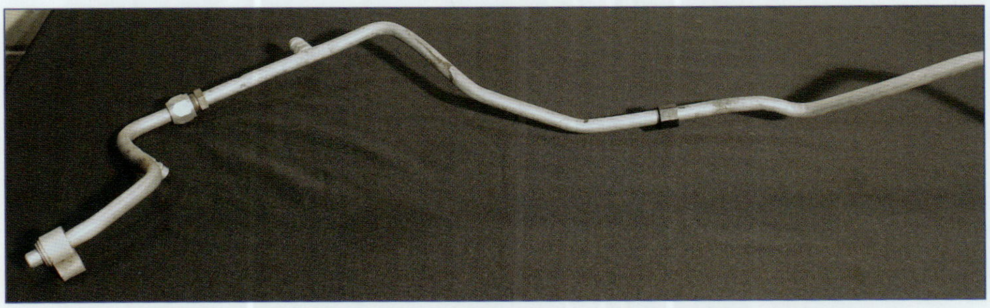

Aluminum lines are used to connect the AC components together. Care should be taken when working around these lines to keep from bending or damaging them, which would cause a leak.

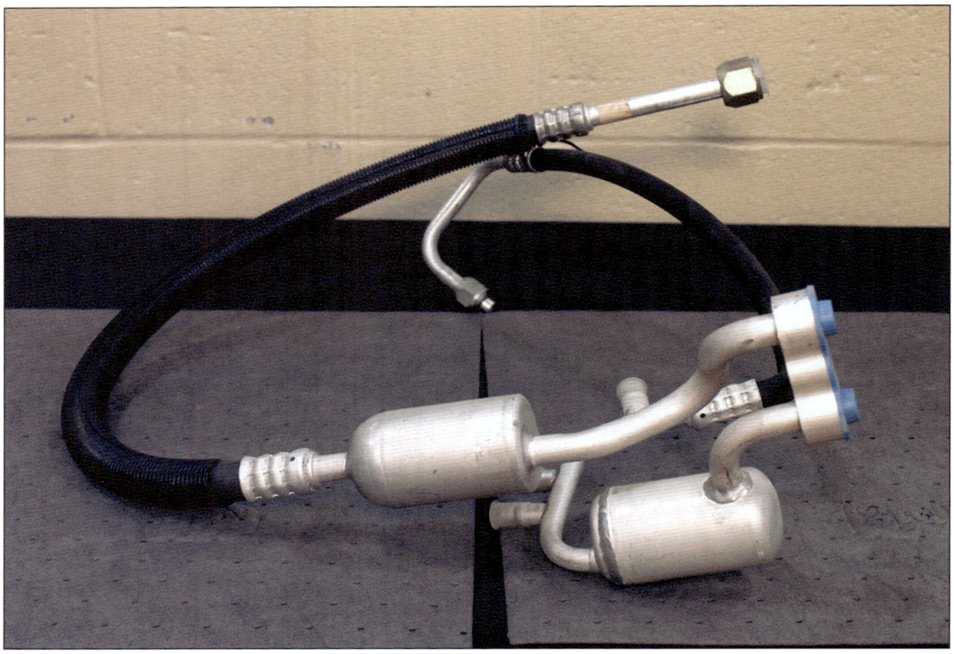

Line and hose assemblies are used in many parts of the AC system to connect the system. These assemblies will be made of aluminum as well as being connected with factory crimps to flexible rubber hoses. The hoses used on these systems are multilayered and provide excellent integrity to prevent refrigerant leaks.

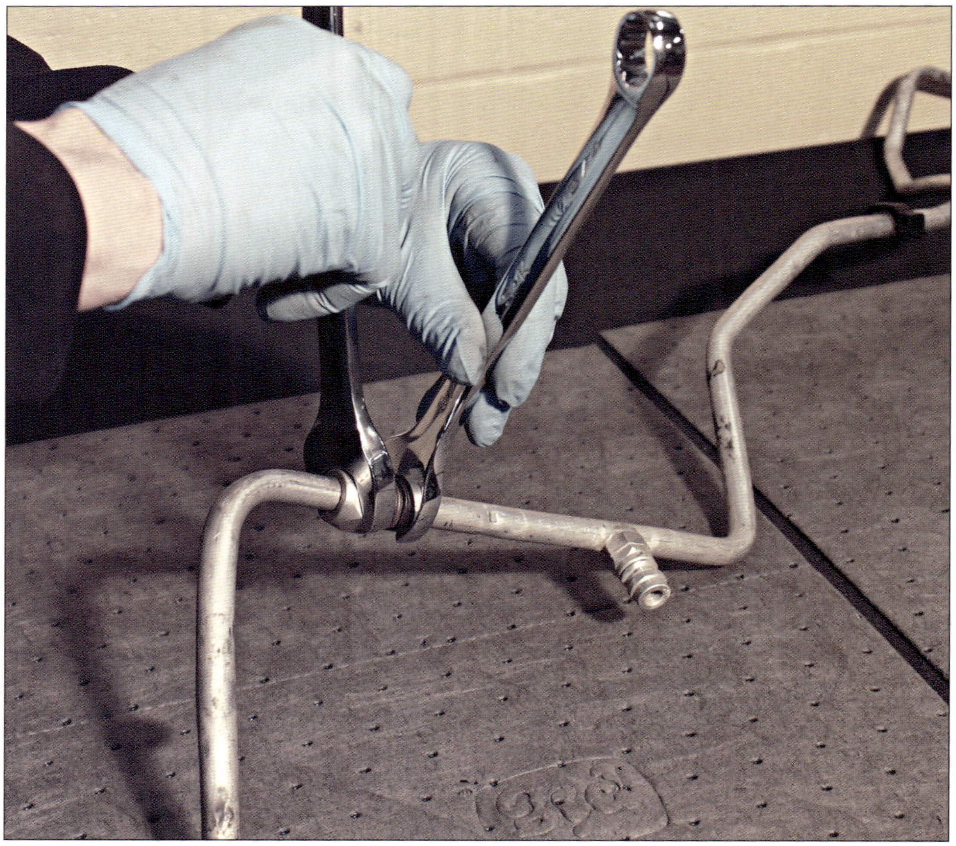

Two wrenches are needed to service the bolted connections on refrigerant lines. The exact size should be used when loosening and tightening these connections to prevent rounding the corners of the hex-shaped fittings. The O-rings should always be replaced when opening up connections in the AC system.

2 Finish loosening the connection by rotating the fasteners by hand.

3 If replacing the line or hose, be sure that new gaskets and/or O-rings are used in every location that is opened during the repair. See the instructions following this for information on the service procedures.

4 Carefully start the assembly of the fasteners by hand by rotating them clockwise. Be sure that the fasteners start perfectly by rotating them by hand two or three revolutions before using tools to finish the tightening procedure.

5 Finish the tightening procedure by using a torque wrench where possible to bring the tightness of the connection to the exact level. Refer to a reliable service source to find the torque specification.

It is wise to use flare nut wrenches on AC lines whenever possible to prevent rounding the corners of the hex-shaped nuts. These tools provide more contact with the surface than standard open-end wrenches.

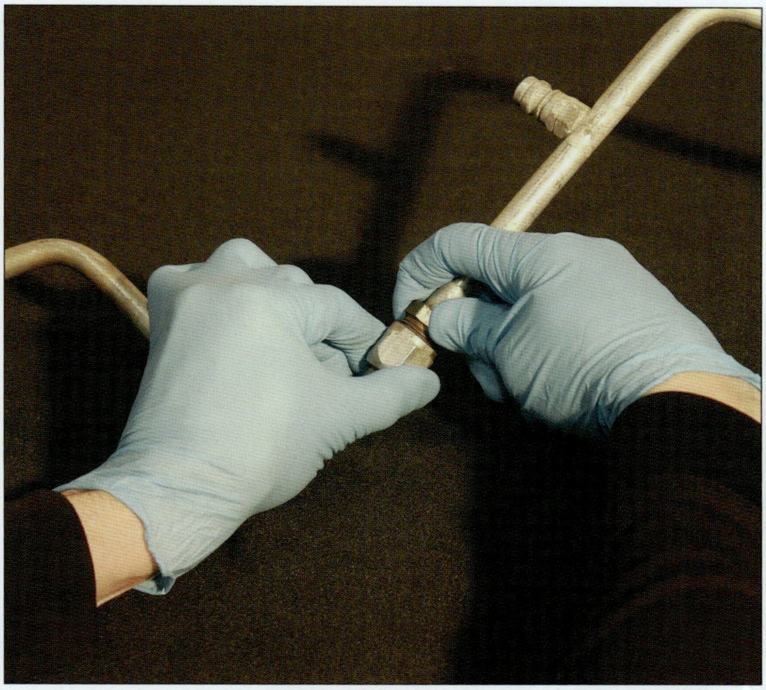

Extra care should be practiced when starting to connect two sections of line together to prevent damaging the threads on the fasteners. It is wise to turn the fasteners by hand two or three turns before using wrenches.

A torque wrench should always be used to ensure that the fasteners are correctly tightened. A connection that is too loose will leak and a connection that is too tight will likely damage the threads. The correct torque should be researched from a reliable source.

Quick-Connect Couplings

Use the following steps when servicing quick-connect-style lines and hoses.

The metal brackets that some manufacturers use to provide an extra layer of protection against leaks need to be removed prior to disconnecting the coupling with the special removal tools.

The brackets should be safely stored after removal to prevent accidental loss. These devices are used to provide an extra layer of protection for quick-connect couplings. The brackets should be installed prior to returning the vehicle to service.

1 Remove the metal bracket from the quick-connect joint if one is in place.

The quick-connection bracket should be removed prior to using the special tool that allows the connection to be disconnected. This bracket provides an extra layer of protection to ensure that the connection will not come apart while in operation. Not all manufacturers use these brackets.

2 Inspect the connection to determine which side of the assembly that the spring is on. Choose the correct size special tool to use on the connection.

The quick-connect coupling should be closely inspected to determine where the spring is located. The side of the connection with the spring is where the disconnect tool lip will need to be inserted.

Several companies make sets of disconnect tools that are made from aluminum. This set has six different sizes and the pieces are very rigid since they are made of metal. Quick-connect couplings are used in other systems, such as fuel supply lines, transmission cooler lines, engine oil cooler lines, and even engine coolant lines.

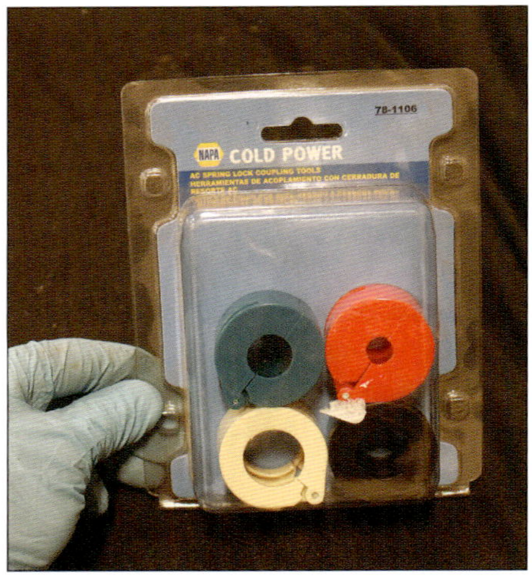

The quick-connect tools typically come in various sizes and are often color coded to assist in choosing the correct tool for each job. These tools are available at most parts supply stores. These tools are made of plastic so they can be damaged if they are dropped or used improperly.

3 Install the special tool with the beveled edge facing the spring.

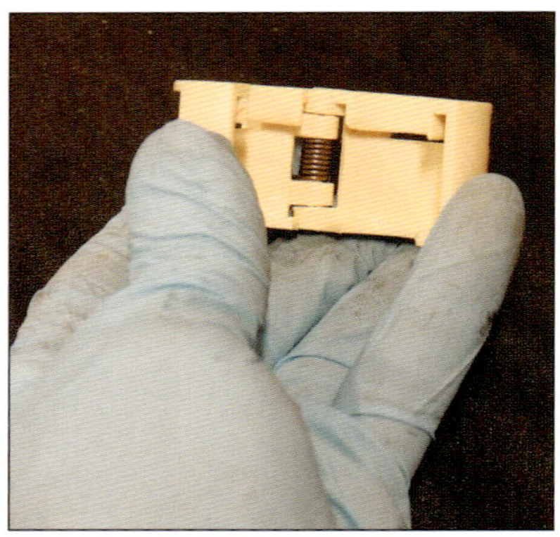

The tool has one side that has a beveled lip. This beveled lip faces the spring in the quick-connect coupling. The tool is spring loaded, so it must be held open when installing it into a quick-connect coupling.

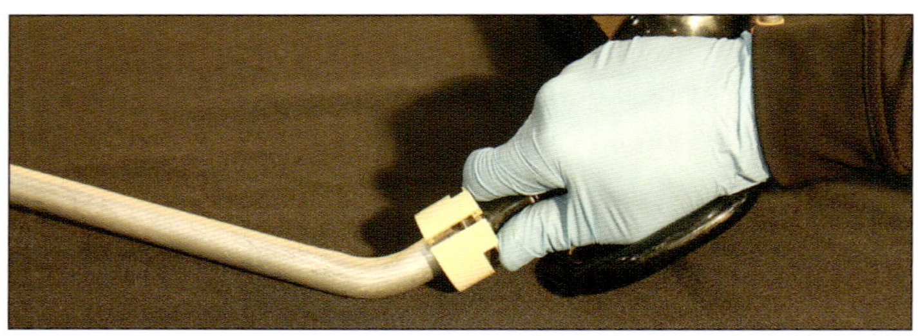

The tool is inserted into the quick-connect coupling with the beveled lip facing the spring in the joint. The lip moves the spring back to allow the coupling to be pulled apart.

4 Push the tool into the joint with one hand while pressing the opposite way with the other hand.

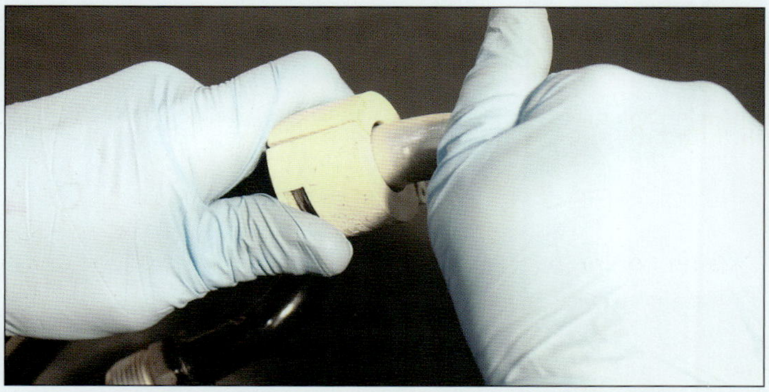

While pushing the tool into the coupling, the other side of the connection can be pulled apart. Once the joint is partially separated, the tool can be removed to allow it to completely come apart. It is sometimes necessary to twist the line to assist in breaking it loose to allow it to be separated.

5 Pull the connection apart.

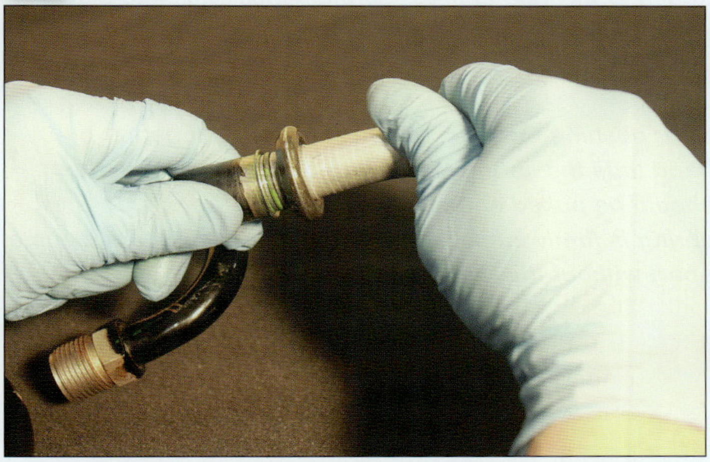

After the quick-connect joint has been disconnected using the tool, the two parts of the assembly can be fully disconnected. Most of these connections have two or three O-rings to allow for better sealing qualities.

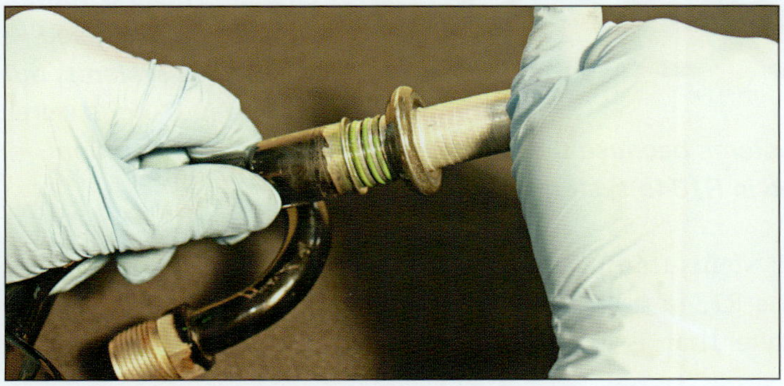

The quick-connect joint is pulled apart after the tool is used to begin the process. The joint typically comes apart easily once the initial separation has been achieved.

6 If replacing the line or hose, be sure that new springs, gaskets, and/or O-rings are used in every location that is opened during the repair.

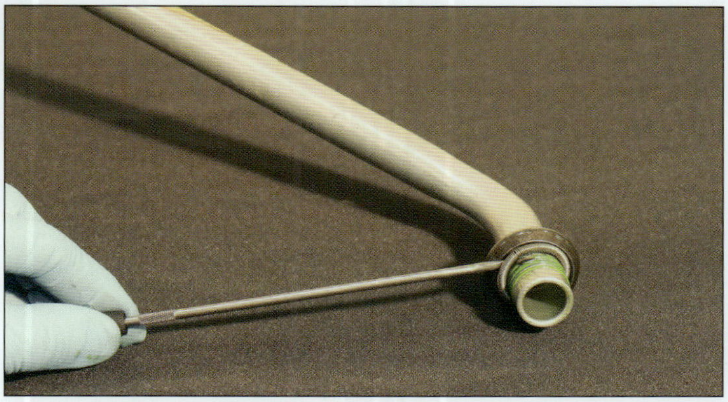

The spring on the coupling can be serviced. A pick can be used to pull the spring out of the housing. Extra caution should be applied to ensure that the correct size replacement spring is used.

Slide the new spring into place using normal finger pressure. This process is typically very simple and does not require the use of a pick or tool.

7 Assemble the connection by carefully pushing the two parts together until an audible snap is heard. After hearing and feeling the spring pop into place, carefully try to pull the connection apart. The connection should not be able to be pulled apart by hand without using the tool.

The new spring should be firmly seated by hand to ensure that it is in the correct position. Once the spring is correctly installed, the coupling can be reassembled without the use of any tools. Always install new O-rings every time a connection is opened for service.

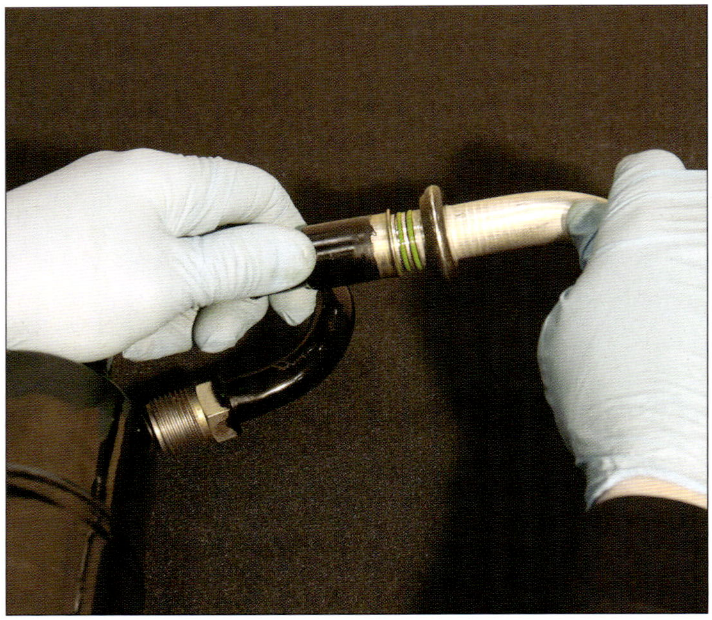

No tools are needed to reassemble a quick-connect coupling. The two parts of the connection can just be pushed together by hand until the spring snaps back into place. Even pressure should be used to prevent putting too much side pressure on the O-rings, which could damage them.

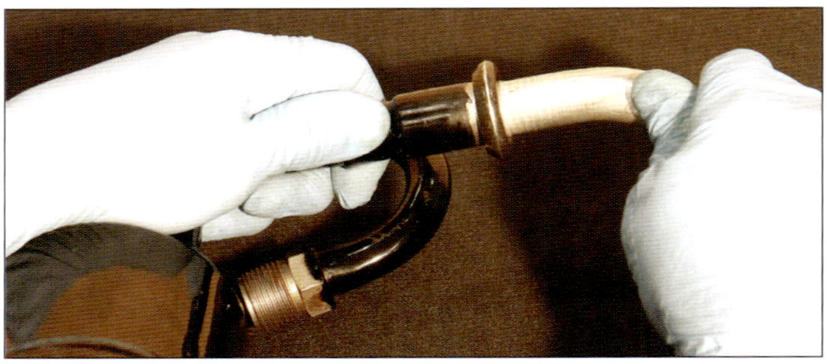

After pushing the quick-connect coupling together by hand until the spring snaps into place, the connection should be pulled on to see if it will hold together. If the spring is firmly in place, then the connection will not come apart without the tool in place.

8 Install the metal bracket onto the connection if one was removed in step one.

Gaskets and Seals

Gaskets and seals are used to provide a leak barrier for the lines, hoses, and the many other parts of the AC system. The person repairing the AC system should always replace the seals and gaskets every time a connection is opened for any reason. It is crucial to use the correct repair technique when replacing gaskets and seals to prevent leaks.

Black O-rings are available in many sizes and should be carefully chosen. These O-rings were commonly used on R12 AC systems, but the green O-rings were needed for R134a systems because they are more resistant to deterioration from the PAG oil used in R134a systems.

O-rings are often used to seal the various components of the AC system together. Black-colored O-rings were used on older systems that used R12. Systems that use R134a used an improved O-ring style that is typically green in color. There are some key points to follow when replacing O-rings on the AC system.

Replacing AC O-Rings

Green O-rings are available in many sizes and thicknesses. It is important to make sure that the exact size O-ring is installed in each connection. If the wrong O-ring is installed on an AC system, the refrigerant will leak at that connection.

1 Carefully remove the old O-ring using a pick or similar tool.

2 Inspect the sealing area for burrs and sharp edges. Use a fine emery cloth to smooth out any blemishes that are found.

A pick or similar tool is needed to assist in removing the O-rings from lines and hoses. The O-rings should be removed without cutting or damaging to make it easier to match up with the new O-ring.

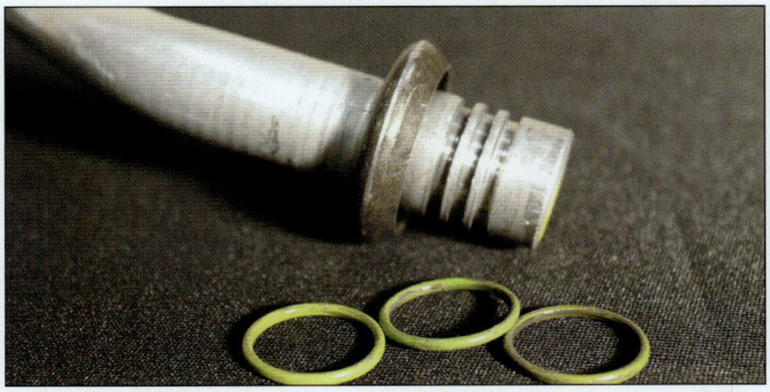

The O-ring grooves need to be closely inspected after removing the old seals. If any burrs are found in the O-ring grooves and flanges, then the area can be cleaned up with some fine emery cloth. Be sure to clean the groove area thoroughly before installing the new O-rings.

3 Find the exact size of replacement O-ring. Extra care should be used to choose the O-ring's exact diameter and thickness to ensure the system will not leak in the future.

The old O-rings should be paired with the replacement items to make sure the fit is exact. The diameter and thickness must be exactly the same as the original O-rings. Using the wrong size of O-ring will cause a refrigerant leak in the AC system.

4 Carefully install the new O-rings into place.

The new O-rings need to be carefully installed onto the line, paying close attention to not cut or damage the surface of the O-ring. Typically, this process can be completed by using the fingers and rolling each one into place.

5 Install a small amount of refrigerant oil on each O-ring.

After the new O-rings are fitted into their grooves, a little PAG refrigerant oil should be added to each one. The oil needs to be spread over the whole surface of the O-ring to assist in the sealing properties of the rubber.

6 Reassemble the connection using the proper technique to ensure a tight and secure connection. See the steps previously on repairing quick-connect-style couplings as well as repairing bolted-style couplings.

Schrader Valves and Check Valves

The service ports on AC systems are provided as a connection point for the manifold set or the AC machine. There is typically a low side service port as well as a high side service port. These service ports have a valve inside the port that is spring loaded and acts like a one-way check valve. There are two styles available: a Schrader-style valve or a ball-style valve.

The low side R12 service port is a threaded port that has a Schrader valve to prevent refrigerant from passing through the port when a service hose is not connected. This port is a 1/4-inch threaded connection.

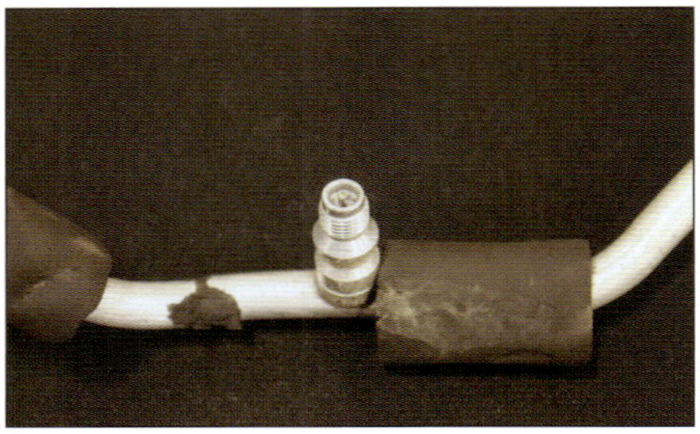

The high side R12 service port is a threaded port that has a Schrader valve to prevent refrigerant from passing through the port when a service hose is not connected. This port is a 3/16-inch threaded connection.

A high side adapter is needed when connecting an R12 manifold set to an AC system because the high side service port is 3/16 inch and the fittings on the R12 manifold set are both 1/4 inch.

The low side R134a service port is a 13-mm quick-connect coupling that has a Schrader or ball-type check valve to prevent the refrigerant from passing through the port. This is the location where the blue service hose is connected, which allows diagnosis and service procedures to be performed on the system.

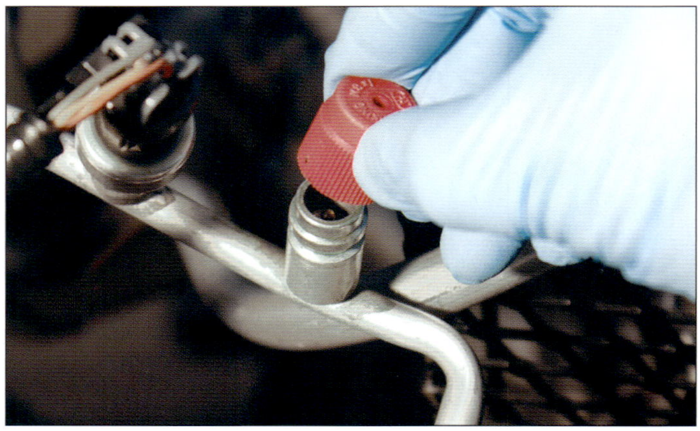

The high side R134a service port has a 16-mm quick-connect coupling with a Schrader- or ball-type check valve to prevent the refrigerant from passing through the port. This is the location where the red service hose is connected to the system to allow diagnosis and service procedures.

The low side R1234yf service port is a 14-mm quick-connect coupling that has a Schrader- or ball-type check valve to prevent the refrigerant from passing through the port. This is the location where the blue service hose is connected to the system to allow diagnosis and service procedures.

The high side R1234yf service port is a 17-mm quick-connect coupling that has a Schrader- or ball-type check valve to prevent the refrigerant from passing through the port. This is the location where the red service hose is connected to the system to allow diagnosis and service procedures.

Schrader valves for the service ports are available in several sizes depending on the make and model of the vehicle. These valves look similar to tire Schrader valves but have special O-rings that seal the refrigerant in the system.

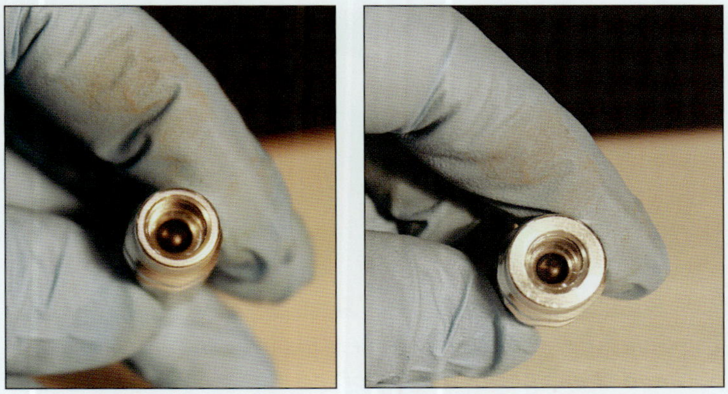

The ball-style check valve is available for low side service ports and is replaced as an assembly. This unit has seals, springs, and a special check ball device that prevents refrigerant from passing through the connection.

Replacing AC Schrader Valves

Use the following steps when servicing Schrader-style valves.

1 Remove the plastic service cap to determine which check valve style is used.

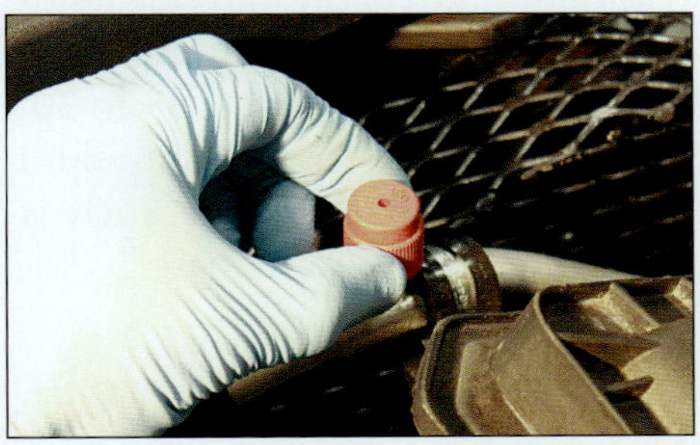

The service ports have plastic caps that need to stay in place except when service needs to take place. These caps prevent dust and debris from entering the service port in addition to serving as a secondary seal device for refrigerant leaks. Close attention should be used when removing the caps to see if any pressure releases when the cap is removed. If pressure is present when the cap is removed, then the check valve is leaking and will need to be replaced.

2 Choose the correct tool to remove the Schrader valve.

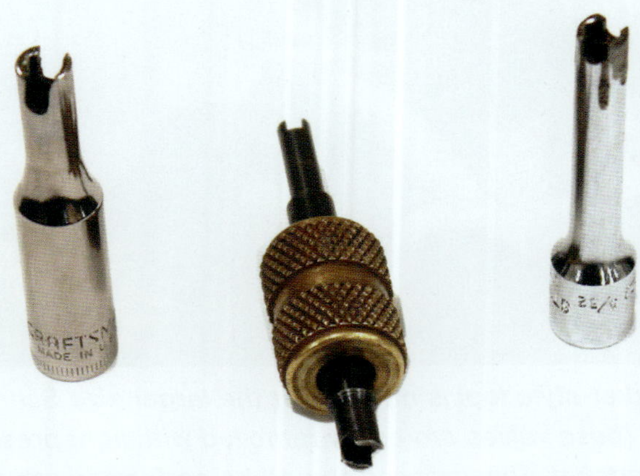

The tools needed to remove and reinstall Schrader valves are available at tool suppliers and parts stores. There are several sizes of valves, so it is important to use the correct size tool when servicing the valves.

3 Install the correct tool into the valve and turn counterclockwise to remove the valve.

The Schrader valve service tool is inserted into the service port and lines up with the top of the assembly to allow for removal. This process can only be performed after the system has been safely recovered. Do not remove the Schrader valve when the system is charged with refrigerant because it will quickly vent out when the valve is removed.

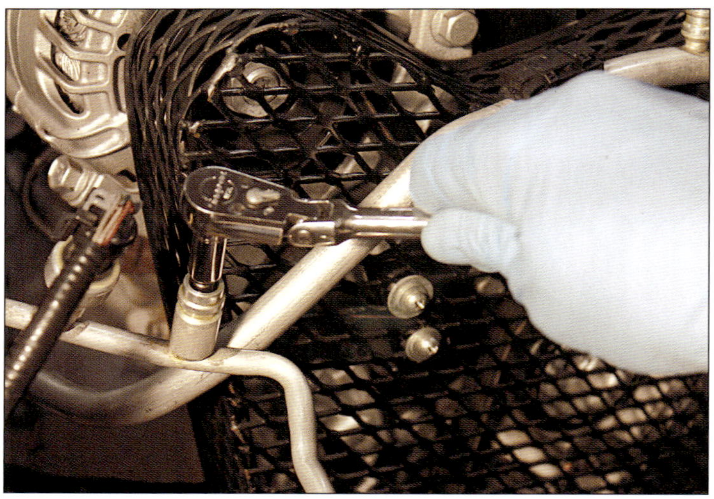

The socket-style tool is needed for the larger size Schrader valves. These valves are easily removed with light pressure on the ratchet. This process should be performed after the system has been safely recovered. If you remove the Schrader valve with the system charged with refrigerant, it will quickly vent to the atmosphere when the valve is removed.

4 Match up the original valve with a replacement valve.

5 Set the new valve back into the opening and use the tool to turn the valve clockwise, being very careful to align the threads perfectly and prevent damage to the threads because of misalignment.

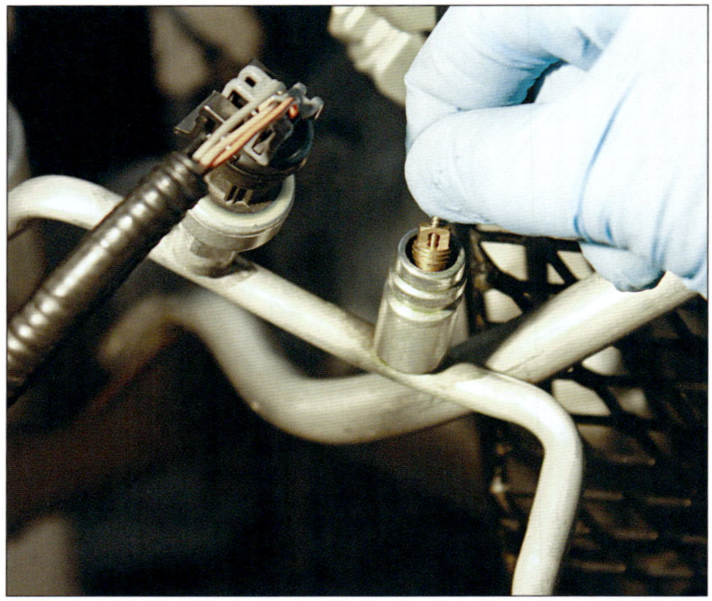

The Schrader valve is carefully inserted into the service port by hand. After setting the valve into the port, the tool is needed to carefully turn the valve clockwise to engage the threads. The ratchet is used to finish the tightening procedure, using care to not overtighten the valve.

6 Tighten the connection to the correct tightness by using mild hand pressure. Use an in-lbs torque wrench if one is available to tighten to the exact specification. The torque value on the valve depends on the diameter of the unit. The range of torque is 3 to 6 in-lbs on the smallest-size valves up to 15 to 30 in-lbs for the largest-size valves. The specification for this torque can be found in a reliable source, such as a service manual or on an electronic database.

Replacing Ball-Style Check Valves

Use the following procedures when servicing ball-style valves.

1 Remove the plastic cap to determine the size and the style of valve that is used.

The ball-type check valve assembly fastens to the line using a threaded connection. When this valve requires service, it is replaced as an assembly. Always install the plastic cap when the repair is completed to help keep debris out of the fitting. The cap also serves as a secondary leak deterrent for the system.

2 Choose the correct size wrench or socket that fits the hex-shaped valve. It is advisable to use six-point tools to prevent rounding the corners on the valve.

3 Choose the correct size of wrench to hold the base of the line or component to assist in breaking the connection loose.

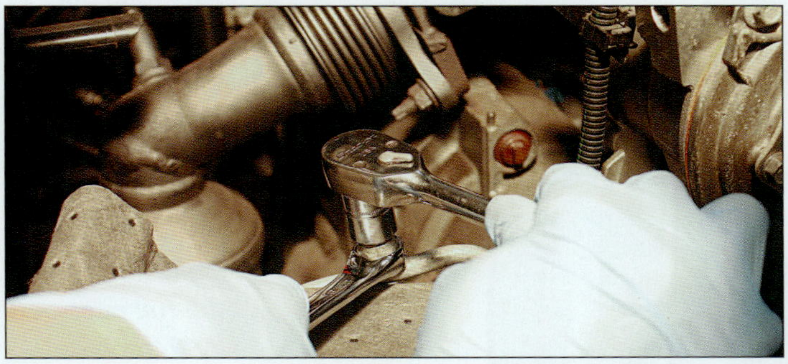

The ball-style check valve is removed with sockets and wrenches as an assembly. This fitting is typically very tight and takes a considerable amount of twisting to break the connection loose, so the correct size tools should be chosen and used.

4 Carefully turn the tools counterclockwise to remove the valve.

5 Choose the correct size of replacement valve.

6 Install a new O-ring along with a little refrigerant oil.

Refrigerant oil should be added to the O-ring on the new valve prior to installing it on the vehicle. The oil helps the O-ring seal and provide good leak prevention for the system.

7 Carefully start the new valve by turning it clockwise by hand.

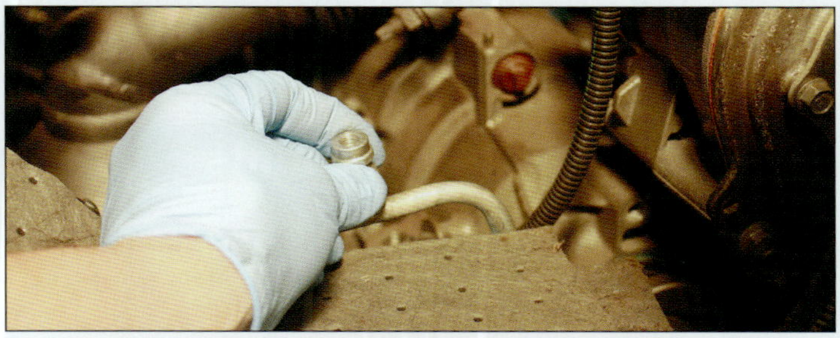

The new ball-style check valve is reinstalled by carefully turning clockwise to engage the threads without cross threading the connection. The new valve should be turned two or three turns before using tools to finish the job.

8 Use a torque wrench to bring the tightness to the specified level. The torque value for these valves are 7 to 10 ft-lbs for the high side and 5 to 7 ft-lbs for the low side.

A torque wrench should be used to finish tightening the ball-style check valve to ensure that the unit is installed at the correct tightness. If this repair is left too loose, the system will likely leak, and if the fitting is tightened too tight, the threads could be damaged.

Component Flushing

It is sometimes necessary to clean out the AC system with a flush substance. If the AC system has had a failure that released debris into the system or if the system is being retrofitted from R12 to R134a, it is advisable to flush out the system.

The parts of the system that are permissible to flush during a retrofit include the lines and hoses, the evaporator, and the condenser. Keep in mind that the condenser should not be flushed if any particles are present in the system. The parts of the AC system that are not flushable include the compressor, the dryer device, and any hose that has a muffler or filter incorporated.

The condenser must be replaced to ensure that it is open and clear any time that debris or particles have been present in the system due to the tiny passages that condensers have.

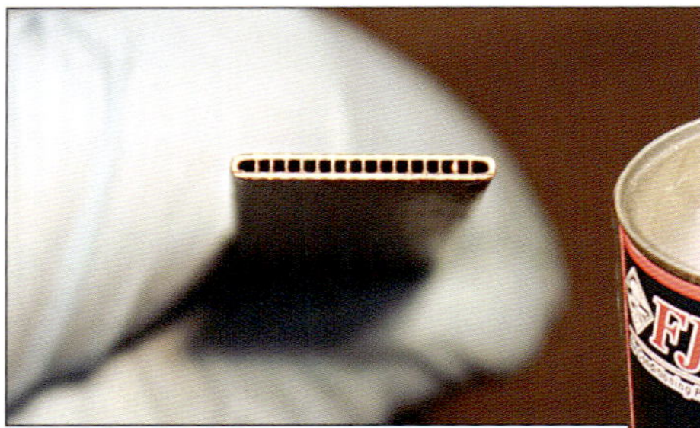

The internal passages on late-model condensers are very small, which means that the flush process will not remove particles that get trapped in the condenser. These condensers must be replaced if foreign debris enters into them.

AC flush solvent is available from several different manufacturers in various size containers. This solvent is used to remove old oil and other contaminants from lines, hoses, and heat exchangers in the AC system. A special injection kit is needed to flush AC components using air or nitrogen pressure.

The flush substance can be purchased in various sizes from most parts supply stores. Below are some key points to follow when flushing parts of the AC system.

Flushing AC Components

1 Install the flush hose to the flush container. Firm finger pressure is recommended for the tightness of this hose.

The flush hose must be firmly installed prior to adding the flush solvent into the vessel. The flush hose is equipped with a rubber-tipped blow nozzle that is used to control the flush process very well.

2 Add the flush solvent to the flush tool. Using a funnel and wearing some type of gloves is recommended in order to prevent spilling the flush solvent or getting it on your hands. This flush vessel holds one quart of liquid.

The flush solvent is added to the container. Be careful to not spill any solvent. The container is typically filled up to the full capacity to provide enough solvent to do a good job of cleaning the system.

3 Install the top to the flush tool. Firm finger pressure is recommended for the tightness of the top.

After adding the flush solvent to the container, the top is installed to the unit. The O-ring should be in good shape to prevent a loss of pressure when the unit is connected to the pressure source.

4 After making sure that the flush hose is firmly connected, connect the flush tool to a shop air source or a pressurized nitrogen source. It is recommended to use confident and firm techniques when connecting the pressure hose to prevent having the chemical escape and be sprayed out of the vessel.

5 Position the line over a drain pan to prevent the flush solvent from spilling on the floor or on the ground.

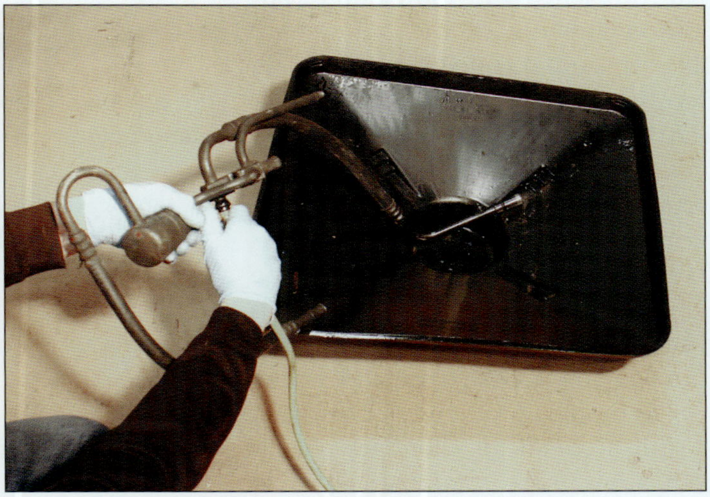

The flush nozzle should be inserted into the opening on the line to be flushed while the other end of the line is directed to a catch pan. The valve should be activated to force the flush solvent through the line. This process should be repeated for each component that needs to be flushed. If several different parts of the AC system need to be flushed, then the container will have to be refilled to complete the process.

6 Carefully blow pressurized flush liquid into the line or component that is being flushed. It is recommended that small bursts of solvent be pushed through the component instead of just giving it full throttle. Using this technique will prevent high pressure from building up in the component and solvent being sprayed out onto the person doing the flushing.

7 The used flush substance can be stored in the container that holds the used refrigerant oil.

8 The correct type of refrigerant oil should be added back into the AC components before reassembling the system. Consult service information for the amounts.

The pressure hose is connected to the pneumatic adapter on top of the flush container. Once the pressure is turned on, the vessel is ready to be used to flush the components. Care should be taken to not accidentally hit the handle on the flush nozzle, which would cause the flush to be quickly released.

An evaporator odor eliminator substance is available to help eliminate the odor that occurs when bacteria is allowed to exist on the evaporator core. This substance can be directly applied to the evaporator core if possible or it can be directed into the duct box drain tube and sprayed up into the opening. The user should closely follow the directions that the chemical manufacturer provides to get the best results.

Cleaning the Evaporator Core

Some vehicle manufacturers have had problems with an unpleasant odor originating in the AC system. This unwanted smell can originate from bacteria on the evaporator core. The environment of the evaporator core includes darkness, temperature changes, and lots of moisture, which promotes bacteria to grow on the surface of the component. This causes the odor to be sent out to the vents when the blower is turned on. The two ways to repair this problem include replacing the evaporator core or treating it with a chemical. There are several companies that make the chemical product. There are a couple of ways that this substance can be used on an AC system.

Apply Chemical onto the Evaporator Core

Adding the chemical directly onto the evaporator core surface is a very effective method of treating the bacteria problem. This method of treating the evaporator core will often not be possible due to the lack of an access point to get a clear shot near the evaporator core. The steps are listed below.

Spraying Cleaner Directly into the Evaporator Core

1. Gain access to the blower motor, blower resistor, or evaporator temperature sensor. This can usually be done by removing the glove box or by removing the trim panel on the passenger-side footwell area.
2. Remove the component that is the easiest to access and store the fasteners in a safe place.
3. Shine a light in the opening that was created by the part removal. The evaporator core should be visible from this location.
4. Install the nozzle hose onto the spray can and direct it inside the duct box.
5. Spray the whole surface of the evaporator core with the chemical.
6. Reinstall the component that was removed.
7. Wait several minutes for the chemical to attack the unwanted bacteria.
8. Roll the windows down. Start the vehicle and turn the blower to the highest setting for several minutes.

Using Cleaner Indirectly at the Drain Tube

Add Chemical through the Duct Box Drain Tube

1. Insert the nozzle of the chemical cleaner into the duct box drain tube.
2. Depress the nozzle valve to fully add all of the chemical into the duct box.
3. Roll the windows down on the vehicle.
4. Wait several minutes and then start the vehicle and run the AC for several minutes.

The process of adding the chemical to the AC system is a fairly effective method of killing the bacteria on the evaporator core. A few manufacturers have designed their AC systems to run the blower motor for several seconds after the vehicle has been shut off in order to dry off the evaporator core, which reduces the chances of having this problem occur.

Another method that any operator can follow is to run the AC system in the fresh air mode as much as possible. The action of pulling in fresh air from outside the cab assists in keeping the bacteria from growing on the evaporator core's surface.

Metering Devices

Metering devices are used on AC systems to create a restriction that causes the refrigerant to change

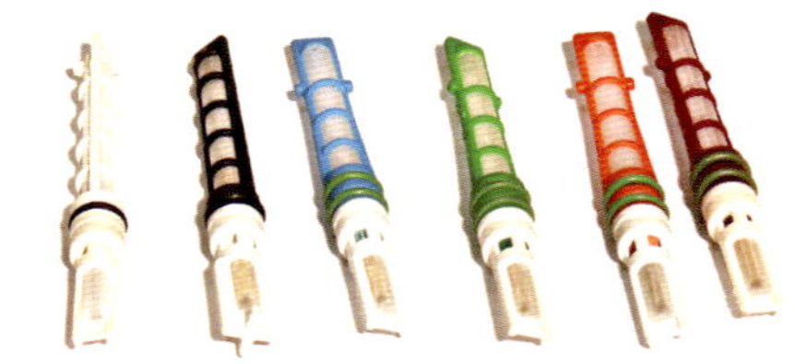

Orifice tubes are available in several sizes, and care should be taken when replacing them in order to install the correct one for the vehicle being repaired. Each size of orifice tube is recognized by a unique color. It is wise to always check the orifice tube each time the system is open for repairs to find out if the system is dirty or has foreign materials flowing through it. The dirt or foreign material will get stuck at the orifice tube since it has a screen.

Thermal expansion valves are available in two styles. The standard valve (left) has a thermal-sensing coil that connects to the evaporator core exit line and is typically located inside the duct box. The block-style valve (right) is self-contained and is typically mounted at the entry point of the evaporator core and can usually be serviced without removing the duct box.

Some manufacturers design the system with the orifice tube near the entry point of the evaporator. This access point typically is accessible with little obstruction or disassembly required. Make sure that the orifice tube is installed with the arrow facing the direction of normal refrigerant flow.

from a high-pressure liquid into a low-pressure liquid. The most common types of metering devices are the orifice tube and the thermal expansion valve. The operation of these devices is covered in depth in chapter 3.

Orifice Tube

The orifice tube is a metering device that is located inside the liquid line and can be found at some point between the condenser exit and the evaporator core inlet. It is recommended to remove the orifice tube any time that the system is recovered to inspect it for debris.

If the orifice tube is covered with debris, then the health of the system is not good and major repairs will need to be made. It is recommended that the orifice tube should be replaced any time it is removed. Here are the steps to follow when replacing the orifice tube.

Replacing the Orifice Tube

1 After recovering the AC system or verifying the system is empty, disconnect the lines at the orifice tube location. The connection may be a bolted connection or a quick-connect connection.

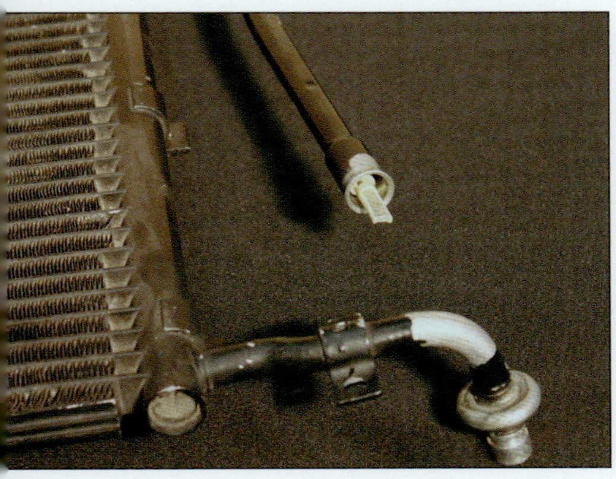

Orifice tubes can be located at the exit line of the condenser. This access point generally requires a little disassembly of the front section of the vehicle such as a headlight housing or front trim bezel. The O-rings or gaskets always need to be replaced whenever an AC system is open for any type of service.

2 Use small needle-nose pliers or a similar tool to carefully pull the orifice tube from the line.

The orifice tube can be removed from the mounting location by using small needle-nose pliers. The orifice tube generally can be removed without much resistance. However, if the tube does not come out easily, then some lubricant can be sprayed into the opening. Having the lubricant in place will assist in removing the old orifice tube.

3 Inspect the orifice tube for debris and foreign materials.

4 Choose the correct replacement orifice tube and apply a couple drops of refrigerant oil at the O-rings on the orifice tube. Orifice tubes are available in several different sizes, which are differentiated by color. Use the correct orifice tube for the given vehicle.

5 Install the new orifice tube into the line with the arrow on the device toward the evaporator core.

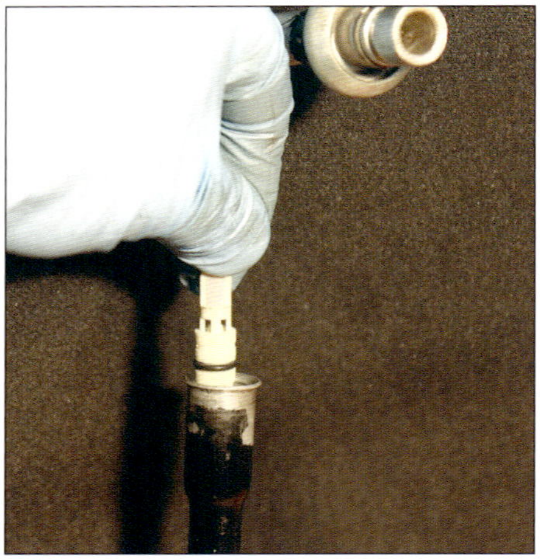

The new orifice tube is installed back into place by hand with the arrow on the orifice tube facing away from the condenser. The arrow faces in the direction of normal refrigerant flow. New O-rings need to be installed each time the system is being repaired.

6 Replace the O-ring on the line as well as apply a couple drops of refrigerant oil to the O-ring.

7 Reassemble the connection using the correct techniques. See the previous section on servicing the AC lines and hoses.

Replacing the Standard-Style Thermal Expansion Valve

The thermal expansion valve is a metering device that can have two different designs. The standard type is usually located inside the duct box and requires major effort and steps to replace. The block-type valve is usually located somewhere near the firewall and is much easier to replace when needed. See chapter 3 for more details about the operation of this component. Below are the steps to follow when replacing the standard-style thermal expansion valve.

1 After recovering the refrigerant or verifying that the AC system is empty, follow the procedures to remove the duct box from the vehicle. This is a very labor-intensive procedure that should only be done by someone with a strong mechanical ability and a complete set of technician's tools.

2 Remove the top/cover of the HVAC duct box to gain access to the evaporator core and thermal expansion valve.

3 Remove the insulating tape from the thermal element.

The thermal expansion valve capillary tube needs to be removed from the exit line of the evaporator core. This part of the valve is insulated with sticky insulating tape that must be removed during the process.

4 Use the correct wrenches to unbolt the thermal expansion valve from the evaporator core plumbing. The final steps of removing the fasteners can be done by hand.

5 Install the correct O-rings or seals to the new thermal expansion valve. Refrigerant oil should be added to the O-rings, but any metal gaskets should be installed dry.

The thermal expansion valve must be disconnected by removing the hex fasteners. The O-ring needs to be replaced before the new valve is installed. The fitting needs to be torqued to the correct tightness during installation to ensure a quality repair.

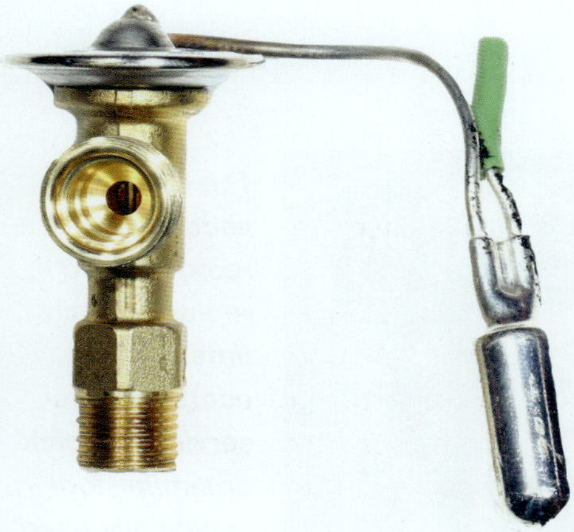

The new thermal expansion valve should be inspected to make sure it is the correct model for the vehicle being repaired.

6 Install the thermal expansion valve into the correct position. Close attention needs to be paid when installing the temperature-sensing bulb onto the evaporator exit line. The fasteners need to be tightened to the correct torque using a torque wrench.

7 Reassemble the duct box, paying close attention to the position of each duct door being in a normal location of travel. If the box is assembled with one of the doors outside the normal area of travel, then the box will have to be opened back up to correct this problem.

8 Reinstall the duct box back into the vehicle, paying close attention to assembling all fasteners back into their original location.

9 The AC system can be evacuated and recharged before being returned to service.

After torquing the fasteners for the thermal expansion valve, the sticky insulating tape needs to be applied around the capillary tube area to ensure that the tube firmly touches the evaporator exit line.

Replacing the Block-Style Thermal Expansion Valve

Replacing the block-style thermal expansion valve is much less invasive and does not require the removal of the duct box assembly. Below are the steps for replacing the block-style thermal expansion valve.

1 After recovering the refrigerant or verifying that the AC system is empty, remove the bolts that hold the line assembly to the valve.

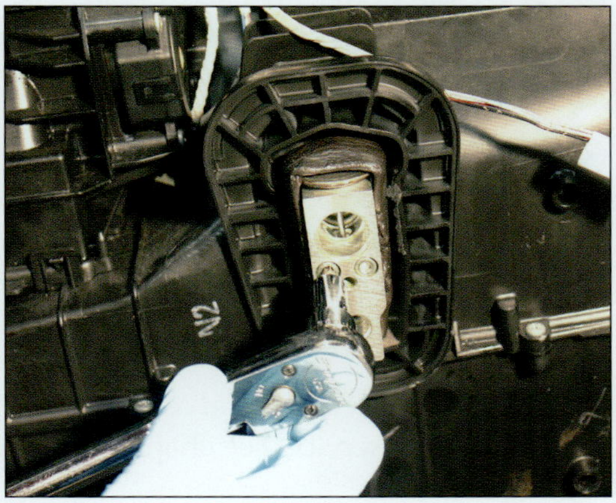

After picking the correct Torx socket size, the fasteners for the thermal expansion valve can be removed by turning the ratchet counterclockwise.

2 Remove the bolts that hold the valve to the evaporator core. These bolts are often very tight and can sometimes be seized, so lots of patience is needed to prevent a broken bolt. If the bolt seems to be seized, use a heat gun or small propane-powered

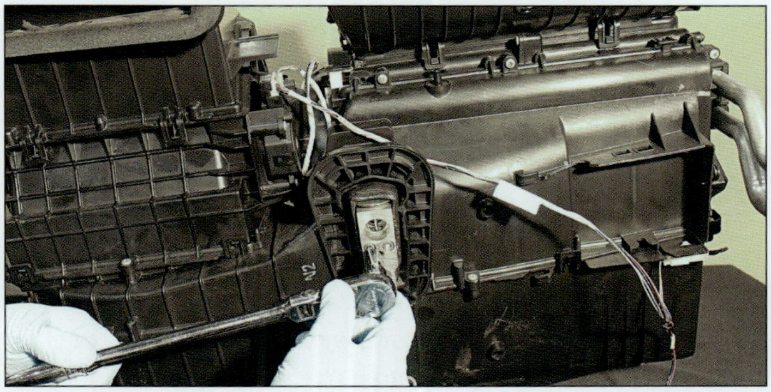

The fasteners for the thermal expansion valve are often very tight, so extra care should be taken when removing them. It is advisable to firmly push the Torx socket into the fastener to cause it to grab the sides very well.

heater to apply direct heat to the bolt to aid in the removal process.

3 Remove the valve and match up with the new one to make sure you have the correct part.

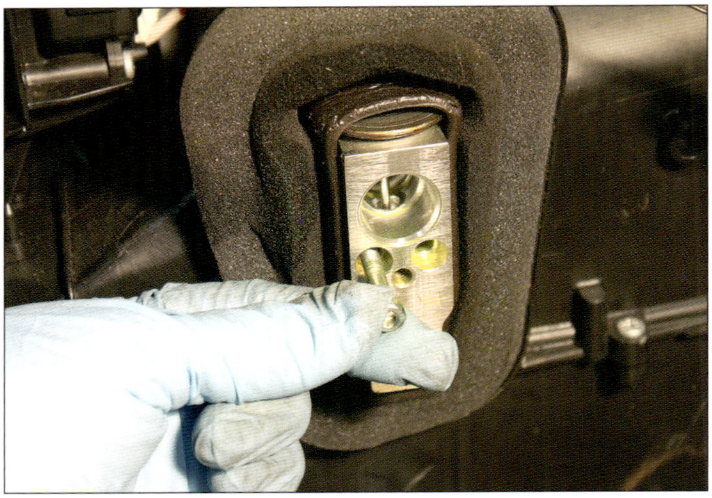

Once the fasteners have been loosened with the Torx socket and ratchet, they can be removed by hand. The fasteners should be stored in a safe place to prevent them falling into a place that is hard to get to.

The thermal expansion valve is separated from the evaporator core by gently prying it away from the housing and pulling by hand. Sometimes it may be necessary to use a flat screwdriver to press against the valve to get it loose from the mounting location.

4 Install new gaskets or O-rings to the new valve and then install it back onto the vehicle.

The O-rings should be removed and replaced each time an AC component is serviced. A pick or similar tool is typically used to get under the O-ring to aid in the removal.

The new O-ring should be carefully installed on the evaporator core inlet line. These O-rings can be installed by hand, but they should be closely inspected to make sure that it is not cut or damaged during installation. The O-rings should be lubricated with refrigerant oil prior to installing the new valve.

5 Tighten all bolts to the correct torque using a torque wrench.

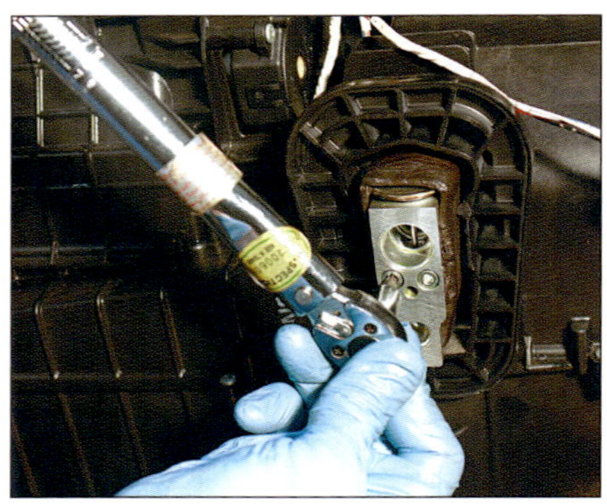

After installing the new thermal expansion valve into place, the fasteners are installed by hand. The last step of tightening the fasteners requires using a torque wrench, which helps attain the proper tightness of the fasteners. Correct torque on the fasteners ensures a quality repair that is not likely to leak or damage the threads.

6 The AC system can be evacuated and recharged before being returned to service. See chapter 5 for details of this process.

Dryer Devices

AC systems use some type of drying device to absorb and store any moisture that is present in the refrigeration system. This section provides information on how dryers are serviced.

Accumulator Dryer

Accumulator dryers are used on vehicles that have an orifice tube as a metering device. The main operation of accumulator dryers is covered in chapter 3. The accumulator dryer is located in the low side of the AC system at some point between the evaporator core and the compressor and is typically close to the firewall of the vehicle.

It is important to remember to install the accumulator dryer as the last step when making an extensive AC system repair because the dryer contains a desiccant that will absorb moisture as soon as it is uncapped from shipment. Another key point to remember is to add about 1 ounce of refrigerant oil to the device prior to installing it on the vehicle.

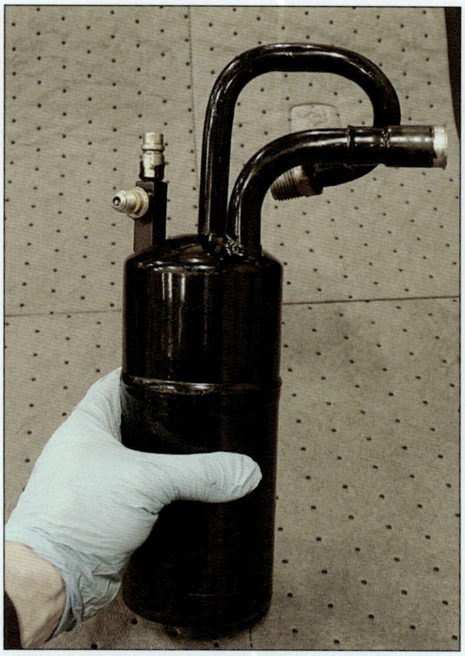

Many accumulator dryers use quick-connect couplings to connect to the lines and hoses of the AC system. As with the hex fasteners, the O-rings should always be replaced and lubricated with refrigerant oil during service procedures.

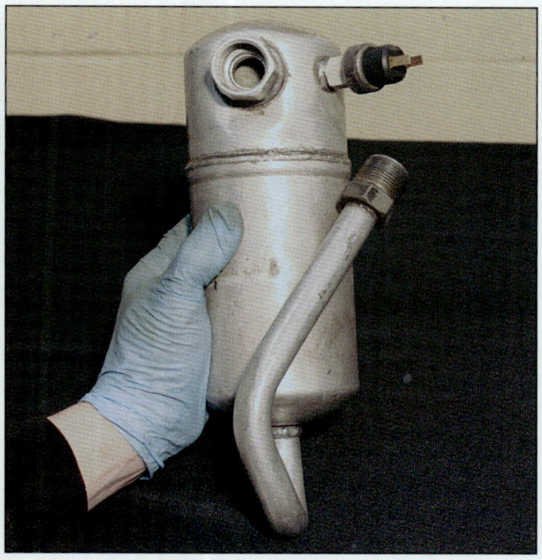

Many accumulator dryers use hex fasteners to connect to the lines and hoses of the AC system. The O-rings should always be replaced and lubricated with refrigerant oil during service procedures.

Accumulator dryers can be mounted with bolted connectors or with quick-connect couplings. The installer should follow the same techniques as when installing bolted lines and hoses as well as quick-connect lines and hoses. New O-rings should always be used with a couple drops of refrigerant oil rubbed on them. New gaskets should always be used and installed if that is the type of seal that is required. Extra care should be taken to ensure that the lines and hoses that connect to the accumulator dryer are installed with high quality workmanship.

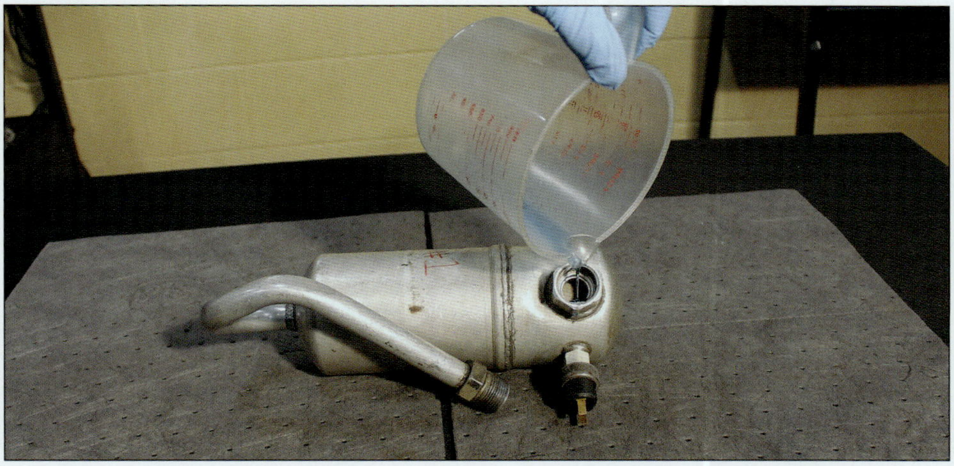

Refrigerant oil should be added to the accumulator dryer prior to installing it on the vehicle. It is important to make sure the correct viscosity and type of oil is used in each AC system to prevent the wrong oil from being installed into the system.

Receiver Dryer

Receiver dryers are used on vehicles that have a thermal expansion valve as a metering device. The main operation of the receiver dryer is covered in chapter 3. The receiver dryer is located in the high side of the AC system at some point after the condenser and before the thermal expansion valve.

Many late-model vehicles have begun combining the receiver dryer into the condenser. This has become

The receiver dryer is used on systems with a thermal expansion valve and are located at some point in the high side of the system between the exit of the condenser and the inlet of the evaporator core. The lines that connect to this dryer are held in place with bolts that should be torqued during installation.

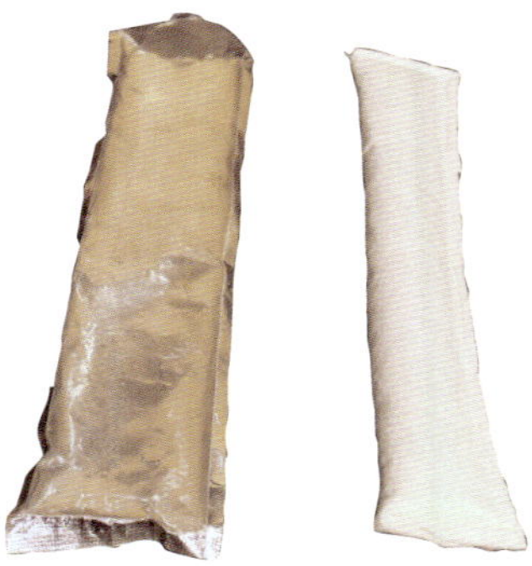

The replaceable desiccant pouch is shipped in a sealed bag to prevent the unit from absorbing moisture during storage and shipment.

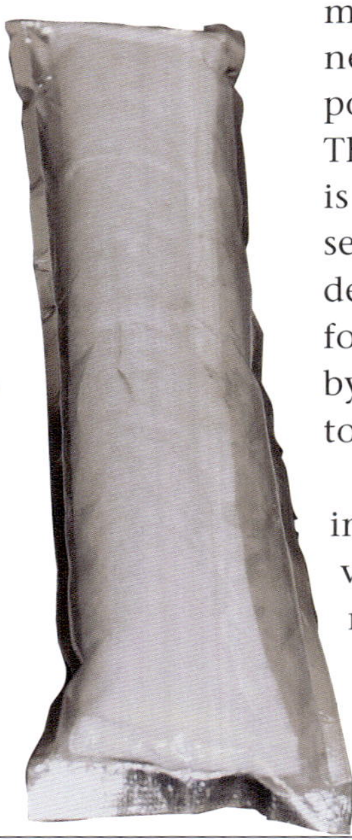

AC systems that use a dryer that is combined with the condenser may use a replaceable desiccant pouch. These systems would have a removable plug at the bottom of the condenser to allow access to the replaceable desiccant pouch.

New receiver dryers and accumulators come from the parts supplier with caps installed at the ports that connect to the lines and hoses. These caps are used to keep the vacuum trapped in the device, which prevents any contamination from air.

popular because it allows the manufacturer to weld the connection, which reduces the leak potential of the receiver dryer. The disadvantage to this design is the dryer assembly can't be serviced without replacing the condenser. Some manufacturers allow for the desiccant pack to be replaced by removing a plug from the bottom of the dryer housing.

The receiver dryer should be installed as the last step in the service routine so the desiccant will not draw an excessive amount of moisture from being left open to the atmosphere for a long time. The receiver dryer is shipped in a vacuumed state and is sealed with caps that must be removed prior to installation. It is important to remember to add some refrigerant oil to the receiver dryer prior to installation. The same high-quality installation and sealing techniques should be followed when installing the receiver dryer as the ones that were discussed above, covering lines, hoses, and accumulator dryers.

Compressor

The AC compressor is the heart of the system and must work at a high level in order to provide reliable and long-lasting performance. The action of replacing the compressor is one that should be done with quality and accuracy. In addition, the compressor is one of the most expensive components in the AC system, so good repair techniques and workmanship should always be exercised.

It is wise to order a kit when replacing the AC compressor. It includes the compressor, dryer device, and metering device. Replacing the dryer and metering device during a compressor replacement improves the performance and durability of the system. Many compressor manufacturers and vendors will not support a warranty on the compressor unless a thorough repair has been made that includes replacing these items.

AC compressors are available at most auto parts stores as well as car dealerships. One aspect of replacement compressors that has become popular in the aftermarket sector is selling AC compressors as a kit. The kit contains a new compressor along with a new metering device and dryer device. Many of the kits also come with an oil that has an additive called Ice 32, which is highly recommended by many of the companies in the aftermarket sector. Below are the steps to follow when replacing the compressor.

Replacing the AC Compressor

1 After recovering the AC system or verifying the system is empty, the compressor removal process can begin.

2 Remove the fasteners for the suction/discharge line.

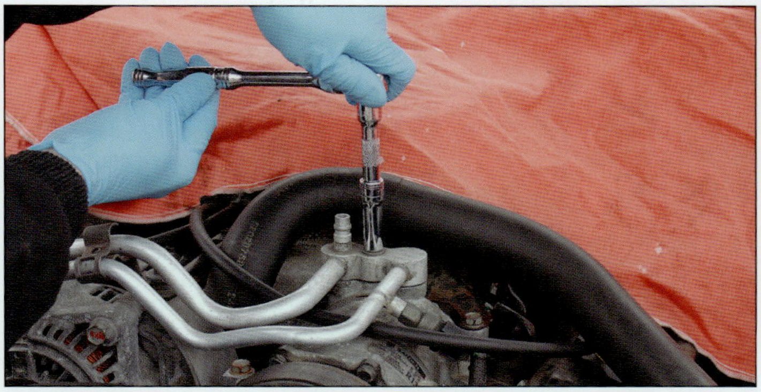

After recovering the refrigerant from the system with an approved machine, the AC lines at the compressor can be removed. This suction/discharge line is held in place with a bolt.

3 Remove the drive belt.

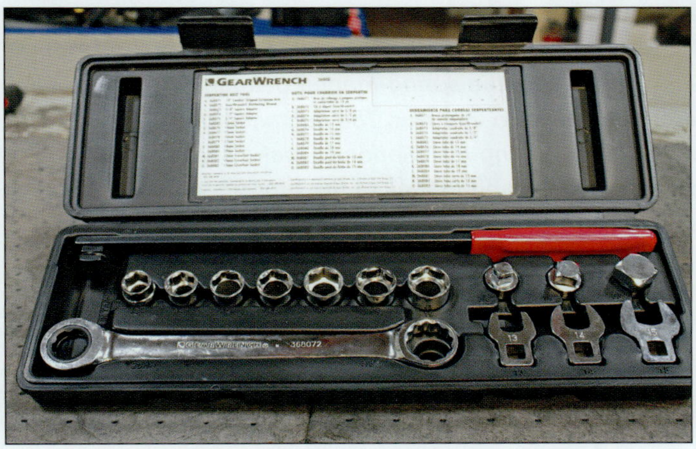

A belt removal kit is often needed when removing and installing serpentine drive belts. These kits are specially made to make it easier to gain access as well as have the required leverage to make belt service much easier.

After choosing the correct parts of the belt service kit, the tool is installed on the belt tensioner to release pressure on the belt and allow it to be removed from the belt train. Close attention should be paid to identify the correct routing of the belt. There will nearly always be a belt diagram on a decal under the hood to assist in the belt installation.

4 Remove the electrical connections of the compressor.

5 Remove the compressor mounting fasteners.

The compressor coil and the pressure switches must be carefully disconnected by releasing the locking tabs and pulling the connector apart. It is easy to break these plastic connectors, so caution should be used to prevent damage.

6 Inspect the old compressor next to the new compressor. It is important to make sure that the correct unit is used. The shape of the body, the diameter and number of belt grooves, the electrical connector, and the location of the suction/discharge port should be closely checked.

The new compressor should be closely inspected to make sure it will fit properly. The recommended way to ensure that the new compressor is correct is to lay it next to the old compressor and closely look at all parts of the items to make sure that the new unit will fit properly. Key parts of the units to check closely include the location of the holes for the mounting bolts, the diameter and number of grooves on the pulley, the location for mounting the suction/discharge line, and the connectors for the compressor clutch coil.

7 Follow the directions for the compressor manufacturer concerning the refrigerant oil in the new compressor.

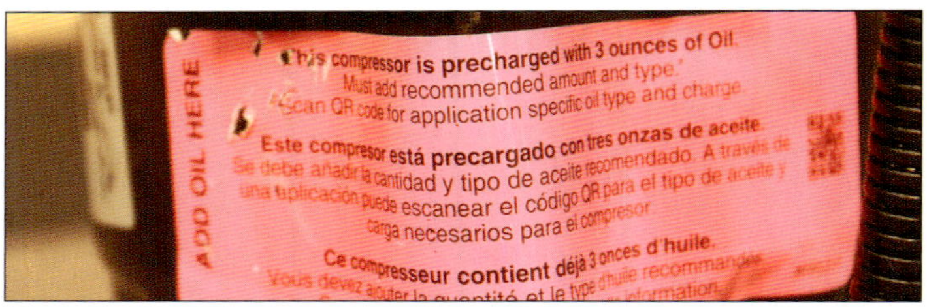

Most new compressors will have a tag or a sticker on the compressor body that give instructions on what to do concerning refrigerant oil. These instructions should be followed to ensure that the oil level and type will be used for the system. If there is not an oil tag with the new compressor, then the old compressor should be drained into a measuring container. The amount that was drained from the old compressor should be added to the new compressor. If the amount was less than 2 ounces, then 2 ounces of new oil should be added to the new compressor.

8 Reinstall the compressor using the correct mounting fasteners. Get all of the fasteners started by hand before torquing any of the fasteners to specifications. It is very important to closely follow the exact torquing procedures to prevent putting the body of the compressor in a bind and causing early failure of the unit.

9 Reinstall the electrical connections to the compressor. Make sure that each connection is securely installed and locked into place.

10 Install the compressor belt and adjust it to specifications if it is adjustable. Check the belt for proper routing and alignment into the correct grooves.

The belt tool is used during the belt installation. This tool aids in releasing the spring-loaded belt tensioner by giving strong leverage to the user. The belt should be closely inspected following installation to make sure that it is routed correctly and that all of the grooves are aligned on the pulleys and belt.

11 Install the suction discharge line, being sure to use new gaskets and seals. Torque the fasteners to the correct level.

12 Install the rest of the parts from the compressor kit using the correct techniques as listed in this chapter.

13 The AC system can be evacuated and recharged before being returned to service. See chapter 5 for details of this process.

Condenser

The condenser is the heat exchanger located in front of the engine radiator. It provides a location for the gaseous refrigerant to cool down and condense back to a liquid. Replacing the condenser typically involves removing some trim panels and fascia components along with moving the radiator enough to gain access to the mounting bolts and lines for the condenser. Here are the steps for replacing the condenser.

Replacing the AC Condenser

1 After recovering the AC system or verifying the system is empty, the condenser removal process can begin.

2 Remove the necessary upper trim bezel fasteners to gain access to the radiator and condenser mounting fasteners.

The trim covers need to be removed with the necessary tools required. Some trim covers are held in place with bolts, while others are held in place with plastic clips. A door trim panel tool is useful when removing the plastic clips.

3 Remove the inlet and outlet lines that connect to the condenser using the correct tools required for this process. Quick-connect couplings will require the use of the removal tools to get the connections apart.

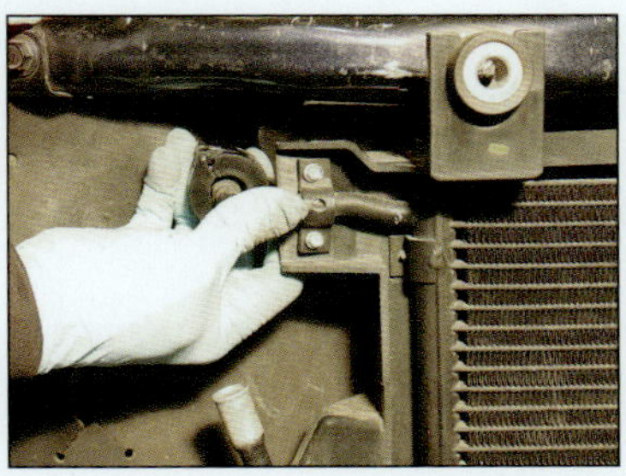

The quick-connect removal tool needs to be inserted into the quick-connect coupling with the beveled lip facing the spring. Once the tool is fully inserted, the joint can be pulled apart and serviced.

4 Remove the condenser mounting fasteners and remove the condenser from the front side of the radiator.

After using the removal tool on the quick-connect coupling, the line can be pulled away from the condenser. It is sometimes necessary to twist the line to assist in breaking the O-rings loose from the housing.

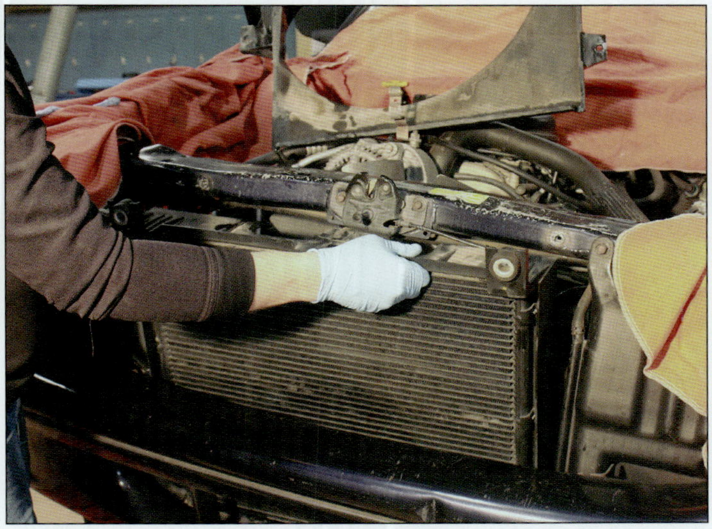

After removing the mounting fasteners from the condenser, the fan shroud, and the radiator, the condenser can be lifted from the front of the vehicle. This particular vehicle required the radiator to be removed prior to removing the condenser.

5 Inspect the new condenser for proper design characteristics to make sure it matches the old unit.

6 Add 2 ounces of the correct refrigerant oil into the condenser inlet passage.

The correct viscosity and type of refrigerant oil should be added to the new condenser prior to installation. A reliable repair database will provide the exact amount of oil to add, but if that is not available, add 2 ounces to the new condenser.

7 Install the new condenser with the old fasteners and torque them to the correct specifications.

The new condenser is installed by reversing the sequence that was used during removal. All of the O-rings and seals should be replaced and lubricated with refrigerant oil. The quick-connect couplings should be firmly connected until a snap is heard. Each connection should be pulled on to make sure that the spring is firmly in place.

8 After replacing the O-rings and gaskets, install the inlet and outlet lines to the condenser, being careful not to pinch an O-ring and making sure the quick-connect coupling snaps together properly. The retaining bracket should be installed onto the coupling properly.

The retaining brackets should be installed after the quick-connect coupling is snapped together. These brackets provide an extra layer of protection to prevent refrigerant leaks.

9 Reposition and reinstall all radiator mounting fasteners as well as all trim panels and fasteners.

All of the trim bezels and seals need to be installed along with the fasteners that hold these in place. All of the fasteners and connectors should be double-checked to make sure that all are in place prior to recharging the AC system and returning the vehicle to service.

10 The AC system can be evacuated and recharged before being returned to service. See chapter 5 for details of this process.

Evaporator Core

The evaporator core is the heat exchanger located inside the duct box that causes the heat to be removed from the air that passes by it, which produces cool and dry air. Below are the steps for replacing the evaporator core.

1 After recovering the refrigerant or verifying that the AC system is empty, follow the procedures to remove the duct box from the vehicle. This is a very labor-intensive procedure that should only be done by someone with a strong mechanical ability and a complete set of technician's tools.

Once the duct box has been removed from the vehicle, the top of the unit can be removed to gain access to the evaporator core. It is wise to pay close attention to the linkages, actuators, and the number and location of fasteners that are removed during this process.

2 Remove the top/cover of the HVAC duct box to gain access to the evaporator core. Pay close attention of the position of the duct doors during disassembly because these doors will need to be in the normal area of travel when putting the assembly back together.

The duct box top is gently lifted away from the unit to allow access to the evaporator core and heater core. Pay close attention to the position of all of the duct doors to assist in making sure that they are in the correct location when the unit is put back together.

3 Remove the evaporator core from the duct box.

4 Inspect the evaporator core closely and make sure the new unit is the correct unit to use for this vehicle.

5 Add 1 ounce of the correct refrigerant oil to the inlet side of the evaporator core.

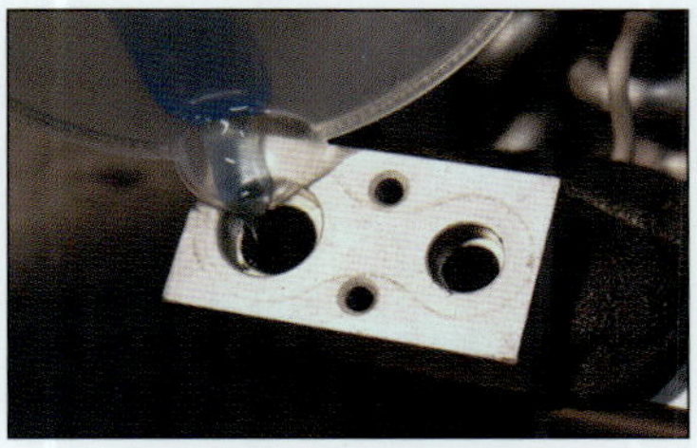

The correct viscosity and type of refrigerant oil should be added to the new evaporator core prior to installation. A reliable repair database will provide the exact amount of oil to add, but if that is not available, add 1 ounce to the new core.

6 Reinstall the evaporator core back into the duct box. It may be necessary to remove the insulating material from the old evaporator core and install it onto the new core. This insulation assists in sealing the unit and prevents duct box air from bypassing the evaporator core.

The new evaporator core is gently inserted back into the duct box housing while making sure that the foam seals are in place to prevent any air from bypassing the core.

7 Reinstall the duct box cover while paying close attention to the position of the duct box doors.

The duct box top is reinstalled and attached with the fasteners. It is important to make sure that all of the duct doors and linkages are in an acceptable position during assembly to allow for proper operation and movement of each component.

8 Reinstall the duct box assembly back into the car and then install all fasteners, hardware, electrical connections, lines, and hoses.

9 The AC system can be evacuated and recharged before being returned to service. See chapter 5 for details of this process.

Retrofitting R12 Systems to R134a

Vehicles that were built with AC systems that used R12 as the refrigerant were used from the beginning days of mobile AC units on cars and trucks up until 1992. R12 was a very reliable refrigerant that did a great job of cooling the cab of vehicles. When it became evident that the release of chlorofluorocarbon (CFC) into the atmosphere was causing deterioration of the atmospheric layer called the ozone, a new refrigerant was introduced to mobile AC systems.

Beginning in 1993, all cars and trucks sold in the United States contained R134a. Slowly, the supply of R12 was reduced, which caused the cost of this substance to rise quickly. This circumstance caused the need to change these older systems over to the R134a. This section of the chapter will provide details on how to perform a retrofit correctly on these older vehicles.

Pre-1993 Vehicles

Vehicles that are in the age range of 1992 back to about 1975 that are still in service are not very plentiful, but there are still a few thousand of them on the road. When a vehicle in this age range is still being driven and the AC system is needed or desired, then a decision must be made on how to proceed with repairing it.

First of all, if a vehicle in this age range still has a functioning AC system, then consider yourself very fortunate. No repairs need to be made except for items such as belts and cleaning the condenser coils. Most vehicles in this era with AC will have an inoperative system that must be diagnosed and repaired. Normal diagnosis procedures such as the ones discussed in chapter 4 can be used to troubleshoot problems in the AC system.

After determining what is at fault in the AC system, it must be decided whether or not to perform a retrofit of the system while repairing the other faults. Nearly always, the correct decision is to perform a retrofit of the system during the repair process. The steps below cover the retrofit process.

Performing a Retrofit Procedure

1 Perform the repair of the faulty AC parts that were found during the diagnosis process. All AC parts that were replaced during this step should have the correct viscosity PAG oil added to them during installation along with new O-rings, gaskets, and seals. PAG oil is synthetic hygroscopic oil specifically designed for compressors in R-134a systems. The viscosity of the oil can be determined by consulting the service information for the AC compressor brand and type.

This retrofit kit comes with three cans of R134a refrigerant, oil, a charge hose, service fittings, and the decal. The box states that this process can be completed in 10 minutes, but to do it right it will take a couple of hours.

This retrofit kit comes with the service fittings, caps, and the decal. This kit will need to be accompanied with more parts, such as O-rings, gaskets, and seals in order to perform a retrofit that can be relied on for long-term quality operation.

2 If the compressor was not replaced in the previous step, then remove it and drain all of the oil out of it. Add 2 ounces of PAG oil or the amount that was drained previously (whichever is greater) into the compressor. Turn the compressor by hand after adding the oil and then reinstall it.

3 Remove all lines and hoses that were not already replaced in step one. Inspect all hoses for signs of wear or leakage and replace any hoses that do not pass the inspection. Flush all the lines and hoses as well as the condenser and evaporator core if they were not replaced in step one. Add at least 1 ounce of PAG refrigerant oil to the condenser and the evaporator core.

4 Replace all O-rings, gaskets, and seals, and then reassemble each connection except for the metering device.

5 Replace the block thermal expansion valve or the orifice tube, paying attention to lubricating the rubber O-rings and seals with PAG oil.

6 Replace the dryer device while replacing all O-rings, gaskets, and seals.

7 Install the quick-connect adapters onto the Schrader-style service ports that were used for the R12 system. If the new service adapters have Schrader valves or check valves, then the old Schrader valves or check valves must be removed. Having stacked Schrader or check valves can cause the system to leak.

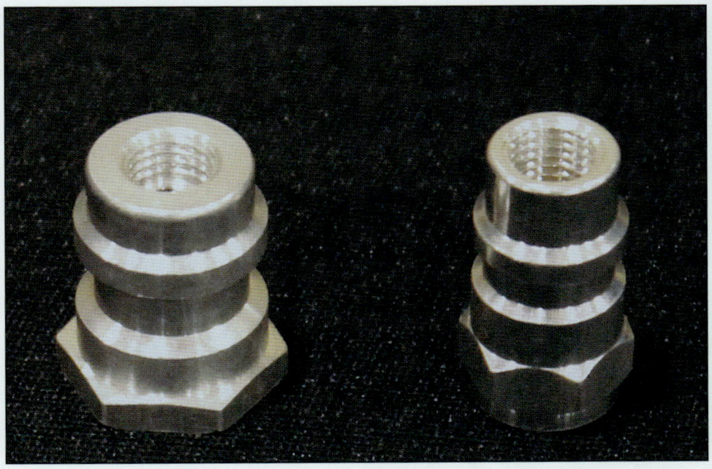

The quick-connect service fittings will be attached to the R12 service ports by screwing them onto the threaded ports. The old Schrader valves must be removed when the new adapters are equipped with Schrader valves to prevent having stacked Schrader valves.

8 If compressed nitrogen is available, then add about 100 psi of pressure to the system to quickly check for any large leaks that may be present. A hissing sound and a loss of pressure will be observed if any large leaks are present. These leaks should be repaired before moving forward in the process.

9 Connect a vacuum pump to the system and evacuate the system for at least 30 minutes. The low side gauge should drop to 25 inches of Hg (mercury) within 10 minutes of vacuum pump run time. If the system does not pull down to a deep vacuum, there is likely a leak that must be found and repaired.

10 Recharge the AC system with R134a to about 85 percent of the original weight. Start the system and test the performance by watching the pressures and duct temperatures.

11 Add the retrofit decal in a visible location under the hood. The decal should give details of who performed the work, and it should list the type and amount of refrigerant and refrigerant oil.

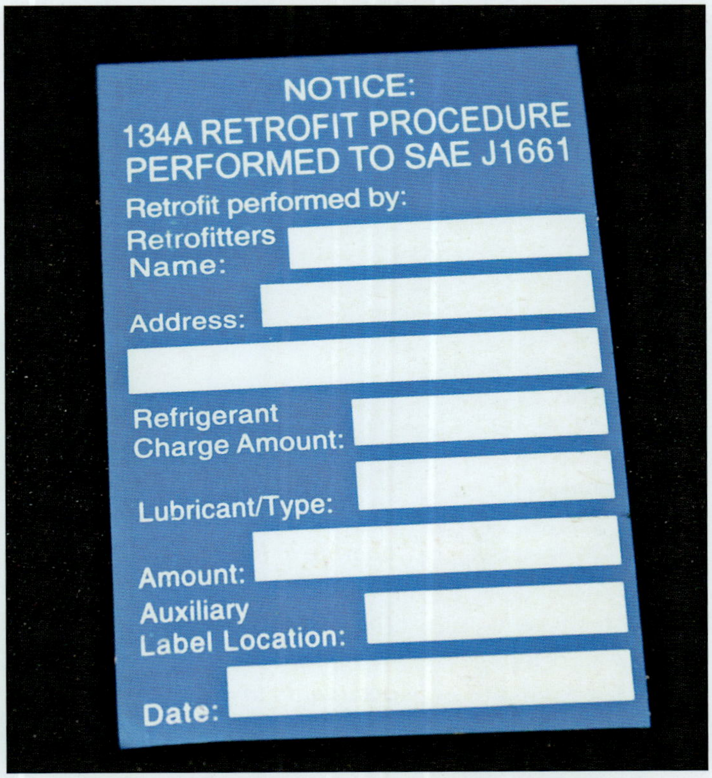

The retrofit decal must be installed in a conspicuous location prior to putting a retrofitted vehicle back into service. The decal provides important information about the AC system for anyone who may service the system in the future.

Restored and Classic Vehicles

Attending a car show that has many classic cars, muscle cars, and street rods that have been preserved or restored is a very high level of entertainment for people who love and admire these awesome machines. Owners of these vehicles often drive extended distances when attending car shows or when just cruising and enjoying their cars and trucks. Having a functioning AC system is a very valuable asset to these vehicles when they are operated in hot weather.

A great aspect of performing a serious restoration of an old vehicle is that the AC can be restored to excellent levels of performance by completing a repair/retrofit of the system. In addition, a complete AC system can be added to these vehicles that did not have AC as an option when it was originally built.

Performing a retrofit on an antique or classic car is very much like doing it on any vehicle that was originally equipped with an R12 system. The first order of business when repairing and retrofitting an old car or truck is to diagnose the obvious

Classic cars are often equipped with air-conditioning to make them more comfortable to operate in hot weather.

The HVAC control head allows the occupants to control blower speed, mode of the air distribution, and the temperature of the air. Having an operational AC system provides much more comfort for the owner and the passengers of a classic car.

Classic cars are often driven on long trips and having a functioning AC system makes the trip more comfortable. This Bel Air has been driven on several long trips and it has performed flawlessly and kept the driver and the passengers cool and happy.

problems that exist in the system and be sure to repair those problems during the repair process. Since this repair is going to be expected to be at a higher level than a repair on a daily driver, more attention is going to be placed on replacing all of the hoses and very likely replacing the compressor with a reliable new unit.

Taking these items into consideration, the repair process is exactly like the retrofit steps listed previously. Extra care should be taken in the fit and finish on a repair like this, so adding some nice chrome clamps and braces adds a level of polish to the end result.

The duct port on the driver's side of this classic Chevy delivers cool and refreshing air to the cab when the AC system is operating.

It is popular to install aluminum condensers and radiators on classic cars to provide a sleek appearance. It is also common to install electric fans to push air through the condenser to improve the performance of the AC system.

The fit and finish on the condenser and receiver dryer is excellent and will provide long periods of reliable operation of the AC system.

The AC compressor assembly has been replaced with a new unit to provide long-lasting, reliable operation. This system uses a V-style belt to pull the compressor. These belts are typically adjusted manually by moving the compressor in a groove. It is important to not put too much pressure on the belt by adjusting it too tightly.

CHAPTER 7

Electrical Operation and Repair of the HVAC System

The AC system has always relied on electricity to perform the job of controlling comfort in the cab of cars and trucks. Parts of the HVAC system requiring electricity have included the AC compressor clutch coil and the blower motor for many years. This chapter will cover the operation and repair techniques needed to repair the electrical and electronic components of the AC system.

Electrically Controlled Components

In recent years, many advances have been made in the AC system and now the system has become a lot more electrified and electronically controlled.

Compressor Clutch

The AC compressor clutch is driven by an engine drive belt on most internal combustion engines. The compressor pulley rotates at all times when the engine is running, but the front clutch plate only rotates when power is sent to the stationary coil mounted to the front of the compressor body. When power is received at the coil, a magnetic field is produced; it pulls the front clutch plate into the face of the pulley, which causes the front plate to begin rotating. The front clutch plate is mechanically connected to the internal pumping components of the compressor, which causes the refrigerant to be pressurized and pumped throughout the AC system.

The method to deliver power to the compressor clutch coil that is used on most vehicles is through a

The front of the compressor is comprised of a front clutch plate, a pulley, and a stationary coil. When the coil is energized, it creates a magnetic field that pulls the front clutch plate into contact with the pulley, which causes the internal parts of the compressor to begin pumping refrigerant.

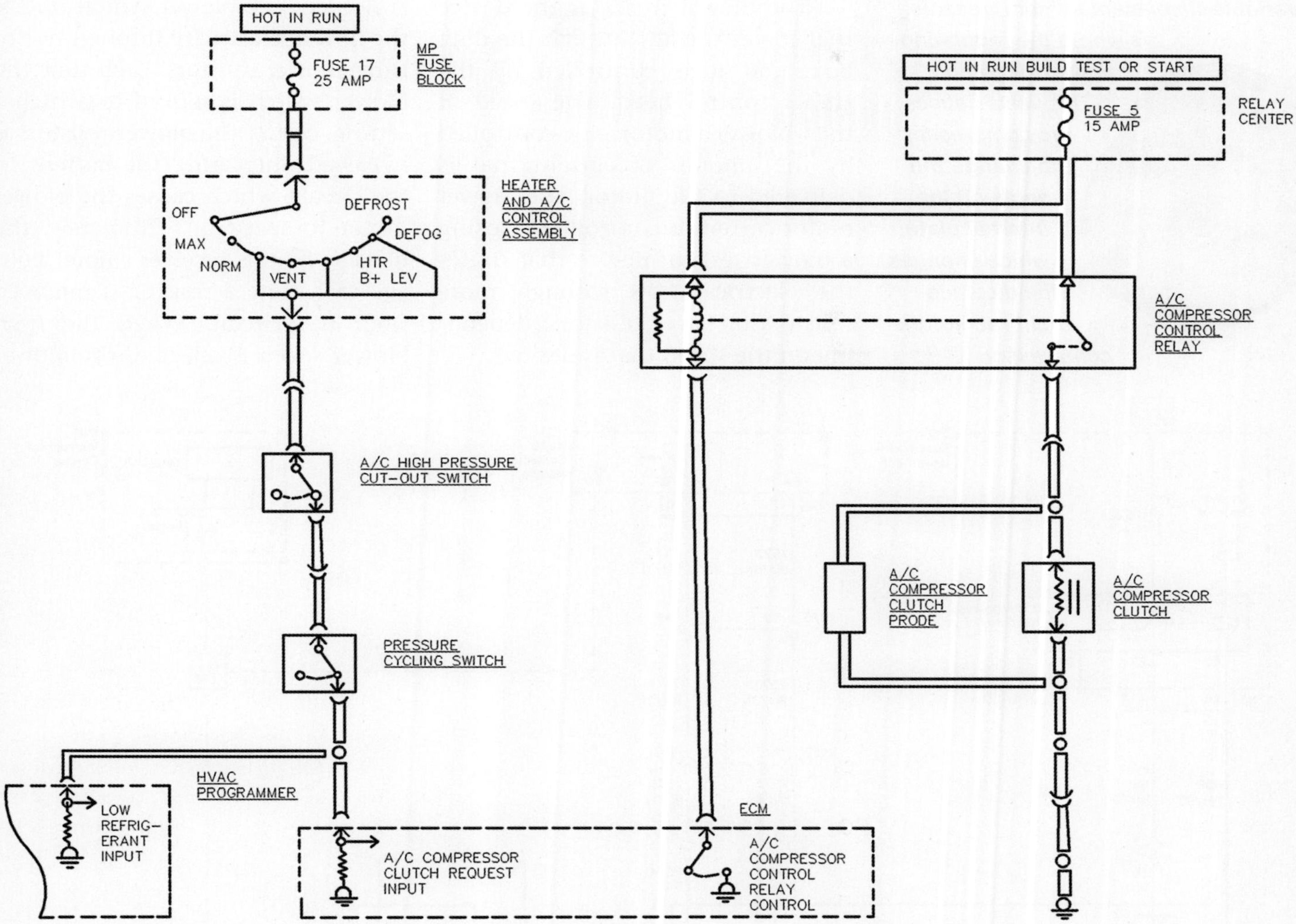

Having a wiring diagram for a circuit that is not functioning is a valuable tool. The main components in the circuit above include the AC compressor clutch coil, the AC compressor control relay, the ECM, the pressure switches, the heater, and AC control assembly and the fuses. Using a wiring diagram, digital multimeters, and some other testing tools can help troubleshoot electrical problems in the AC system.

relay that is controlled by the engine control module. The engine control module looks for an input from the HVAC control head that is routed through switches or sensors that notify the engine control module that the AC compressor can be energized.

A more modern method of controlling the AC compressor operation involves not only turning the compressor on and off but also controlling the amount of work that the compressor performs. These compressors are called variable-displacement style and have been used for many years in a mechanical form. More modern designs are now being used that control the output of the compressor by using a solenoid that controls the compressor piston stroke.

The solenoid receives signals from the engine control module based upon the requested AC needs. These compressors are able to work at full capacity when the heat load is high but can be throttled back when the cab begins to get cool. The advantage of these styles of compressors is that the clutch does not have to be cycled on and off to control evaporator freeze up.

The rear center portion of a variable-displacement compressor is where the regulating valve is located. This valve causes the compressor to change the angle on the internal plate, which changes the displacement ratio of the compressor.

Blower Motor

The blower motor is the device that forces the air through the duct box, and it is controlled by the HVAC control head. The speed of the blower motor is controlled by the amount of current that is delivered to the motor. The blower motor current is controlled by using a blower resistor device that routes the electrical flow through more resistors or fewer resistors, depending on the speed that is desired.

When a very low blower speed is needed, the blower switch directs the flow of electricity through two or three blower resistors. Each time the blower switch is moved to a higher setting, one of the blower resistors is bypassed, increasing the current in the circuit, which causes the blower motor to speed up. Ultimately, the blower motor receives more voltage each time a resistor is removed from the circuit. When the high blower speed is selected, the blower

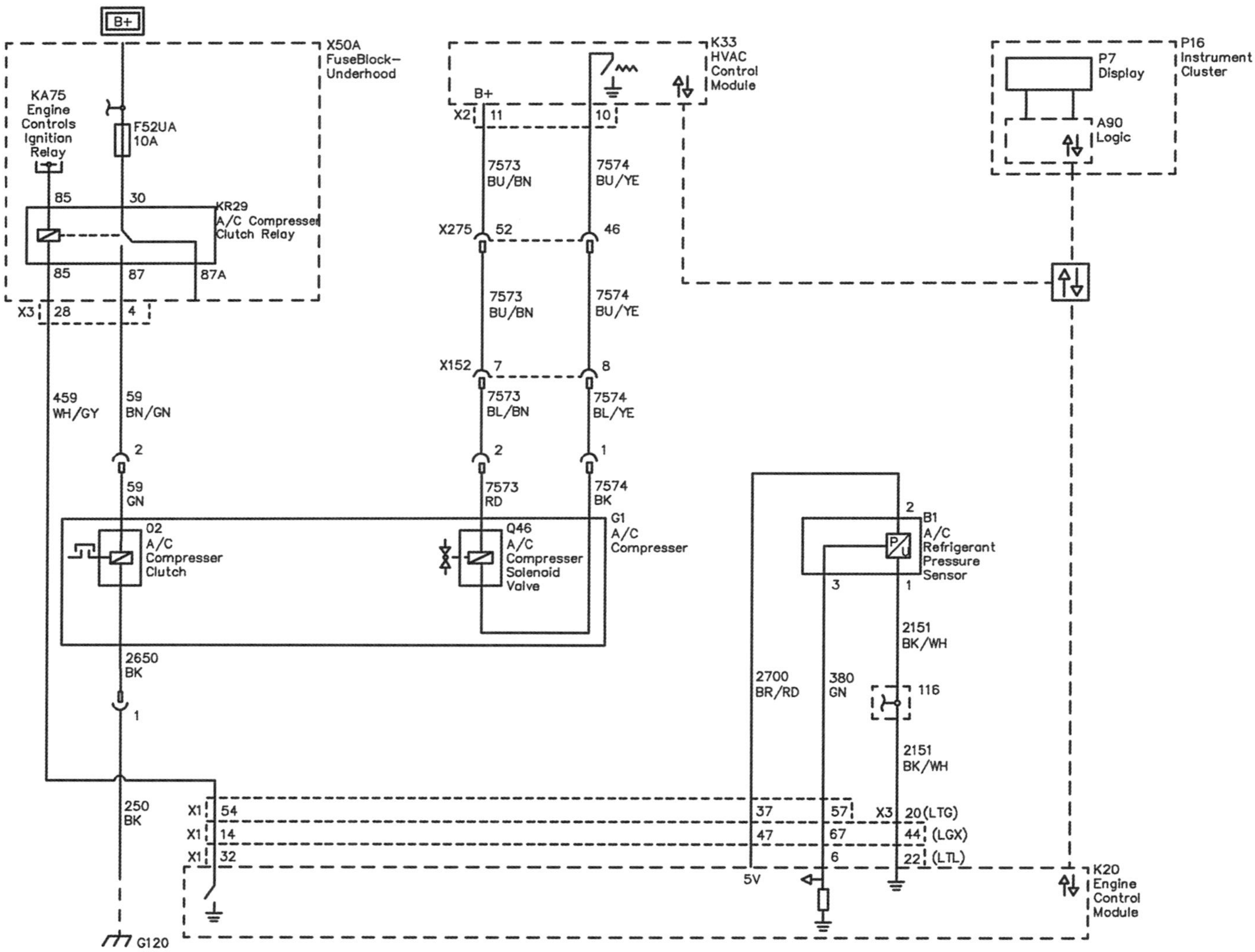

The wiring diagram in more advanced systems is helpful in troubleshooting these more modern systems. The main components in the circuit above include the AC compressor clutch coil, the AC compressor solenoid valve, the AC compressor clutch relay, the HVAC control module, and the AC refrigerant pressure sensor. These more advanced systems often require the use of scan tools and oscilloscopes to correctly diagnose and repair.

resistors are all bypassed and the blower motor gets full system voltage.

Blower motor systems in late-model cars and trucks use a pulse width modulated–style system. These blower motors are controlled by varying the length of the pulse width signal that is sent to the motor. These systems use a blower control module instead of a blower resistor to accomplish the task of controlling blower speed. Different testing techniques are required to diagnose and repair these and will be covered later in this chapter.

The blower motor operates on 12 volts DC and is mounted in the duct box. The impeller sometimes needs to be transferred to the new motor when replacing the blower motor. The impeller sometimes gets debris, such as tissues or paper from the glove box, caught in it, which causes it to make an audible noise that is undesirable.

A pulse width modulated blower motor will have more than two terminals and wires connected to the assembly. These types of blower motors require different testing techniques and strategies.

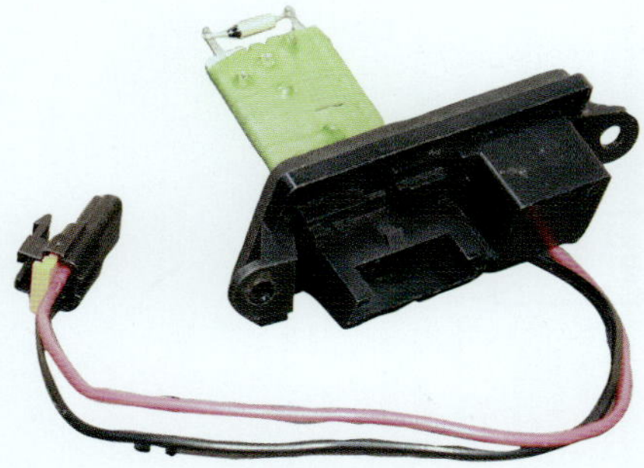

The blower resistor is used on 12-volt DC blower motor systems. This device is typically mounted in the duct box near the blower motor to allow for the airflow to keep it cool.

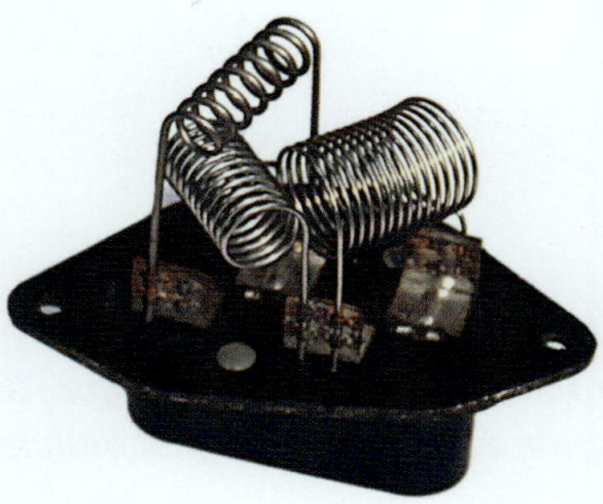

The blower resistor is used on 12-volt DC blower motor systems. This device uses wire wound resistors and is typically mounted in the duct box near the blower motor to allow for the airflow to keep it cool.

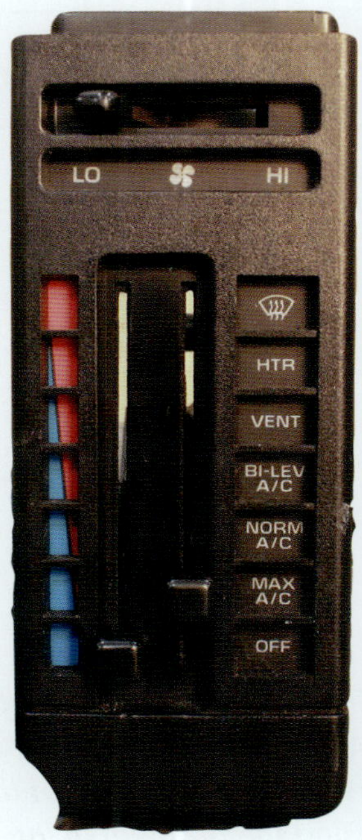

The climate control head allows the occupants of the vehicle to control the airflow in the duct box by controlling the distribution point, the temperature, and the velocity of the air being moved into the cab. The different modes the manual climate control systems include defrost, floor, and vent positions.

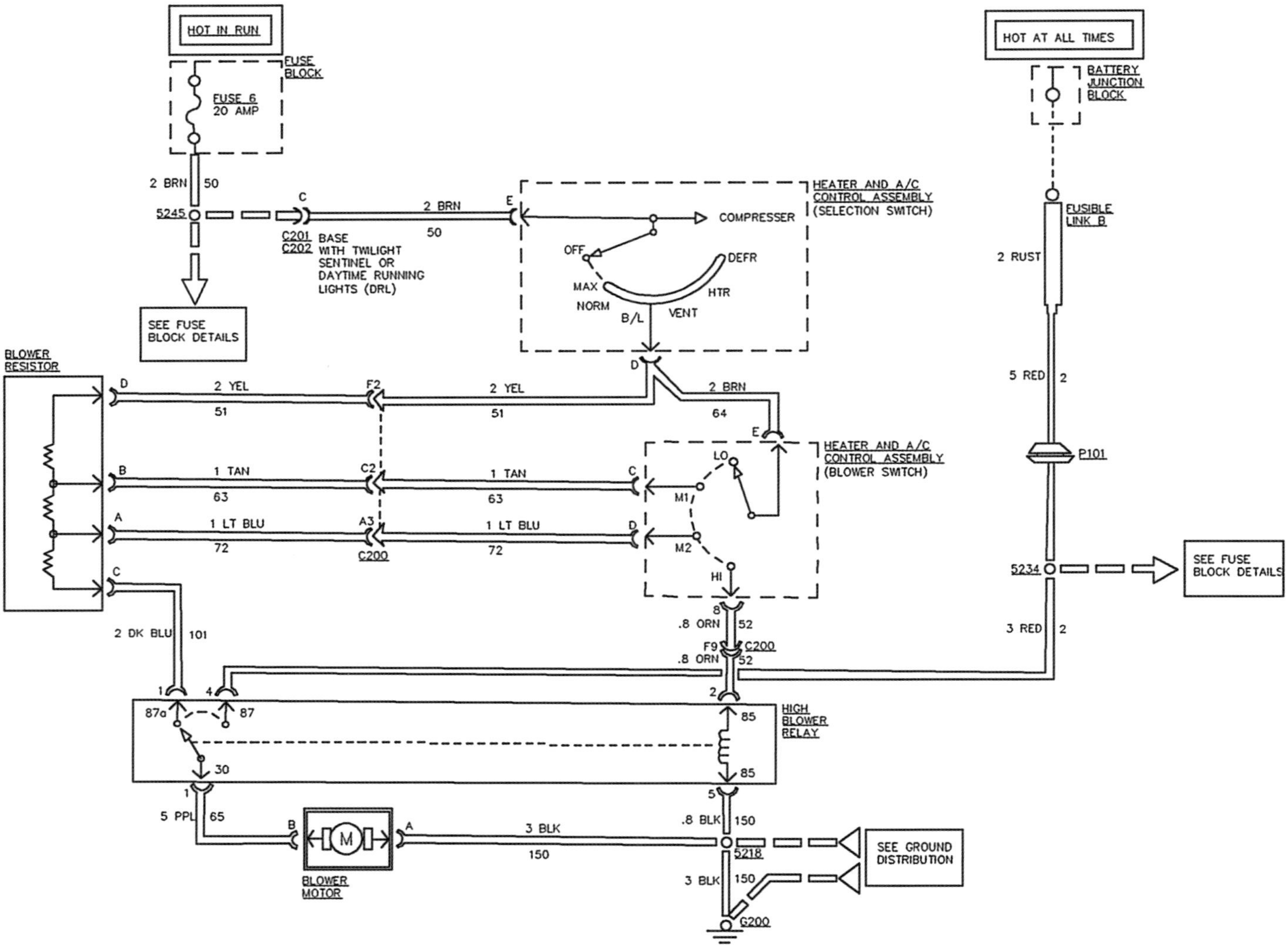

The blower motor wiring diagram is a valuable tool to use when troubleshooting a blower motor problem. The key parts of a blower motor system include the blower switch, the blower resistor, the blower relay, and the blower motor. The switch and resistor are in the power side of this system. Using a blower wiring diagram along with a digital multimeter provides a method to find the problem in the system.

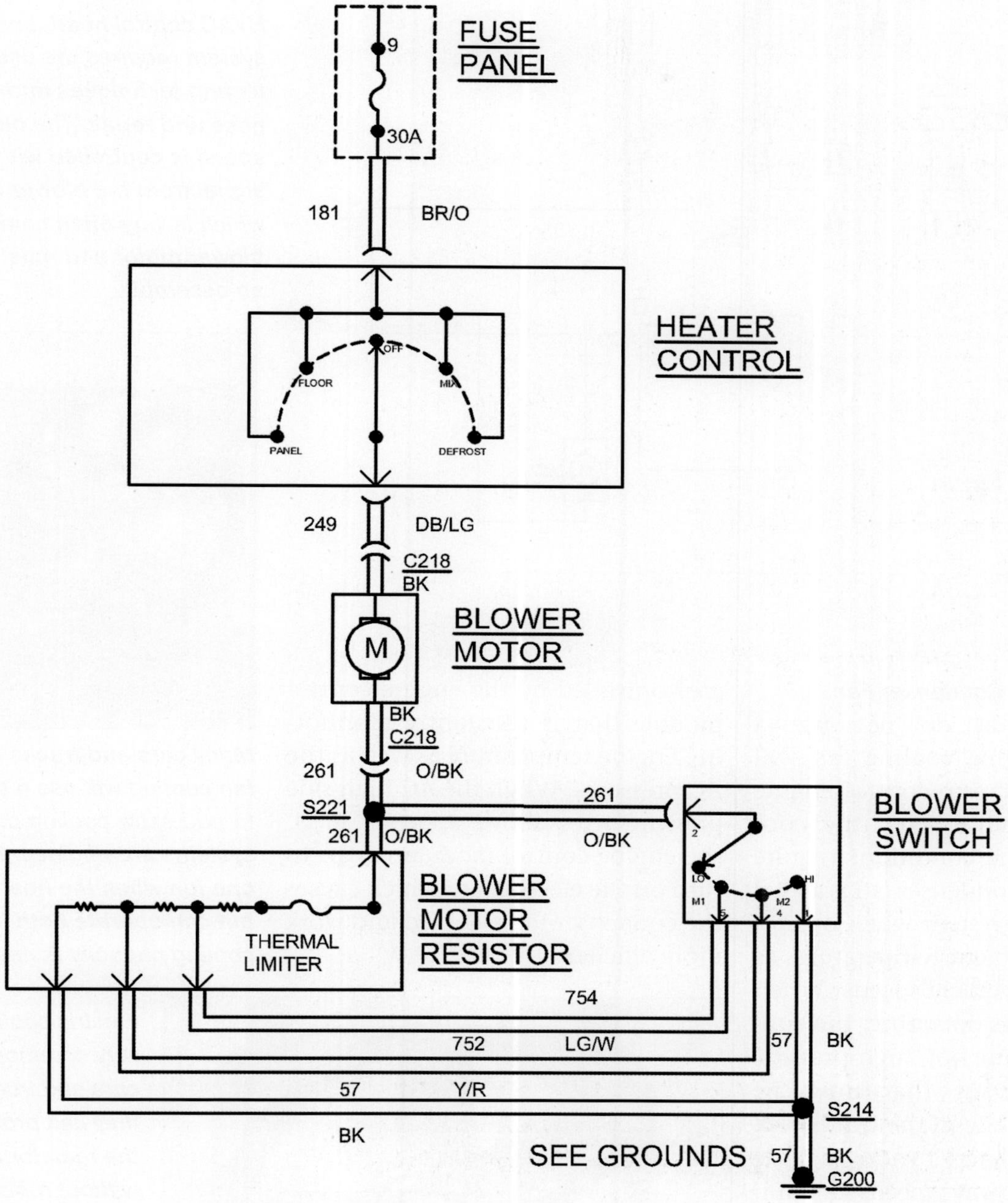

The blower motor in this wiring diagram is controlled with the switch and the blower resistor located on the ground side of the motor. The diagnostic procedure for this type of blower motor is different due to voltage being supplied to the hot side of the motor any time the heater control is turned on.

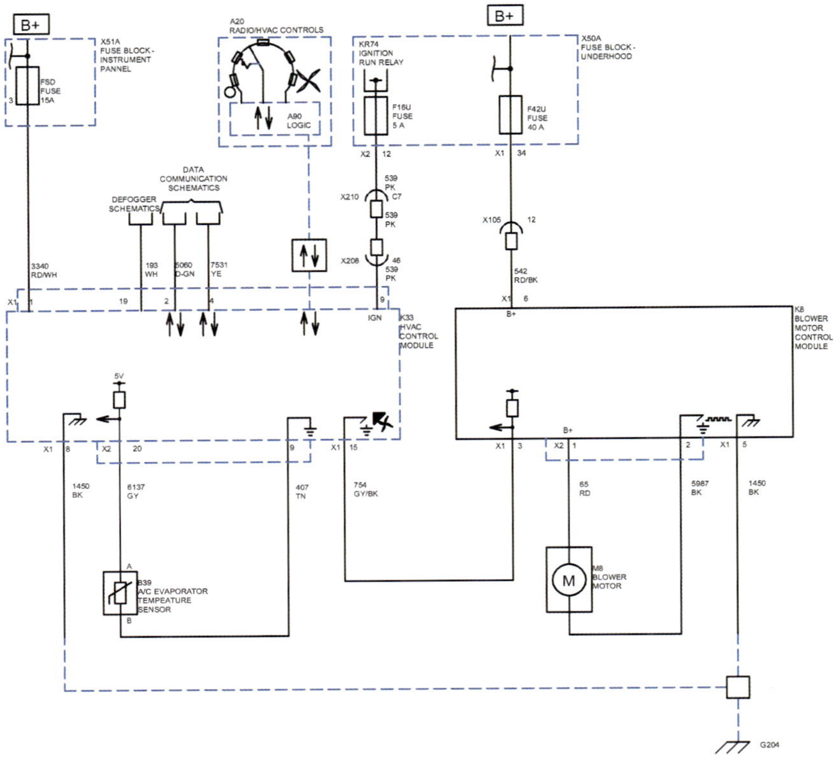

The main components in the circuit include the pulse width modulated blower motor, the blower motor control module, the HVAC control module, the HVAC control head, and the fuses. This system requires the use of advanced testing techniques and tools to diagnose and repair. The blower motor speed is controlled with a pulse width signal from the blower control module, which is very often combined with the blower motor and must be replaced as an assembly.

Many cars and trucks that use electric fan cooling will use a dual fan setup to add extra cooling capacity. These systems are engineered to operate one fan when the heat load is lower but can operate both fans when extra cooling capacity is needed.

Engine Fan and Condenser Fan

Vehicles that do not use a belt-driven engine cooling fan will use an electric fan to control engine temperature and to cool the condenser when the conditions require it. The engine/condenser fan is a vital part of the AC system when operating in high ambient temperatures as well as at low vehicle speeds. When the AC system is operating, the condenser is receiving hot, high-pressure gaseous refrigerant that must be cooled down while in the condenser. The airflow created by driving the vehicle at highway speeds is sufficient to allow this heat exchanger to work very well. When the vehicle is slowed down or stopped, the engine fan must provide airflow across the condenser.

The electric engine fan is typically controlled by a relay or a fan module. Both of these components are controlled by the engine control module that is constantly monitoring engine temperature as well as the AC pressures. When the AC high side pressure rises above a preset level, the engine control module signals to turn on the electric fan, which causes the condenser to be cooled and work more efficiently.

Electric cooling fans are very common on late-model cars and trucks because they can provide cooling for the radiator and condenser without robbing horsepower like belt-driven fans did. The fan assembly should be fastened in a secure method to the front part of the vehicle. The fan shrouds should be closely checked to ensure that they are installed correctly.

Electric actuators are commonly found on cars and truck duct boxes. These small bidirectional motors are connected to the duct doors and cause movement of the door when voltage is sent to the motor from the HVAC control module. These actuators sometimes need to be recalibrated if battery power is lost on the vehicle. This calibration can be commanded with a scan tool or by pressing a sequence of buttons on the HVAC control head.

Duct Doors

The duct box doors located inside the duct box can be moved by a cable, a vacuum actuator, or an electric actuator. Diagnosis of all of these types of mechanisms will be covered later in this chapter. Below is a quick description of how these systems operate.

Cable-Operated System: A cable is used to connect a moveable arm on the control head to a moveable arm on the duct door. When the control head arm moves, it causes the duct-door arm to move, which moves the duct door.

Vacuum Actuator System: Vacuum is supplied to the control head, which directs the vacuum to vacuum actuators through colored vacuum hoses. The vacuum actuators are connected to the duct doors and are typically spring loaded to a fixed position. When vacuum is directed to the vacuum actuator, the device moves the linkage, which moves the duct door.

Electric Actuator System: The duct doors are operated by small electric motors that are directly mounted on the doors. These actuators are reversible and move the doors back and forth as directed by the control head.

Diagnosing Electrical Problems

The electrical systems that are needed to allow the AC system to operate smoothly are very important. Using a logical approach will go a long way when trying to diagnose electrical problems in the AC system. It is a wise strategy to test all of the functions of the HVAC system to see what works and what does not work. For example, if there is no operation from any of the HVAC systems, then the problem is likely to be a main power problem, such as a fuse or a main ground.

Here are some steps to perform when testing the HVAC system for electrical functionality.

Testing the Electrical Operation

1. The control head should light up and respond to changing the settings.
2. The mode settings should change as the knobs are moved to the various positions.
3. The blower speeds should change as the switch is moved to various positions.
4. The AC compressor should click on and off as the AC switch is cycled.

Visual Inspection

The visual inspection is a powerful tool to use when trying to spot problems in the AC system. Some of the mechanical items that are easy to inspect include the hoses, belts, fluid levels, caps on service ports, and wet spots on AC components. In addition to checking these items, it is wise to look for problems in the electrical components of the AC system.

Here are some steps to keep in mind when checking the AC electrical items.

Electrical Inspection Items

1. Check to see if the AC compressor is connected properly.
2. Check to see if the AC pressure switches and sensors are connected securely.
3. Check the underhood wiring harnesses to see if there is any sign of a previous shoddy repair, such as the harnesses not being installed back into the correct clips and brackets.
4. Try lightly wiggling the connectors of the pressure switches and sensors that can be accessed easily.

Vacuum actuators can be used as a method to move the duct doors on older cars and trucks. These devices are typically connected to a duct door with some type of linkage and will be operated by sending vacuum through a hose to cause movement. These actuators are spring loaded to a fixed position and the vacuum causes them to create linear movement, which causes the duct door to move.

Poor connections on the AC system components can sometimes be found by gently wiggling the connectors while the system is turned on. If the system cycles on and off when a connector is gently moved, then a bad connection exists at that point and must be repaired by replacing the terminals or the connector.

AC Clutch Testing and Repair

After determining that the AC compressor is not operating when the system is turned on, it is necessary to test the electrical components of the AC system. This section provides details on how to test many of these electrical items that are used to energize the AC compressor. Multiple testing methods are provided to give readers more than one option.

Fuses

Fuses protect electrical circuits from excessive current flow and are located in fuse panels and power distribution centers. If a circuit has a surge of high current, then the small metallic bar inside the fuse melts to cause an open circuit. It is easy to replace a blown fuse when one is found. The correct amperage fuse should always be used. Adding a fuse that is higher than the manufacturer rating poses a risk for an electrical fire. See the following steps for methods of testing fuses.

12-volt Unpowered Test Light Method: Ground the lead of the test light to a known good body, chassis, or battery ground. Turn on the ignition switch and touch both metal tabs on every fuse in the fuse boxes and power distribution center. Good fuses will cause the test light to light up at both tabs. A blown fuse will only light the test light on one tab. If the light does not light up on either tab, then another test technique can be used.

Digital Multimeter (DMM) Voltmeter Method: Turn the DMM to DC volts and ground the black lead to a known good body, chassis, or battery ground. Turn on the ignition switch and touch both metal tabs on every fuse on the vehicle. Good fuses will have voltage available at both tabs and blown fuses will only have voltage on one of the tabs. If there is no voltage on either tab, then another technique can be used.

Power Probe Method: Connect the Power Probe to power and ground. Turn on the ignition switch and touch both metal tabs on every fuse on the vehicle. Good fuses will have voltage available at both tabs, and blown fuses will only have voltage on one of the tabs.

DMM Ohmmeter Method: Disconnect the vehicle battery. Turn the DMM to the ohmmeter setting and then touch both tabs on every fuse on the vehicle. Good fuses will have very low resistance and blown fuses will have an OL reading, which means that the fuse is open.

DMM Continuity Method: Disconnect the vehicle battery. Turn the DMM to the continuity setting and then touch both tabs of every fuse on the vehicle. Good fuses will cause the meter to make an audible *beep* to show a complete circuit, and blown fuses will give no audible response.

Fuses are available in many physical sizes as well as amperage ratings. Items from left to right are: a mini fuse, a standard ATC-type fuse, a maxi fuse, a fuse element, a fuse cartridge, and a fusible link. Fuses generally range in amp ratings from 2 amps up to more than 100 amps and are used in accordance with the expected load of the circuit that they will be protecting.

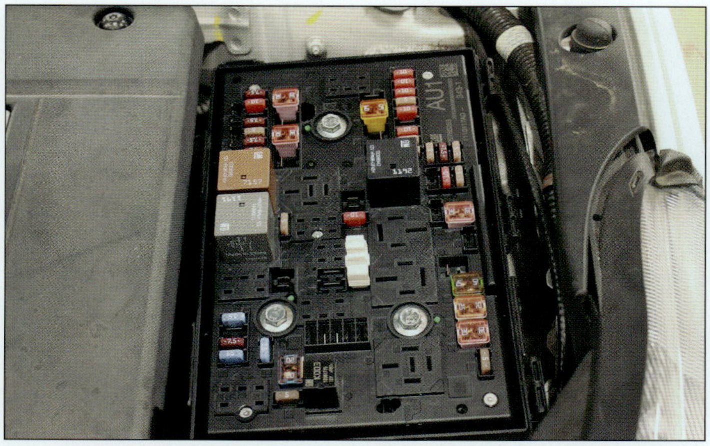

The power distribution center is located under the hood and it houses the electrical components in a convenient location that is usually easily accessible. This power distribution center has mini fuses, cartridge fuses, and relays. The electrical components can easily be tested and serviced in this central location.

The fuse panel is located inside the vehicle and it contains mini fuses of various amperages. Some fuse panels will also have some relays, depending on the manufacturer. Having the fuses located in this central location provides a way to quickly test all of the fuses without having to search for each fuse in a different location.

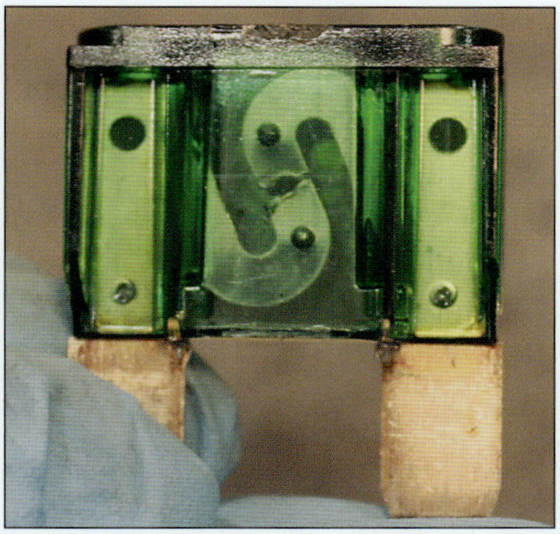

A fuse is designed to be the weak link in an electrical circuit to protect the system against too much amperage. The metallic strip inside the fuse will get hot and melt to create an open circuit when the amperage in the circuit rises above the amperage rating of the fuse. A blown fuse will show a break in the metallic strip inside the fuse. The continuity of the fuse should always be tested if a fuse is suspected to be blown but the metallic strip appears to be good.

A blown fuse will often appear to be burnt in the area of the metallic strip. This is caused by the strip melting when the current is increased to levels that exceed the rating of the fuse.

Fuses can be tested with a 12-volt unpowered test light by grounding the test light at a known good ground and then touching both metallic tabs on each fuse. A good fuse will cause the test light to illuminate at both test points. An open fuse will only illuminate the test light at one of the points. The ignition switch needs to be on when testing fuses.

Fuses can be tested with a digital voltmeter by connecting the ground lead of the meter to a known good ground and then touching both metallic tabs on each fuse with the probe of the red lead. A good fuse will have voltage at both test points, but an open fuse will only have voltage at one of the points. The ignition switch needs to be on when testing fuses.

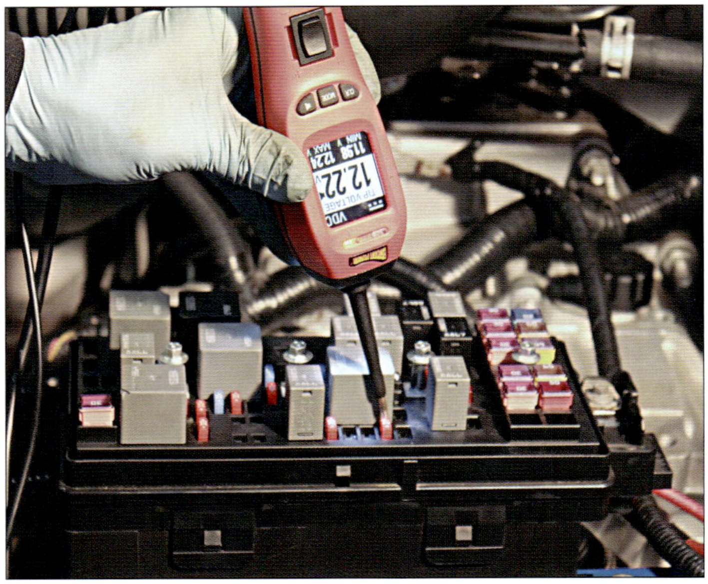

Fuses can be tested with an electronic testing device, such as a Power Probe. This tool needs to be connected to power and ground and then it can be used to measure voltage at the tip of the tool. With the ignition switch turned on, the tip of this tool needs to contact both metallic tabs on each fuse. A good fuse will have voltage at both test points, but an open fuse will only have voltage at one of the points. This tool also has a light that projects toward the tip, which is handy when using the tool in dark areas.

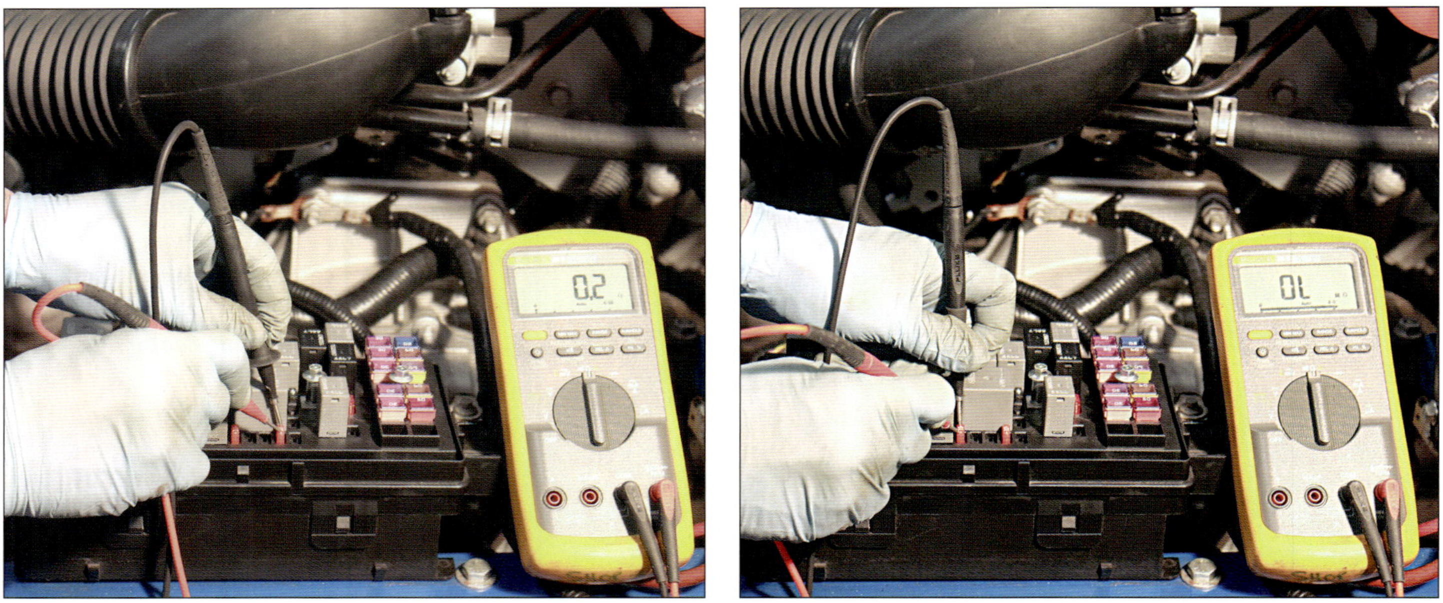

Fuses can be tested with an ohmmeter without removing them from their mounting location. After disconnecting the battery, the ohmmeter leads should be inserted at the metallic tabs on each fuse to measure the resistance of the device. A good fuse will have a very low reading on the meter, and a bad fuse will have an OL reading on the meter, which means the fuse is blown (open).

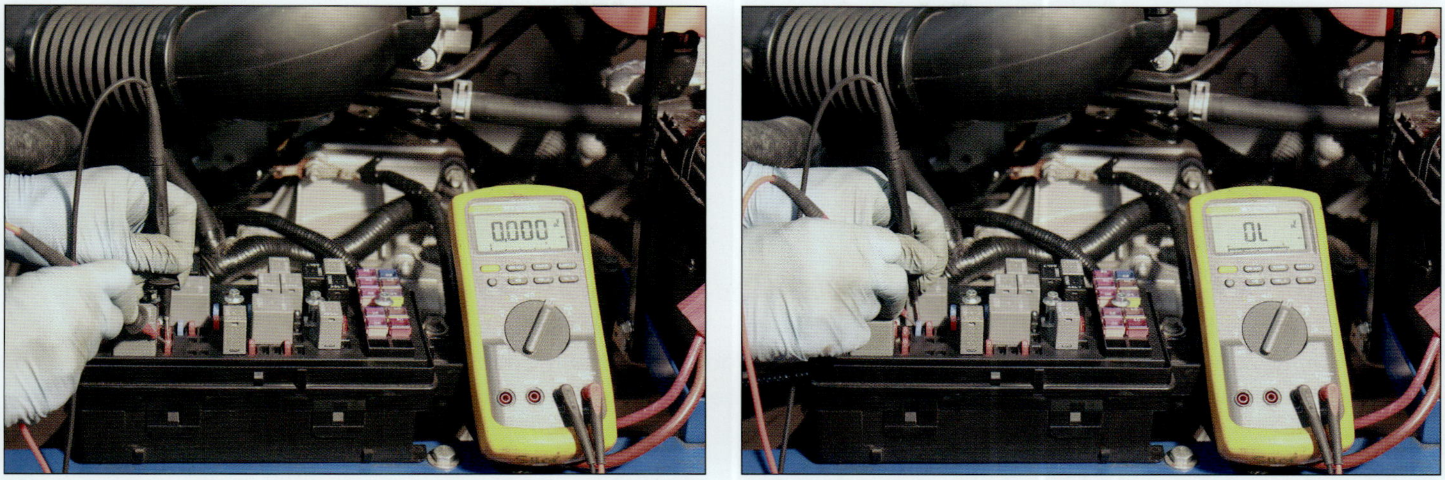

Fuses can be tested with the continuity tester on the digital multimeter without removing them from their mounting location. After disconnecting the battery, the test leads of the meter should be inserted at the metallic tabs on each fuse to test for continuity of the fuse. A good fuse will cause the meter to make an audible sound as well as have a 0.0 volt reading on the display. A bad fuse will cause the meter to have an OL volt reading on the display. No audible sound will be present when testing a bad fuse.

Circuit breakers are used to protect circuits and are located in the fuse block or in the power distribution center. The circuit breaker on the left is a manually resetting style and the one on the right is an automatically resetting style.

Circuit Breakers

Circuit breakers are used for protection on circuits that draw increased amounts of amperage during normal operation, such as the blower motor. Circuit breakers are available in two styles: automatically resetting and manually resetting. When the bimetallic strip heats up due to increased current flow, the circuit breaker moves to open the circuit. Automatic circuit breakers cool down and then reconnect the power to the circuit. Manual resetting circuit breakers have to be manually pressed to reconnect the power to the circuit.

Control Heads

The control panel is the device that allows the front-seat occupants to select the desired operation of the HVAC system. The control head has settings for the mode, the temperature, the air source, and the blower speeds. The era of the vehicle will determine what kind of service can be performed on the control head.

Older vehicles had some serviceable parts on the control head, such as the blower switch or the vacuum switching valve. However, more recent vehicles have control heads that are fairly electronic in nature and will likely need to be replaced as an assembly if problems occur. The main point to check on a control head that does not work is to make sure it has power and ground supplied to it.

Vehicles with automatic temperature control have very advanced control heads, and it is often possible to use the control head to retrieve diagnostic trouble codes from the control head by pressing a series of buttons. This is a handy diagnostic strategy that will assist in finding problems with these advanced systems.

Another handy routine that is often available on these advanced systems is calibrating the duct door actuators. This is accomplished by depressing a series of buttons on the HVAC control head. These routines are available on most reliable service information databases.

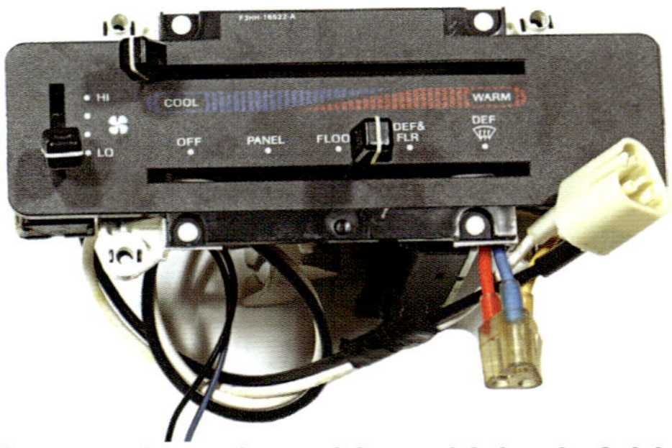

The HVAC control head on older vehicles is fairly reliable and very simple in design. These control heads often have a vacuum switching valve to control the vacuum-operated duct door actuators. The blower motor control switch can sometimes be a serviceable component on this era of control head.

More modern HVAC control head designs mainly control electrical operation of the system and are typically not serviceable. If these control heads develop a problem, then the complete assembly must be replaced.

Relays

Relays are magnetic switches used in the AC system to send power to loads that draw lots of current, such as the compressor clutch and the blower motor. After testing the fuses, the relay is a very good place to begin testing because it can be accessed easily at the relay box or power distribution center. Below are some strategies that can be used when testing electrical circuits at the relay.

HVAC systems that automatically control the desired temperature in the cab are called automatic temperature control. These systems use HVAC control heads that have digital displays and operate in an advanced method.

Tips for Testing Relays

1. Listen for a click when the circuit is turned on and off.
2. Substitute a known good relay in place of the relay that is not working.
3. Use a toggle switch relay to see if the circuit can be energized with the toggle switch.
4. Use a fused jumper wire across the load side of the relay to see if the circuit can be energized by bypassing the relay.
5. Test the relay in a static method by using the ohmmeter on the DMM. The coil should have about 60 to 100 ohms and the normally open contact should be OL, which means the contacts are not connected.

The power distribution center is a convenient location for various sizes and types of fuses as well as the many relays that are needed on late-model vehicles. Power distribution centers are located under the hood, while the fuse panel is located inside the vehicle. Some vehicles will have multiple power distribution centers and fuse panels. This power distribution center has ISO relays as well as half ISO relays. Half ISO relays are smaller and take up less space, which is popular on newer vehicles that have many more electronic options. ISO relays have standardized pin configurations that have been spelled out by the International Standards Organization.

There are several pin configurations for relays that are used on various manufacturers' vehicles. There are four-pin relays that have two terminals for the coil and two terminals for the load side contact. Some relays use one more terminal that operates as a normally closed switch. The larger relay is an ISO relay and can deliver about 30 to 40 amps to a load, while the three smaller relays are half ISO style and can deliver about 20 amps to a load. The smaller relays are popular because of their smaller-size body and how more of them can fit in a power center.

Bypass relays are very handy to use when troubleshooting relay-powered circuits. This set contains six of the most common pin configurations being used. These devices can be used by substituting them for the relay that is being diagnosed.

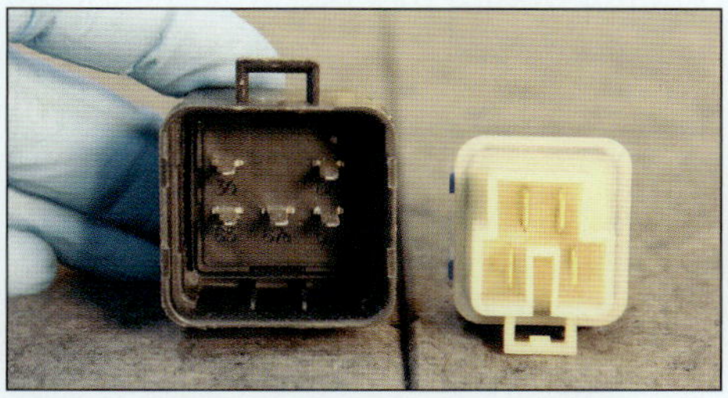

These relays are configured a little different than the ones in the photo above. The relay on the left is a five-pin relay and the relay on the right is a four-pin relay.

Bypass relays can be used to easily turn on relay-powered circuits during the diagnosis process. These devices are installed in place of the stock relay and then are turned on with a toggle switch mounted on top of the unit. If the load turns on when the toggle switch is flipped, then the load side of the relay circuit is functional.

The bypass relay is being used in the power distribution center to activate the AC compressor clutch. The original relay was removed and the bypass relay was installed instead. The toggle switch is switched to on, which should supply power to the AC compressor clutch.

By pressing the toggle switch on this bypass relay, the circuit is energized. This is a logical location to use when diagnosing circuits that are powered by a relay because it breaks the circuit in half and energizes the load side of the circuit. If the load turns on with this technique, then the control side of the circuit should be tested.

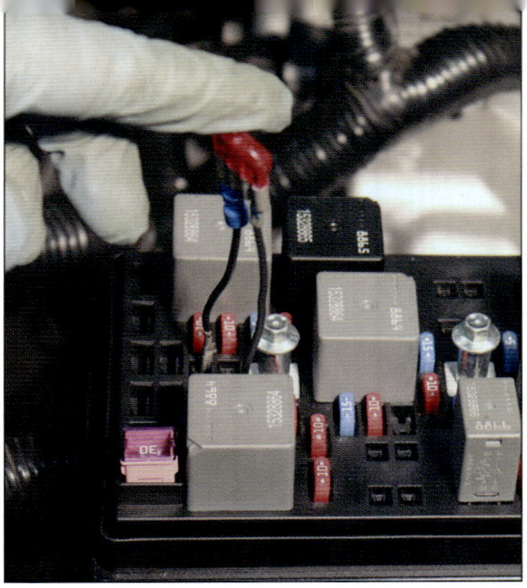

A fused jumper wire can be used to bypass switches and relays. This fused jumper is installed in terminals 30 and 87 of this four-pin relay. This action safely supplies power to the AC compressor clutch. Never connect any jumper wires in terminals 85 and 86 because damage to the power distribution center can occur.

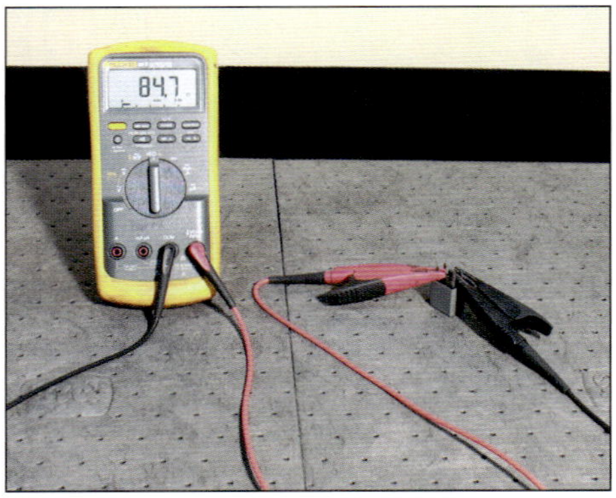

Relays can be bench tested with an ohmmeter. This relay coil is being tested and the reading is within the normal range of 70 to 90 ohms.

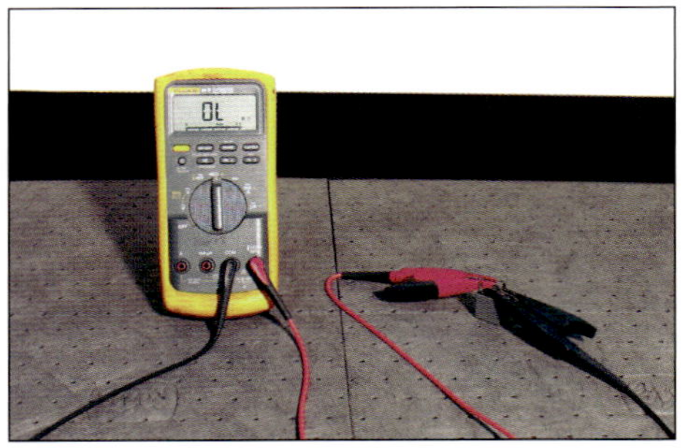

The "normally open" contacts of this relay are shown to be "OL" on the ohmmeter, which means that the contacts are open. A low ohmmeter reading during this test would indicate a shorted contact on the relay.

Pressure Switches

The AC system often uses pressure switches to sense pressure in the high side of the system as well as the low side of the system. The high side switch is located at some point in the high side of the system and is connected into the system by either threading onto a line or directly into the body of the compressor. The high side switch is typically a closed switch at pressures below about 375 psi, at which point the contacts open and cause the compressor to turn off for a few seconds to allow the pressure to drop to safer levels.

The low side switch is located at some point in the low side of the system and is connected into the system by either threading onto a line or other low side component. The low side switch is typically a closed switch at pressures above about 25 psi, at which point the contacts open, causing the compressor to turn off for a few seconds to allow the pressure to rise. The low side switch assists in controlling the temperature in the evaporator from getting too cold. This switch also causes the compressor to turn off if the system gets low on refrigerant. Below are some strategies to use when testing pressure switches.

Servicing AC Pressure Switches

1 After verifying the system has pressure, disconnect the electrical connector and connect a fused jumper wire across the terminals of the connector. This will bypass the switch to see if the compressor will turn on. Never perform this test if the AC system has lost all pressure because the compressor will possibly run without any lubricant, which will quickly destroy the unit. A small paper clip can also be used for this procedure, but care should be used to prevent terminal damage.

2 Use an ohmmeter to test the resistance across the switch contacts. The low side switch should have low resistance with the system pressure above 25 psi and the high side switch should have low resistance with the system pressure below 375 psi.

When AC pressure switches are found to be defective, then it is time to replace them with a new unit. Many of these switches are mounted to a line or component that has a check valve underneath it, so it is not necessary to recover the refrigerant prior to replacing it. These switches are made with a raised portion in the center of the switch that presses on the check valve when it is installed on the system.

These switches can simply be turned counterclockwise to remove them from their mounting location. A new O-ring should be installed with the new switch, and the unit should be tightened to specifications with a torque wrench. (There are some switches that screw onto the line or component, but there is no Schrader valve underneath.)

These systems must be recovered prior to removing the switch for service. If a switch is held in by a snap ring, then the system must be recovered prior to removing the switch for service. After replacing these switches, the AC system will need to be evacuated and then recharged with the correct amount of refrigerant.

Testing and Servicing AC Pressure Switches

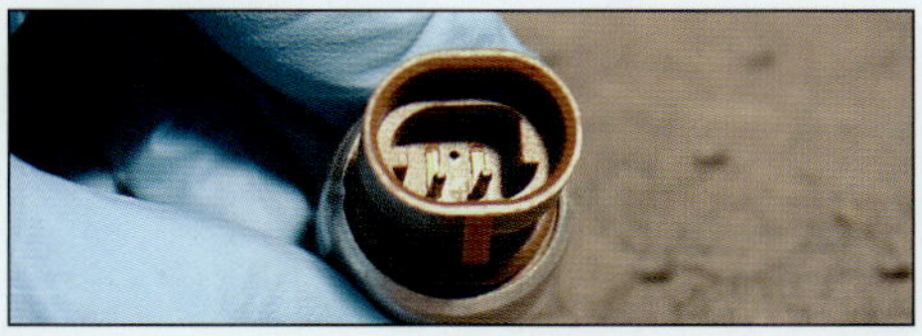

1 *The high side switch has two terminals and is located on a line or a component in the high side of the AC system. The connector for the switch should be closely inspected to make sure the terminals are in good shape and not corroded or damaged.*

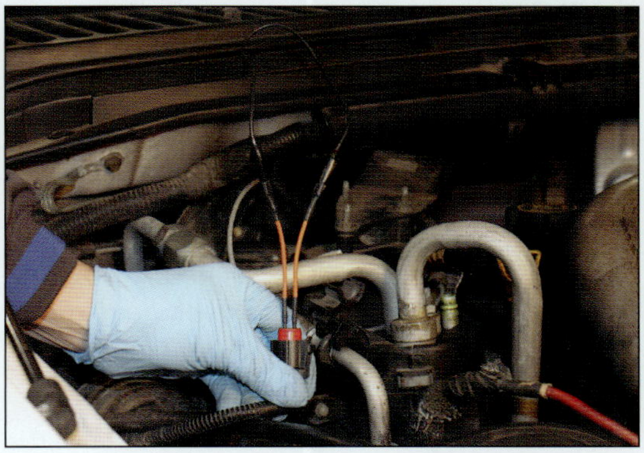

3 *After verifying that the AC system has pressure that indicates the presence of refrigerant, the low side switch can be bypassed to see if the compressor will engage. Using jumper wires that fit into the terminals without damaging them is a method to bypass the switch. This procedure should only be used when testing to see if the low side switch is bad and should not be done for more than a few seconds.*

2 *The low side switch has two terminals and is located on a line or a component in the low side of the AC system. This switch provides protection for the system if the pressures in the low side of the system drop below certain levels.*

4 *Similar to using the jumper wire, a small paper clip that fits into the terminals without damaging them is another method to bypass the switch. It is important to use a jumper device that does not cause the terminals in the connector to spread out when it is installed.*

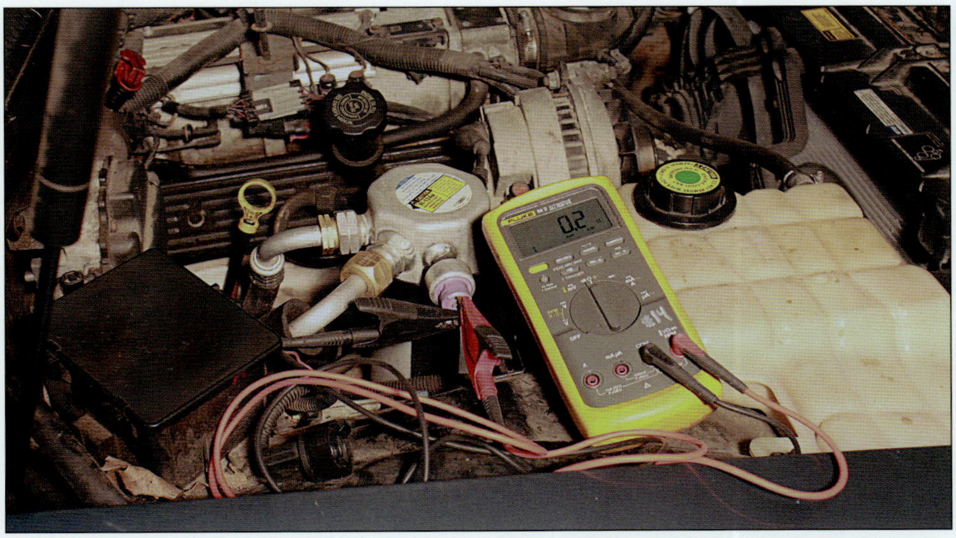

5 *An ohmmeter can be used to test the resistance of a pressure switch. The result of this test will be a very low resistance if the switch is closed and OL if the switch is open. A low-pressure switch should be closed if there is at least 25 psi of pressure in the system. A high-pressure switch should be closed if the pressure is below about 375 psi.*

6 *The bottom side of the low side and high side switches are made with the center portion that protrudes out. This raised portion is what engages the Schrader valve at the mounting location. AC systems with switches like this do not require the system to be recovered when replacing the switch. When this switch is removed, the Schrader valve holds the refrigerant in the system.*

7 *The low side switch is always mounted in the low side of the system and when the metering device is an orifice tube, this switch is often mounted on the accumulator dryer. This switch does have the raised center, which means that the AC system does not have to be recovered to replace this switch.*

8 *The connector needs to be pinched to release the retaining clips to allow it to be disconnected. It is important to be careful when disconnecting any electrical connector to prevent breaking the latches or causing any other damage to the assembly.*

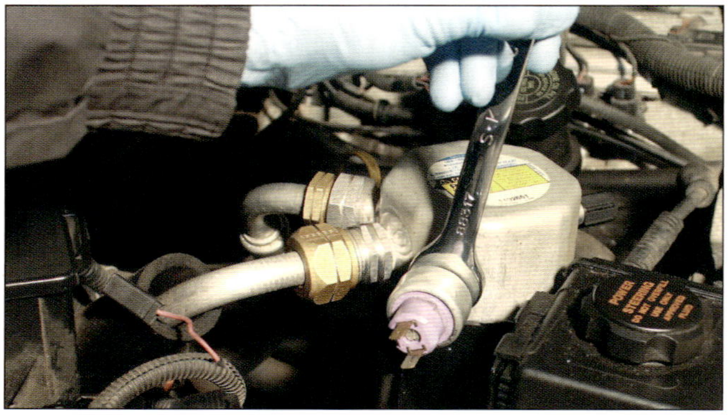

9 *The bottom side of the low side switch has a hex surface that will allow a wrench to be used to loosen the switch for removal. Be sure to use the correct size wrench to prevent rounding the corners off of the hex fastener.*

10 *After the switch is removed, the Schrader valve and O-ring should be inspected for damage. If bubbles or a hissing sound is observed, then the Schrader valve is leaking and will need to be replaced. The refrigerant will need to be recovered if the Schrader valve needs to be serviced.*

11 *The O-ring should always be replaced when replacing any switch or sensor on the AC system. A pick is a useful tool to use to aid in the removal of the O-ring.*

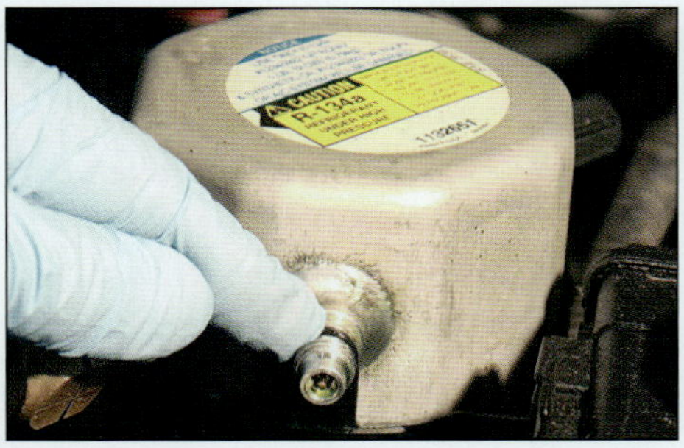

12 The new O-ring can be installed by hand and lubricated with refrigerant oil to aid in sealing. Make sure the correct size and thickness of O-ring is used to prevent a refrigerant leak.

13 The new switch is installed by hand, making sure to not cross-thread the connection. The switch should be turned about three turns by hand prior to using the wrench to finish the tightening process. A wrench is used to tighten the switch back to the correct tightness and then the connector can be reattached. The switch tightness is at a very low torque and should only be turned with mild wrench pressure. A torque wrench should be used if there is doubt on the tightness level. A crow's foot wrench can be used along with a torque wrench to attain the exact tightness. The torque specification can be found in a service manual or on an electronic database.

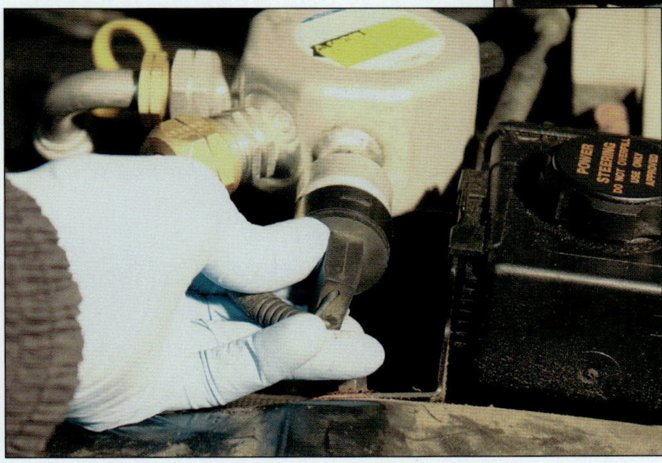

14 The electrical connector is reinstalled by carefully pushing it into place until the latches of the connector snap into place.

Pressure switches that do not thread onto a fitting are typically held in place with a snap ring. These switches always require the refrigerant be recovered prior to removing them from the system. The O-ring should always be replaced when servicing this type of switch.

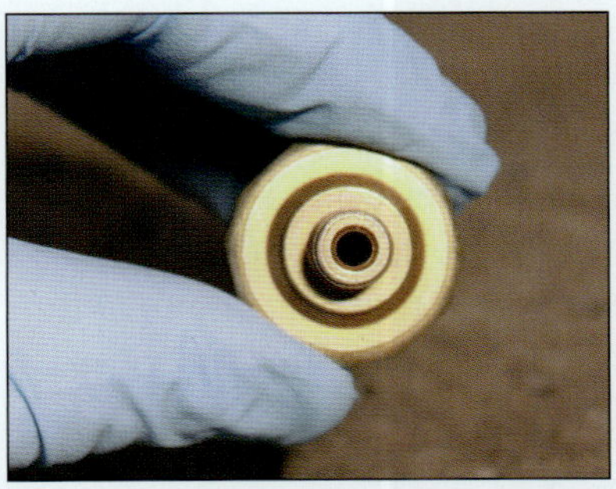

Pressure switches and sensors that do not have a protruding area in the center require the AC system to be recovered prior to removing them from their mounting position. These switches and sensors are not as common as the other type, and anyone who is servicing the AC system should always make sure they are aware of which type a system uses prior to performing service on these devices. The service procedures in the service manual or an electronic database will reveal whether or not the system needs to be recovered when these switches are being serviced.

Pressure Sensors

Pressure sensors are used to monitor pressure in the AC system in a similar way that pressure switches function. The main difference is that these devices must be diagnosed with either a voltmeter or a scan tool. These sensors operate by varying the signal voltage as the AC pressure rises and falls. This signal voltage can be seen on a scan tool or by back-probing the signal wire with a voltmeter. Replacing these devices involves the same techniques and cautions as replacing pressure switches.

The AC pressure sensor connects to the AC system the same way as the pressure switches that have the Schrader depressor. These sensors can be replaced without recovering the refrigerant.

The ambient temperature sensor is typically located at the front side of the vehicle either to the left or right side of the radiator and condenser. It must be a reasonable distance away from heat sources so it can accurately measure the outside temperature, which is used for the fuel injection system as well as for the HVAC system.

The engine coolant temperature sensor is located at some point on the engine that is exposed to engine coolant. This sensor is located at the rear of one of the cylinder heads.

Temperature Sensors

Temperature sensors are used in the AC system to sense temperature and prevent the evaporator from getting too cold and freezing up. These sensors are just thermistors that operate by varying resistance as the temperature rises and falls. The module that controls the HVAC sends a reference voltage to these devices and continually monitors the voltage drop across it as the temperature changes. These sensors can be tested by testing the voltage drop across the sensor with a digital multimeter (DMM) or by using a scan tool and monitoring the sensor input in the data list.

Other types of temperature sensors that are used in the AC system include the ambient air temperature sensor, the cabin temperature sensor, and the coolant temperature sensor. These variable sensors are used to sense temperature in their given location to allow the AC system to operate as designed in a reliable manner.

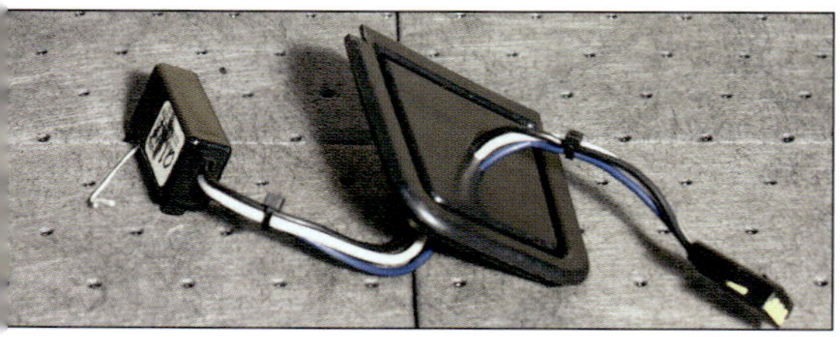

The evaporator temperature sensor is located in the duct box very near the evaporator core. Care should be taken when installing the new sensor to prevent damaging the evaporator core.

AC Clutch Coil

The AC clutch coil is used to create a magnetic field that attracts the front plate toward the pulley to engage the internal parts of the compressor. Below are the strategies to troubleshoot the clutch coil.

Testing the AC Clutch Coil

1. Test for power and ground supplied to the coil. To do this, connect the voltmeter leads to the compressor coil connector by back-probing the terminals. Turn on the AC and measure the voltage drop across the terminals. If source voltage is available, the coil is faulty and needs to be replaced.

2. Test the resistance of the coil. To do this, disconnect the compressor coil connector. Connect the ohmmeter leads across the terminals of the coil. The reading should be 2 to 5 ohms.

3. Run direct voltage to the coil by connecting a fused jumper wire to source voltage and run the other end of the wire to the positive terminal of the compressor coil. This can also be accomplished on the vehicle by jumping across the AC clutch relay with a toggle switch or a jumper wire.

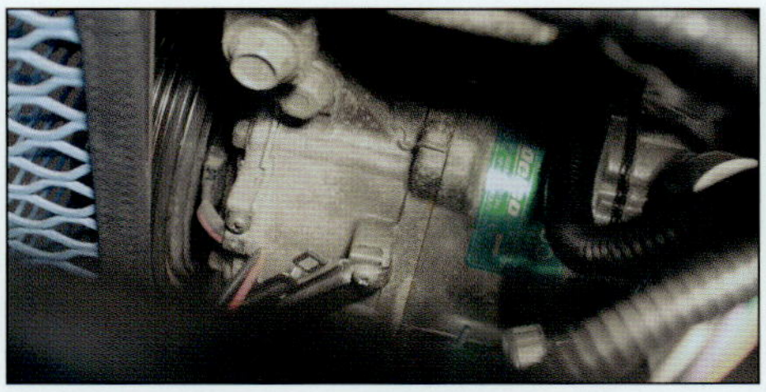

The AC compressor clutch coil is located on the front side of the compressor and is typically serviced by replacing the compressor assembly.

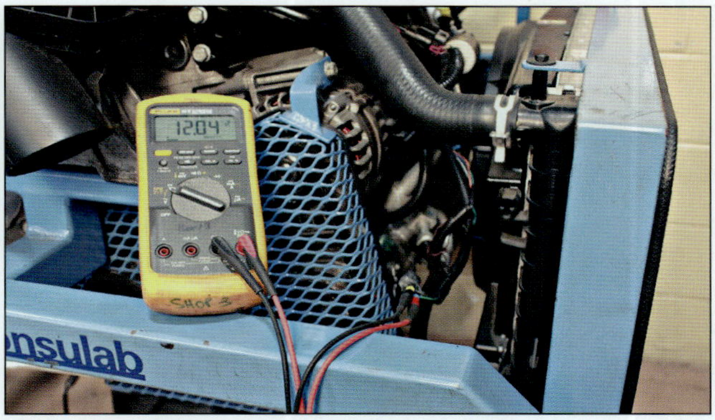

The supply voltage to the AC clutch coil can be tested by back-probing the terminals at the coil connector with the AC commanded on. The voltage reading should be about 12 volts if the system is operating correctly.

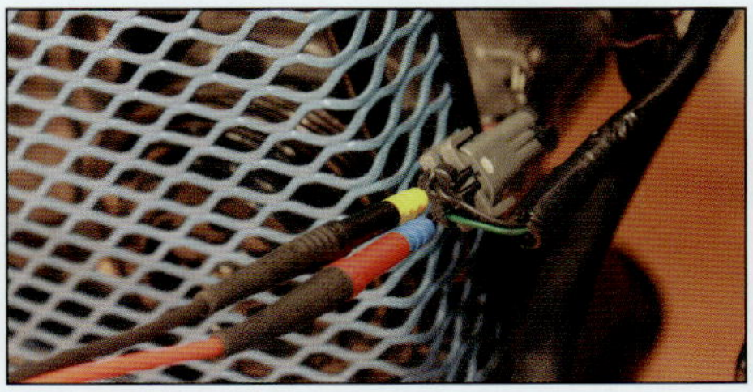

Direct power and ground can be supplied to the AC compressor clutch coil by connecting a power and ground wire to the coil connector. The compressor should make a clicking sound when power and ground are directly connected to the coil.

An ohmmeter can be used to measure the resistance of the AC compressor clutch coil. This test is performed with the coil connector disconnected from the harness. Care should be taken to only use test wires that will not damage the terminals of the clutch coil. The expected resistance for this test is typically between 2 to 5 ohms. Always refer to quality service information for exact specifications.

Duct Box Testing and Repair

It is important to keep in mind that the components located inside and outside of the duct box must function correctly to keep the passenger compartment at a desirable temperature. This section provides details on how these components work and how to troubleshoot and repair them.

Blower Motor

Diagnosing and repairing the blower motor can be done by using good logic and strategy. Blower motor problems tend to fall into two categories: excessive noise and not working at all.

A blower motor that makes an audible unpleasant noise could be caused by an object or piece of paper getting stuck on the impeller wheel. This can be caused by the duct box system pulling the item into the case and it getting stuck on the impeller. The foreign material can typically be cleaned out to eliminate the noise. A faulty blower motor bearing can also cause a noise that has a metallic sound, such as a bad bearing. This can be repaired by replacing the blower motor assembly.

A blower motor that does not work at all needs to be diagnosed. The motor needs to have power and ground in order to operate. If the blower motor does not operate on any speed, then a DMM can be connected to the electrical connector of the blower motor by back-probing the terminals. After connecting the DMM, the ignition switch should be turned on and the blower switch should be set to high. If the blower motor has system voltage dropped across it during this test, then the motor is faulty and needs to be replaced. The steps below list the typical method for replacing a blower motor that is located inside the cab under the dash area.

Replacing a Typical Blower Motor

1. Remove the lower trim panel on the passenger's side.
2. Remove the glove box assembly to gain access to the area behind it.
3. Disconnect the blower motor electrical connector.
4. Remove the blower motor fasteners.
5. Remove the blower motor assembly.

6 Inspect the new blower motor to make sure it is compatible with the vehicle.

7 Install the new blower motor, being careful to not damage the impeller wheel.

8 Install the blower motor fasteners.

9 Connect the blower motor electrical connector.

10 Install the glove box and lower trim panel.

11 Test the blower for proper operation.

Other things that could cause problems with the blower motor include a faulty blower resistor or a faulty blower motor switch. A faulty blower resistor will typically cause the low speeds to not work, but the high speed will usually still operate. The blower switch is not a serviceable part on most vehicles built since about 1995, which would require the complete control head to be replaced if the blower switch is found to be faulty. However, the blower switch was replaceable on many older vehicles, which reduces that cost of repair.

Blower motors on late-model cars that use the brushless DC motors need to be diagnosed with an oscilloscope. These blower motors are not be diagnosed the same way as the older-style motors. The signal that causes these motors to change speeds is a variable pulse width signal that can be viewed using some type of oscilloscope. To test this signal, connect the oscilloscope leads to the signal wire and watch the signal change as the blower speed is changed on the control head. If the signal changes with the switch, then the motor needs to be replaced. If the signal does not change, then the control head is likely defective and will need to be replaced.

The voltage supplied to the blower motor can be tested with a voltmeter connected to the blower motor connector by back-probing the terminals at the blower motor. The voltage drop at the blower motor with the switch turned to high should be near 12 volts.

The voltage drop at the blower motor with the switch turned to medium-high should be about 10 volts.

The voltage drop at the blower motor with the switch turned to medium should be about 7 volts. The voltage drop at the blower motor will be lower each time the blower motor switch is adjusted to a lower setting.

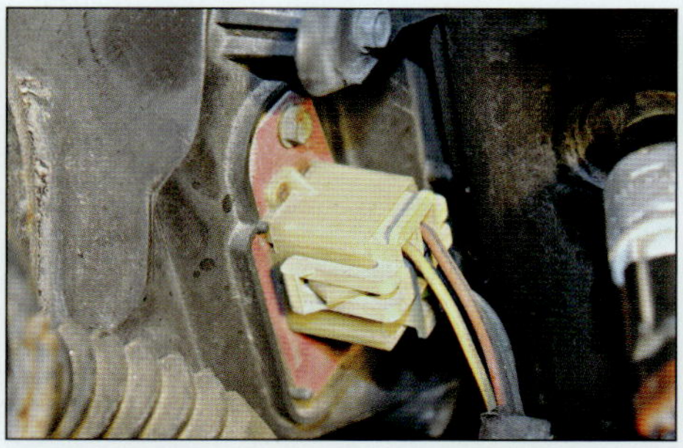

The blower motor resistor is mounted on the duct box near the blower motor. These devices need to be in the duct box so they can be cooled by the passing airflow. If one of the resistors in this device goes bad, then the lower blower speeds will not function correctly.

Old-style HVAC control heads may have serviceable parts, such as the blower motor switch. This blower switch can be unbolted from the control head and replaced.

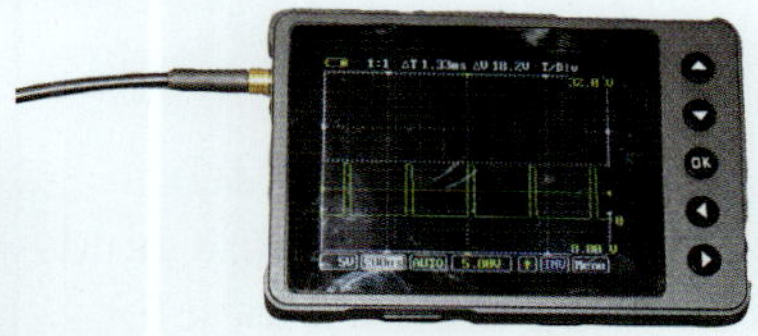

Pulse width modulated blower motors receive a varying square wave signal from the control module to change speeds. An oscilloscope allows this varying signal to be tested accurately. The signal on the oscilloscope is about a 15 percent command, which means the blower motor should operate at a low speed.

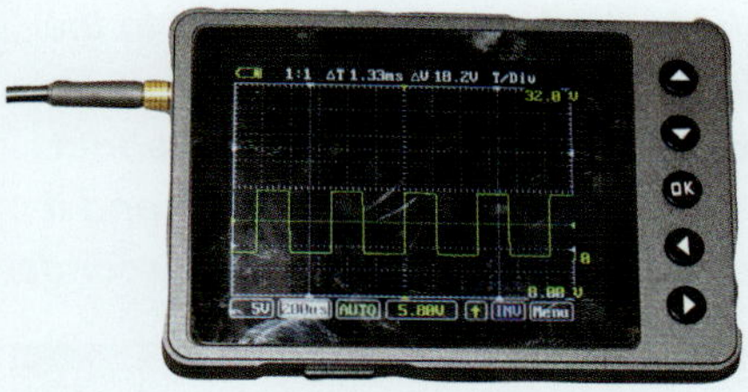

The signal on the oscilloscope is about a 50 percent command, which means the blower motor should operate at a medium speed.

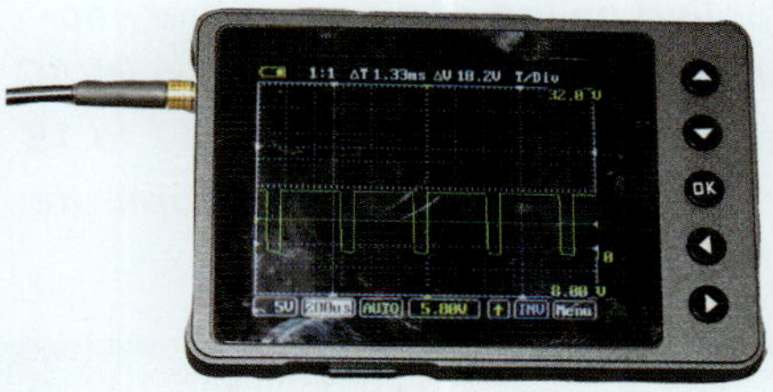

The signal on the oscilloscope is about a 90 percent command, which means the blower motor should operate at a high speed.

Duct Doors

The duct doors control the airflow through the duct box. The types of duct doors include the following examples.

Fresh/Recirculated Air Door: Controls where the duct box air is pulled from. The two positions for this door include fresh air and recirculated air.

Blend Air Door: Controls the temperature of the duct box air by forcing it through or around the heater core. When the blend door forces the air through the heater core, the air is warmed up, but when blend door causes the air to bypass the heater core, the air is not heated. This door can be full hot, full cold, or at any point between these two limits.

Mode Doors: Controls where the air is distributed into the cab. The three mode options include defrost, vent, and floor. Many systems allow for bi-level or tri-level operation, which allows the air to be distributed at two or three locations at once. For example, it is possible to have air coming from the defrost port as well as the floor, or all three locations.

These doors can be moved by either cables, vacuum actuator, or electric actuators. See the steps below for troubleshooting each type of system.

Testing Duct Door Operation

1 Cable-operated duct doors: Quickly move the selector to both ends of the range on the control head and listen for a snapping sound under the dash. If a distinct snap is heard at both ends of the range, then the cable is operating correctly and the door is hitting the limits of travel. If a snap is only heard on one end of the travel, then the cable length will need to be adjusted. The adjustment is correct when both ends of the travel causes the door to move to its limits. A reliable service information database can be consulted to determine how to adjust the cable length. The HVAC control head will need to be removed to replace one of the duct door cables.

2 Vacuum-operated duct doors: Test for vacuum being supplied to the HVAC control head. If no vacuum is present, seek the problem closer to the vacuum source, such as the engine or vacuum pump. Check the one-way check valve operation. Use a vacuum pump at the engine area to see if the system will hold vacuum. Test each vacuum actuator to see if it holds vacuum for a minute. Look for damaged vacuum tubing.

3 Electric-operated duct doors: Test for voltage at the duct door actuator while moving the controls on the control head. If voltage is present and the actuator does not move, it is faulty. The actuator can also be removed from the duct box to see if the duct door can be moved by hand.

These electric actuators also need to be calibrated if vehicle's battery power is lost or the actuator has been replaced. Calibration can sometimes be performed by pressing a series of buttons on the control head or by using a scan tool connected to the vehicle data link connector. Scan tools are very useful in checking the system for faults and running output tests as well.

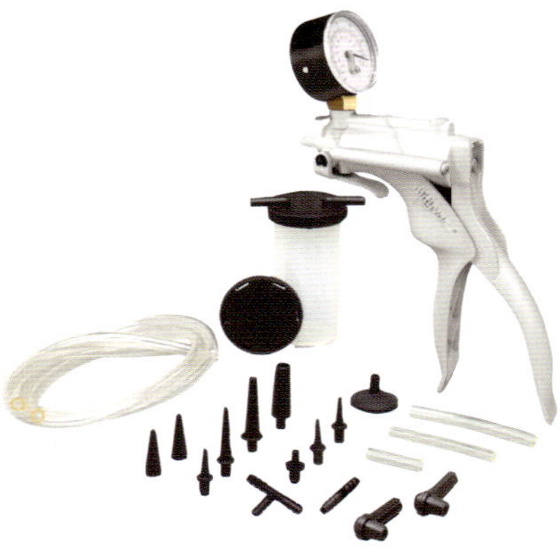

A vacuum pump test kit is handy to use when testing the vacuum-controlled components of the HVAC system. The gauge is useful when trying to measure vacuum levels and the pump can be used to create vacuum to test vacuum circuits and components. (Photo Courtesy Lincoln Tech/Mityvac)

A vacuum gauge or a vacuum pump can be used to measure the vacuum supplied by the engine or other vacuum source. Vacuum-operated HVAC systems need to have about 17 to 18 inches of vacuum present to operate correctly.

A vacuum pump can be used to create a vacuum to test to see if there are leaks in the hoses that connect to the HVAC control head and actuators. The pump should be actuated until about 18 inches of vacuum is created and it should not leak off for several seconds.

A voltmeter can be used to measure the voltage supplied to the duct door actuator. This test is performed by back-probing the terminals at the actuator with the voltmeter leads while adjusting the controls on the HVAC control head. If voltage is present during the test, the control head and wiring is good and the likely problem is the actuator.

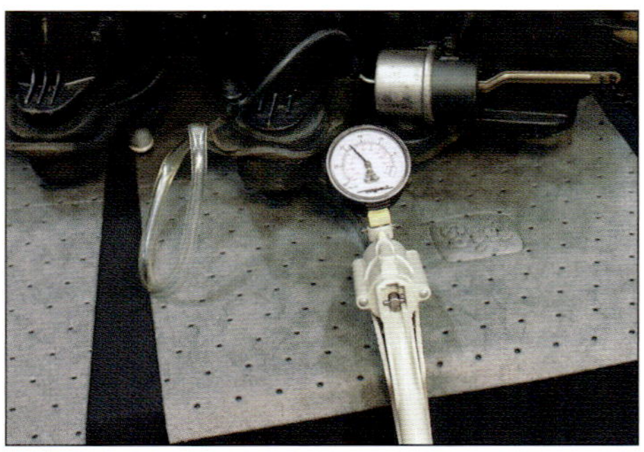

The vacuum actuators on the duct box can be tested by using a vacuum pump to see if each port can be held in place. The hose of the vacuum pump should be connected to each port of the vacuum actuator and then the pump should be actuated to create a vacuum. The vacuum actuator should not leak off for several seconds.

The data link connector is in the location where a scan tool can be connected, which will allow the operator to view data activity and trouble codes as well as perform output tests on the system.

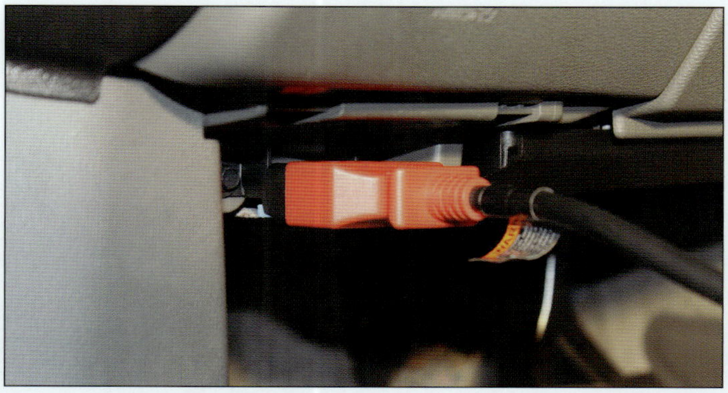

The power cord for the scan tool connects to the data link connector. The operator should be careful when connecting and disconnecting the scan tool to not damage the connector or the scan tool power cord.

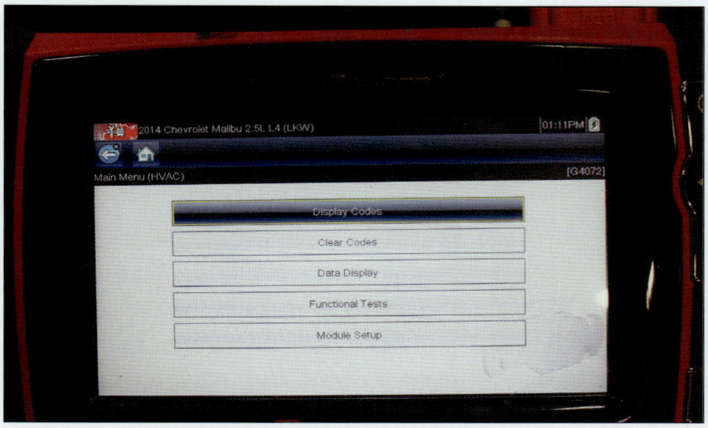

The scan tool allows for many diagnostic functions to be performed by the operator. Having a quality scan tool greatly increases the diagnostic capabilities of someone working on the HVAC system.

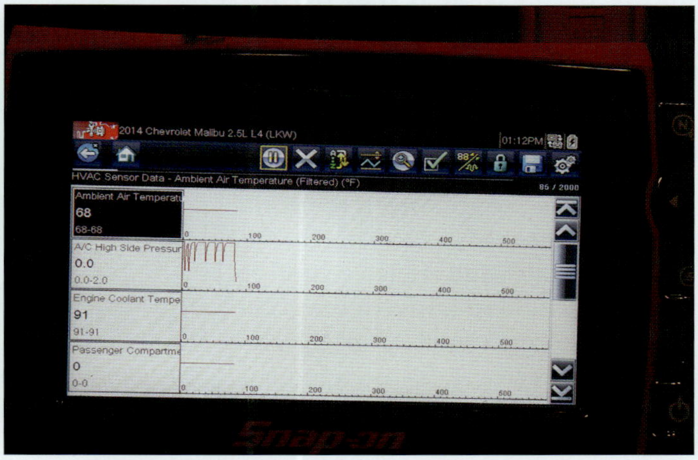

The scan tool allows the operator to view live data from the many sensors and switches that the AC and heating system uses.

Electrical Testing

Electrical testing with a digital multimeter is a valuable skill that will enable a person to accurately diagnose many problems in almost any electrical system. A multimeter is a versatile tool that will measure voltage, amperage, and resistance of an electrical component or electrical circuit with many of them able to make several other electrical tests. This section will mainly focus on using the tool as a voltmeter, an ammeter, and an ohmmeter.

Voltmeter Testing Techniques

The voltmeter is used to measure voltage in a component or a circuit. A simple way to understand how what is being measured is that the voltmeter is measuring electrical pressure. The display on the screen is showing the difference in electrical pressure between the positive (red) lead and the negative (black) lead.

When measuring the voltage on a vehicle battery, the display shows around 12 volts, which means that the difference between the two leads is 12 volts. The voltmeter is very useful when testing to see if an inoperative electrical load is receiving the correct voltage. There are two ways to perform this test: unplug the load and connect the voltmeter to the electrical terminals of the harness as well as leave the load connected and connect the voltmeter to the terminals by back-probing the connector.

Front-Probing with a Voltmeter

When testing for voltage at a connector that is disconnected from the load, it is important to be careful to not cause damage to the terminal by

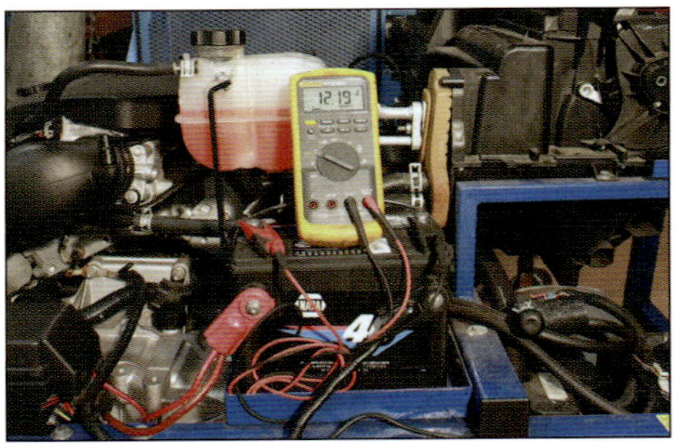

The voltmeter is connected in parallel with the item being tested for voltage. This battery has 12.19 volts of potential. A fully charged battery will have about 12.6 volts.

This set of jumper wires is very comprehensive in that it has many of the popular types of terminals on the jumper wires. The set also has wires that connect directly to the meter to reduce the need for alligator clips. Using these jumper wires greatly improves the accuracy of electrical testing that is done with the multimeter in addition to preventing damage to the terminals.

forcing the meter lead into the terminal. A better method of performing this test is to use the correct test terminal to make the measurement. There are jumper kits available that have many types and sizes of wires that can be used to safely perform electrical tests.

Using safe and reliable testing strategies will help improve the accuracy of the test results and will prevent damage caused to the terminals that will cause problems after the work is completed. These jumper kits come with leads that fit into the meter plugs that directly connect with the wire with the corresponding terminal to the one being tested.

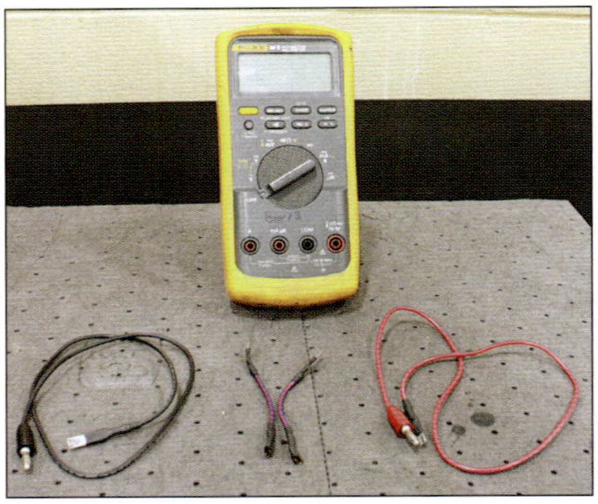

This jumper kit set comes with leads that fit into the meter on one end and a blade-style connector on the other end that mates with the small jumper wire.

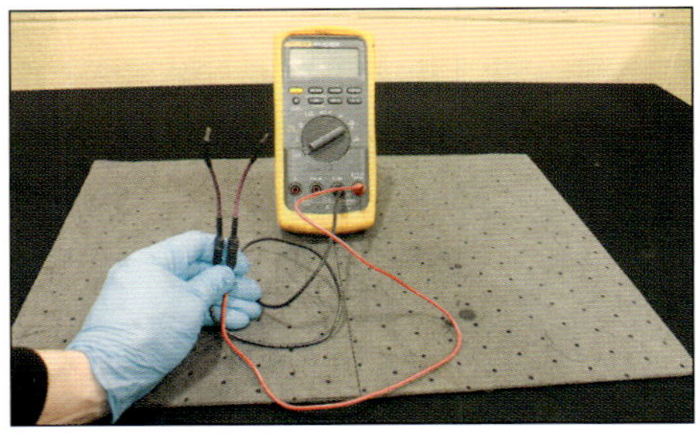

The meter leads are connected into the appropriate ports on the meter and have been connected to the small jumper wires. They can now be used to test electrical components or harnesses without causing distortion of the terminals.

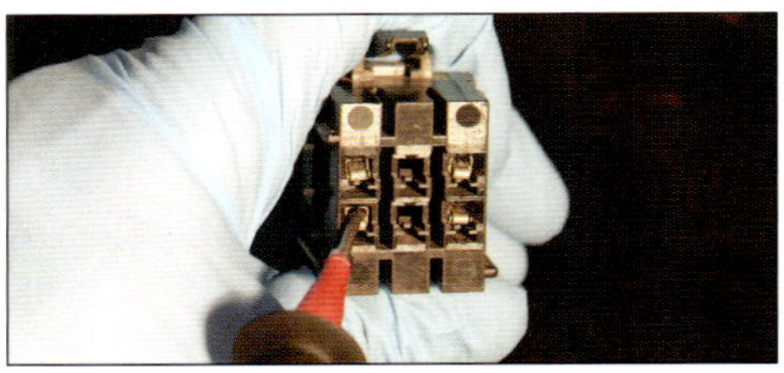

Testing a component or a harness by pressing the meter lead into the terminal is called front-probing. This action can cause damage to the terminals because it will distort the shape of the terminal and can cause a poor connection when it is rejoined with the circuit on the vehicle.

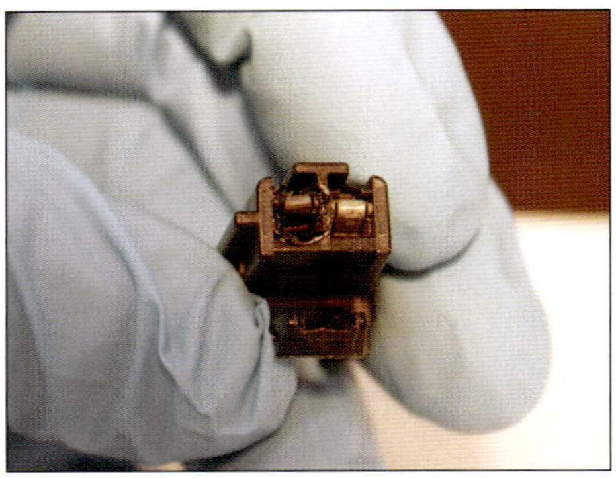

Damaged terminals that have become loose will cause an unwanted point of resistance, which will cause a voltage drop in the connector. This voltage drop will become hot and cause the connector to become burnt and damaged.

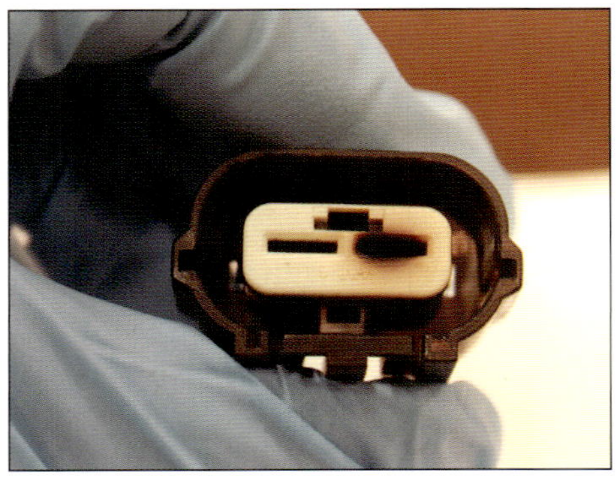

A poor terminal to terminal contact caused this connector to become burnt and damaged. This type of circuit problem will usually begin as an intermittent electrical problem and then eventually cause the circuit to become inoperative.

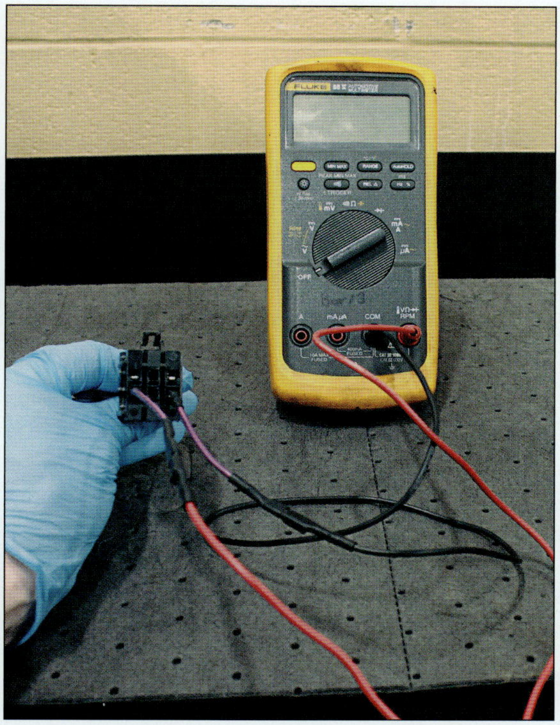

Using the appropriate testing wires and techniques will produce accurate results without damaging the terminals in the circuit.

This kit is a valuable asset to use when electrical circuits need to be back-probed with a voltmeter. These probes fit onto the banana plug–type meter leads, which reduces the need for alligator clips. (Photo Courtesy aeswave.com)

Back-probing with a Voltmeter

Using the voltmeter to measure the voltage in a live circuit is an excellent way to get a true test reading of the integrity of the circuit. To accomplish this task, the voltmeter must be connected to the circuit without the connectors being unhooked. This goal can be accomplished by back-probing the voltmeter leads into the connector body.

One way to do this is to use small probes that connect to the ends of the voltmeter leads. These probes are inserted into the back side of a connector without causing damage to the wire, the terminal, or the weather seal. Another way of back-probing a connection is to use T-pins and alligator clips. Using T-pins can get the job done, but it is important to pay attention to not let the pins touch each other at any time because this will cause the circuit to short out and could damage sensitive electronic components on the vehicle.

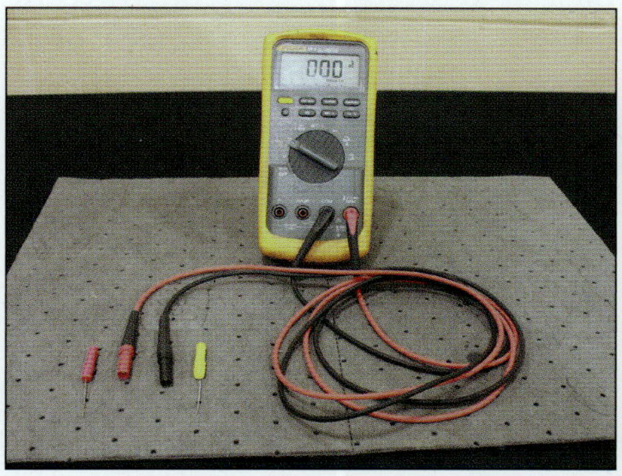

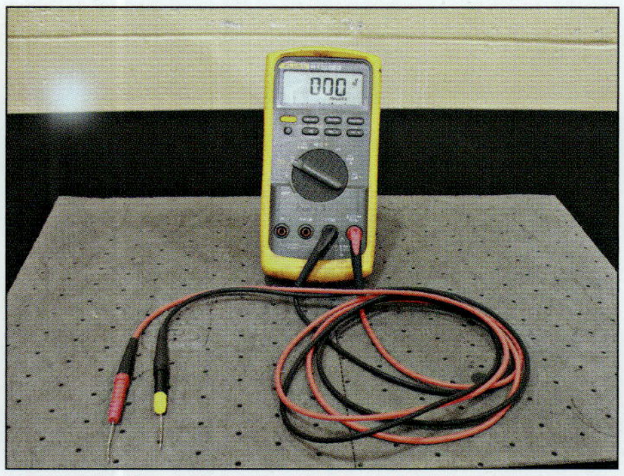

The acupuncture probes can be directly connected to the meter leads, which provides a reliable and firm connection (left). The probes have been connected to the meter leads and are now ready to be used to back-probe an electrical circuit (right).

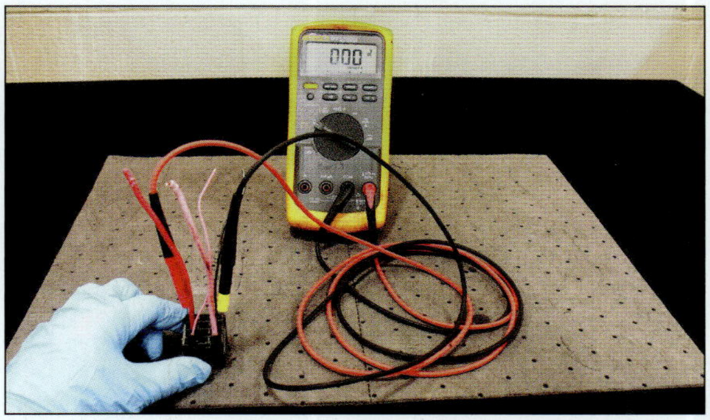

A circuit or component can be back-probed with the acupuncture probes connected to the meter leads by inserting the pins into the back side of a connector. The pins are small and do not damage the wires, insulation, or weather seal of the connector. This test provides valuable results when performed on a live circuit because the load is connected.

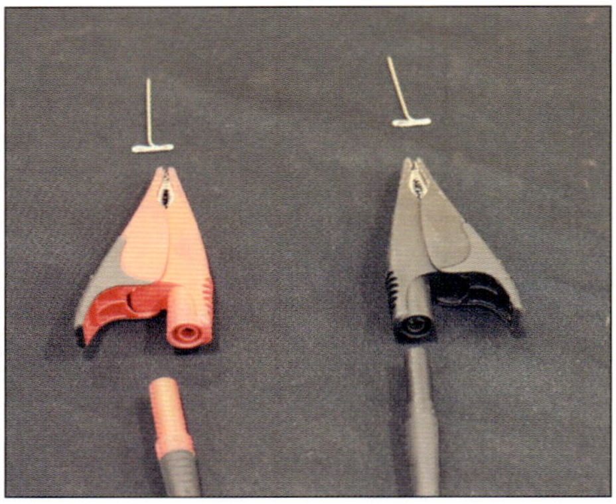

T-pins can be used to back-probe electrical circuits. Alligator clips are needed to connect to the top of the T-pins.

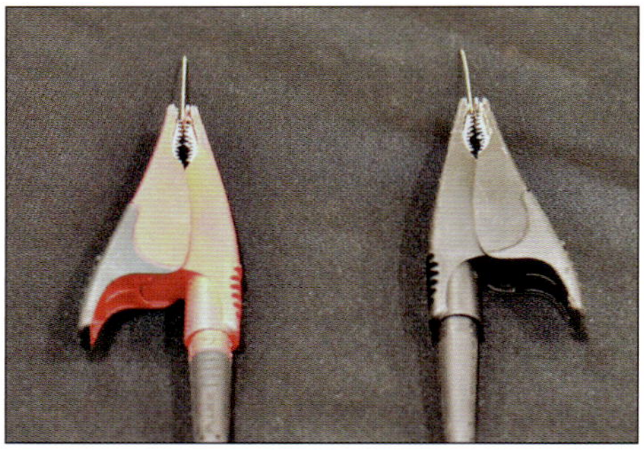

T-pins used with alligator clips on the meter leads will allow the ability to back-probe an electrical circuit.

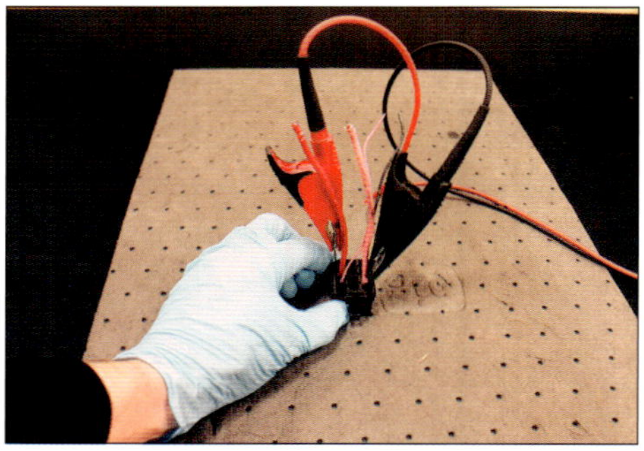

The connector is being back-probed using T-pins and alligator clips on the meter leads. The pins are small and do not damage the wires, insulation, or weather seal of the connector. Care should be taken to prevent the tops of the pins from touching each other, which would cause a short circuit and could damage an electronic component.

The ammeter is connected at the power distribution center to the terminals for the left headlight. The fuse panel is a handy location to test the amount of current in a circuit without having to dig too deep into the harness.

Ammeter Testing Techniques

The ammeter is used to measure the electrical current in a circuit. To measure current in a circuit with the internal ammeter, the operator must insert the meter in series with the circuit while the circuit is fully connected. This allows the electrical flow to pass through the meter, and the display will show how many amps are flowing in the circuit.

The limitation to measuring current this way is the size of the internal fuse in the meter, which is usually about 10 amps. A couple of good locations to insert the meter into a circuit include at a fuse or at a switch. At either place, the device is removed and then the ammeter leads are inserted into the circuit. A key point to remember when using the ammeter is to never connect it in parallel with a power supply or a load. Doing this will cause the internal ammeter fuse to be blown and need to be replaced.

Using an amp clamp is a very powerful way to measure electrical current without having to connect the leads of the meter into the circuit. The amp clamp is able to measure current by simply putting it around the wire to be measured and turning the circuit on. This tool senses the magnetic field around the wire and calculates the current flow. Below are the steps when using an amp clamp with a digital multimeter.

Using an Amp Clamp

1. Plug the lead of the amp clamp into the volt/ohm slots on the meter.
2. Turn the meter dial to the millivolt setting.
3. Turn the amp clamp power button on.
4. Adjust the dial on the amp clamp until the meter display shows zero.
5. Connect the amp clamp around the wire to be tested and turn on the circuit.
6. Observe the reading on the meter display. Even though the meter dial is set to millivolts, the numbers represent the amperage that is flowing in the circuit.

Ohmmeter Testing Techniques

The ohmmeter is used to measure electrical resistance in a component or a circuit. A key point to follow when using the ohmmeter is to only connect it to circuits after the power has been turned off or removed. The ohmmeter can be damaged if it is connected to a powered circuit. It will also provide an incorrect test result.

Common uses for ohmmeters include testing sensors, coils, switches, and wires. It is also a great idea to use jumper wires that correctly fit the terminals of the component or circuit being tested to improve accuracy and to keep from damaging the terminals.

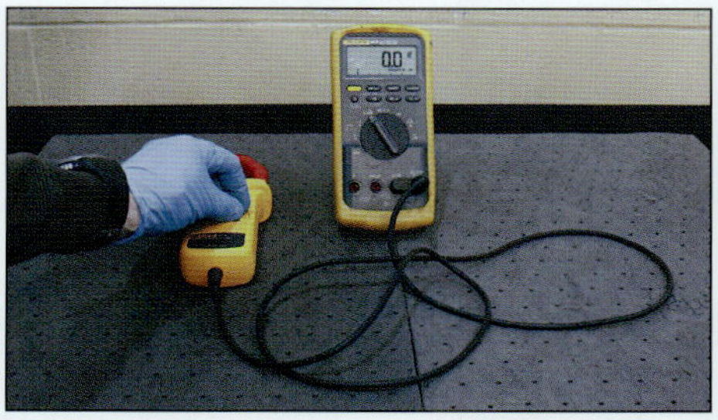

The amp clamp connects to the multimeter at the volt/ohm and ground locations. The meter dial is turned to millivolts and the power button on the amp clamp is turned on. The dial on the amp clamp is adjusted until the display shows zero. The tool is now ready to be used to measure current.

The amp clamp jaws open up to allow it to be put around a wire so that the current in the wire can be measured. The circuit being measured is the blower motor, so the amp clamp is placed around the power wire for the blower motor.

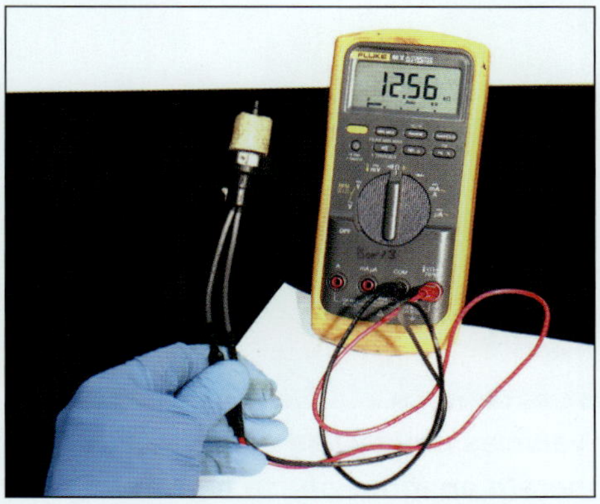

The ohmmeter is used to measure the resistance of the temperature sensor. The correct size jumper wires are being used to make an accurate and noninvasive measurement. This sensor has 12.56 kilo ohms of resistance, which equates to 12,560 ohms.

Hybrid and Electric Vehicle Testing

Hybrid and electric vehicles are very popular in many areas due to their alternative methods of propulsion. Both of these vehicle styles use large battery packs to fully drive or assist in driving the vehicle. These batteries are made up of modules that are connected in series to create a very large voltage.

These vehicles also have unique heating and AC systems. The AC compressor is driven electrically, and the heating system uses electricity to create heat for the passenger compartment. There are some key safety factors that must be followed when maintaining and repairing the HVAC system on these advanced vehicles.

The blower motor is turned on and the meter display shows 16.1, which means that the amperage is 16.1 amps flowing to the blower motor.

Removing and Installing the High-Voltage Service Plug

1 Use approved lineman's gloves when removing and installing the high-voltage disconnect service plug.

2 With the gloves on, lift the handle on the service plug and then pull the handle away from the battery. This will release the service plug from the battery.

3 Place the plug in a safe location while working on the high-voltage system.

4 The plug is installed by placing it into the battery and then rotating the handle toward the battery.

5 Push the handle down to engage the microswitch on the handle. If the handle is left in the upward location, the vehicle will not power up and will set a code for the microswitch.

6 Test the vehicle by powering the vehicle on and checking for fault indicators on the instrument cluster as well as testing the operation of all systems that were being repaired.

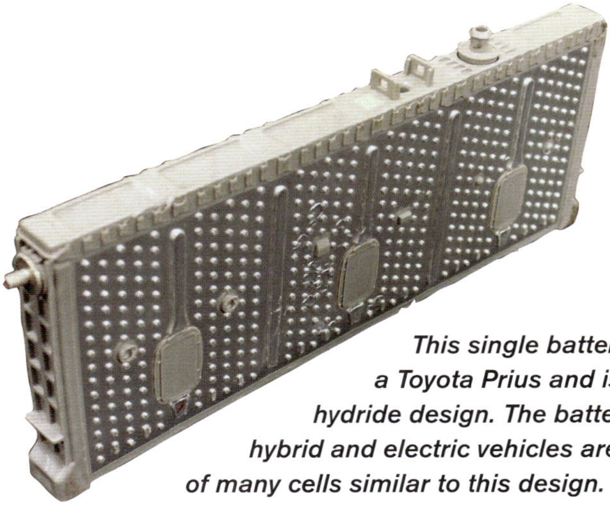

This single battery module is from a Toyota Prius and is a nickel metal hydride design. The batteries that propel hybrid and electric vehicles are typically made up of many cells similar to this design.

The cells of hybrid and electric vehicles are connected in series, which creates a very high-voltage DC battery. The positive terminal of one cell is connected to the negative terminal of the battery next to it.

The battery cover has been removed to provide this view inside of the battery. The cover should never be removed by anyone who has not had training to repair high-voltage vehicles.

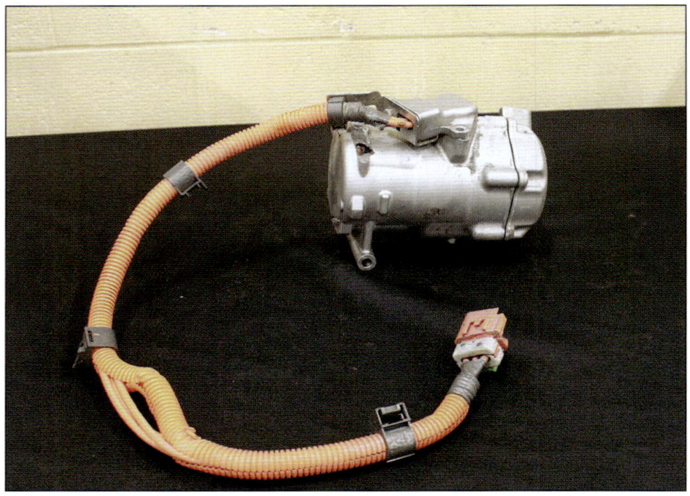

Hybrid and electric vehicles mostly use electric AC compressors that operate on three-phase high voltage. The high-voltage system should be safely turned off and disengaged before any service is performed on any high-voltage components.

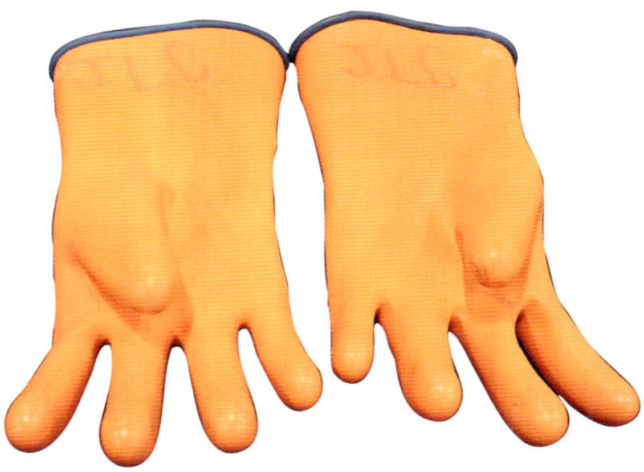

High-voltage lineman gloves are needed in order to work safely around the high-voltage systems on hybrid and electric vehicles. These gloves should be closely inspected before each use to make sure there are no holes or tears in the surface of the gloves.

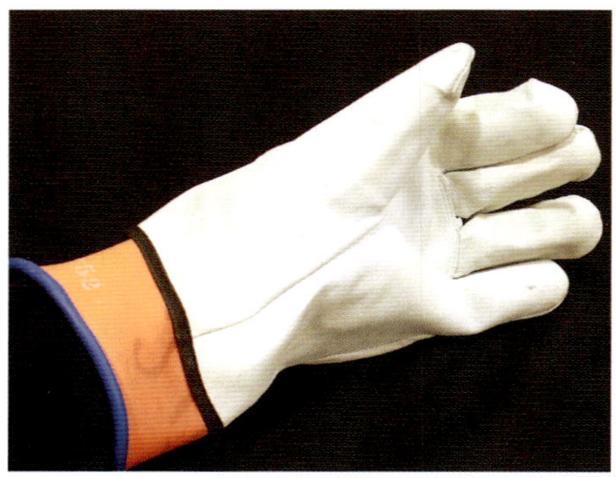

Leather protector gloves are typically worn to cover the rubber lineman gloves in order to reduce the chance of damaging the rubber gloves when working around the sharp edges of a vehicle.

The high-voltage service plug is typically orange in color and designed to be removed whenever the high-voltage system needs repair. High-voltage gloves should be worn when removing or reinstalling this plug.

The upper part of the service plug is the handle and it must be lifted to begin the removal process.

Once the handle is moved upward, then it can be rotated away from the battery to facilitate the removal of the plug.

The service plug is installed using the reverse steps that were used during removal. The last step is to push the handle downward to engage the microswitch on the handle.

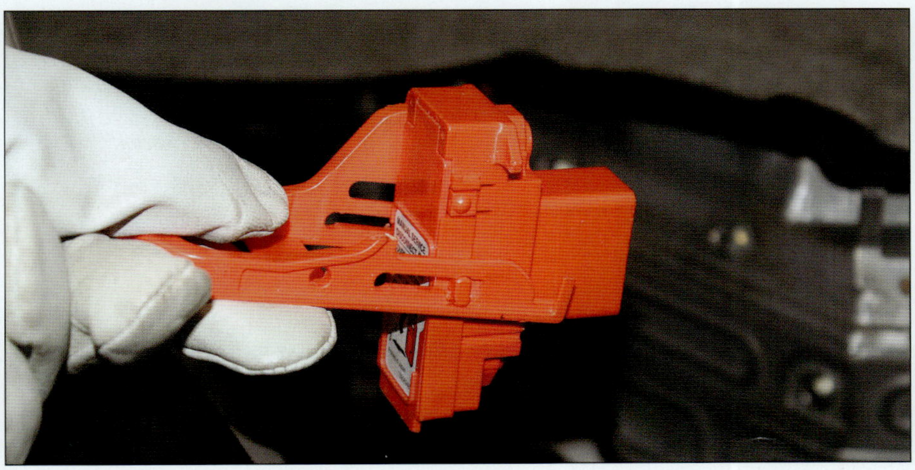

This close-up view of the service plug allows a clear visualization of how the plug is designed. This service plug has a large fuse under the cover that protects the high-voltage system from shorts and other problems.

CHAPTER 8

HEATING SYSTEM

The cabin heating system is an important system that provides comfort for the passengers when the temperature is cool or cold. This system works in conjunction with the engine cooling system to provide the warm air that is desired. The hot coolant that is available within the engine cooling system is the source of fluid that is needed to deliver heat to the duct system. This chapter will cover the operation of these systems as well as diagnosis and repair strategies that are needed to keep the system working at a high level.

Overview

The engine cooling system is a vital part of any internal combustion engine because it works to keep the engine in a safe temperature range under all types of operating conditions. Heat is generated in the engine when the fuel is combusted to produce the energy to create power. Unfortunately, only about one-third of the heat energy contained in gasoline or diesel fuel is transmitted into power. About one-third of the heat energy is removed through the exhaust system, and about one-third of the heat energy is absorbed by the coolant that is pumped through the engine block, cylinder heads, and intake manifold.

This heated coolant is then pumped to a large heat exchanger located in the front section of the vehicle. This heat exchanger is called the radiator and it releases the heat to the surrounding air as it is forced past the core section of the radiator. The engine cooling system is designed to build up pressure as the engine heats up. This added pressure raises the boiling point of the coolant, which is desirable to prevent the system from boiling over during high-load conditions.

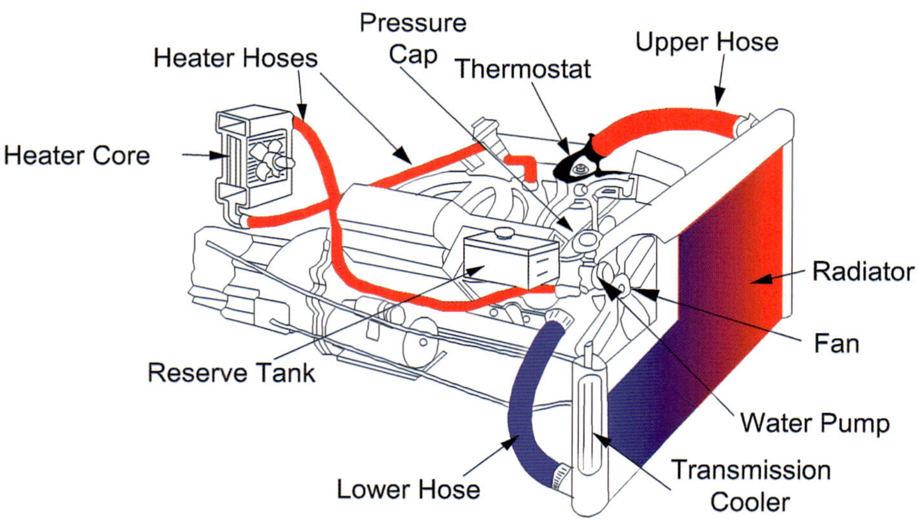

The engine cooling system uses liquid coolant to remove heat from the engine and carry it to the radiator. The cabin heating system uses this hot coolant to heat the cabin by forcing it through the heater core, which is located near the cowl panel or under the instrument cluster in the duct box.

Engine Cooling System Parts

Let's take a look at the different components.

Coolant: The coolant is the liquid medium that is used to transfer the heat from the engine to the radiator. This substance is made of pure water and antifreeze and is composed of approximately a 50-50 mixture. There are several different types of coolant that are used by various manufacturers and it is important to use the correct type when adding coolant to a system. When quality coolant is used, the boiling point is raised while reducing the freezing point of the fluid to safe levels to prevent the substance from freezing when very cold temperatures are present. Care should be taken to never allow the coolant to freeze into a solid, which would likely cause major engine damage.

Water Pump: The water pump is the mechanism that forces the coolant through the engine, which carries the heat out to the radiator. There are several methods used to drive the water pump: the accessory drive belt, the timing belt, the timing chain, or an electric motor. The water pump has a limited life span and will need service if it fails because of leaks or a bad bearing. The pump will leak if the seal fails. Coolant will escape from the weep hole if the seal fails.

The water pump has an impeller that forces the coolant through the engine, heater core, and radiator. The water pump is driven by the accessory belt, timing belt, or timing chain.

The water pump is an important part of the engine cooling system because it moves the coolant throughout the engine as well as through the heater core and the radiator.

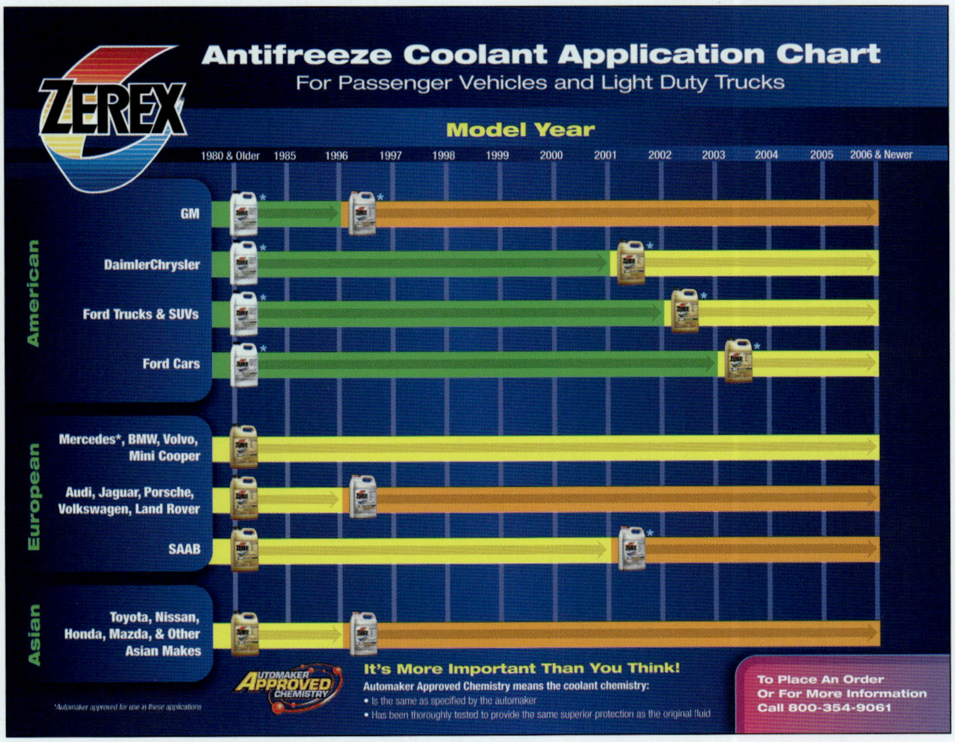

This chart shows the various colors and types of coolant that are available in the marketplace. Caution should be used to make sure that the correct coolant is used in each application. (Photo Courtesy Zerex)

Water pumps that are driven by the timing belt require more work and labor time to replace when they fail. It is wise to go ahead and replace the water pump during the timing belt replacement interval because it is driven by the timing belt and is easily replaced while the timing belt is removed.

The accessory belt is a common way to drive the water pump on many engines. The drive belt tensioner holds constant pressure on the belt to prevent belt slippage. The belt must be removed along with the water pump pulley to gain access to the water pump fasteners.

The thermostat performs a vital job for the cooling system by regulating the temperature of the engine. The thermostat blocks coolant flow leading to the radiator when the engine is below normal operating temperature. This allows the engine to build temperature to reach a level required for optimum efficiency and reduced emissions. The thermostat also contributes to the heating system to produce warm air sooner.

The thermostat uses a temperature-sensitive pellet or spring to regulate coolant flow in the engine. If a thermostat opens too soon or fails in the open position, then the engine will not warm up at the normal rate, which will reduce fuel economy as well as the performance of the heating system.

Thermostat: The thermostat is the mechanical temperature-regulating device that works to allow the engine to reach and maintain normal operating temperature. The thermostat operates by holding coolant in the engine until a specified temperature is reached and then it opens to allow the hot coolant to leave the engine and travel to the radiator. When the heated coolant exits the engine, cooler coolant is allowed to enter the engine, which helps the engine cool down. This process continues with the goal of keeping the engine at a predetermined temperature, which is generally about 180 to 200°F.

Radiator: The radiator is the heat exchanger that is located in front of the vehicle. Hot coolant enters the radiator and it passes through the core while air passes over it, which allows the heat to be removed from the coolant. Radiators are available in downflow and crossflow designs as well as various dimensions and core thicknesses. The size variables of the radiator are dependent on the needs of the engine setup. The radiator cap is an important item that is used to seal the radiator from leaking. An interesting aspect of the radiator cap is that it allows the cooling system to build up pressure as the temperature rises. This design allows for the boiling point of the coolant to be raised, which helps prevent an overheating situation.

The bottom side of the thermostat is exposed to the heated coolant produced by the engine. A thermostat that is stuck closed will quickly cause the engine to overheat and likely boil the coolant.

The radiator is the big heat exchanger located in the front grille area of the vehicle. This crossflow radiator has the tanks located on each side of the core. Coolant enters at the top left side and then flows across the core area, releasing heat to the passing airflow until it gets to the tank on the right side. The coolant exits on the bottom left side when the thermostat opens to allow hot coolant to leave the engine and cooled coolant to enter the engine.

This radiator is a downflow design that has the tanks located on the top and the bottom of the core assembly. Coolant enters at the top tank and then flows downward through the core area, releasing heat to the passing airflow until it gets to the bottom tank. The coolant exits the bottom tank when the thermostat opens to allow hot coolant to leave the engine while letting cooled coolant enter the engine.

The cooling system is designed to allow the heated coolant to build pressure, and the radiator cap operates to allow this pressure to build up to specified levels before releasing to the reserve tank. This added cooling system pressure raises the boiling point of the coolant to help prevent the system from boiling over under high-load conditions. The radiator cap should never be removed while the engine is hot because the pressurized coolant could cause burns if it gets sprayed onto the person removing the cap.

Hoses and Clamps: Radiator hoses and heater hoses are used to connect the various parts of the engine cooling system. Many hoses are designed to have natural bends that allow for direction changes without causing the hose to crimp, which would impede the flow of coolant. The hoses are secured in place with hose clamps that apply pressure to prevent leaks. Hose clamps are available in several sizes and styles, and each one is unique in how it is serviced.

The cooling system hoses are often designed and manufactured with natural bends that allow safe and reliable routing through the engine compartment. The constant tension hose clamps provide long-lasting service without losing any strength or holding pressure.

The upper radiator hose connects to the upper intake area of this engine and is held in place with a constant tension hose clamp. This hose also has some plastic conduit installed around it to provide further protection from the heat in the engine area.

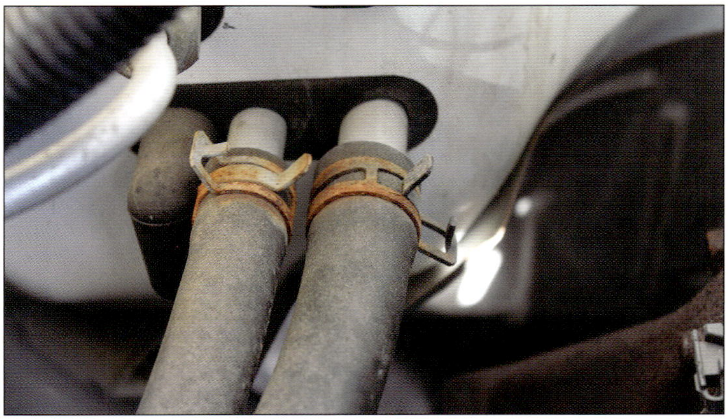

The heater hoses are connected to the heater core at the lower section of the firewall. The hoses are secured with constant tension hose clamps that will provide reliable sealing of the hose connection.

Constant tension hose clamp pliers make servicing this style of clamp quick and easy.

Hose clamps come in many sizes to accommodate the varying sizes of hoses. Two of the most common styles of hose clamps are the threaded style and the constant tension style. A screwdriver or a socket can be used to adjust the threaded style, while pliers or special hose clamp pliers are used to remove and install the constant tension–style clamps.

Many manufacturers use coolant pipes to carry coolant to various parts of the engine. These coolant pipes use quick-connect couplings to connect to other parts of the engine. It is wise to replace these quick-connect coupling connectors when service is required to reduce the chance of leakage after the repair.

Coolant Pipes and Fittings: Many manufacturers are using coolant pipes in place of coolant hoses. These coolant pipes are typically made from light metals or plastic and are connected with various styles of coupling techniques. These coupling processes used by manufacturers allow for quick assembly when the vehicle is being put together. However, these quick coupling devices do not allow for reliable outcomes when it comes time for servicing them. It is recommended that the coupling devices be replaced when they are removed for any service operation.

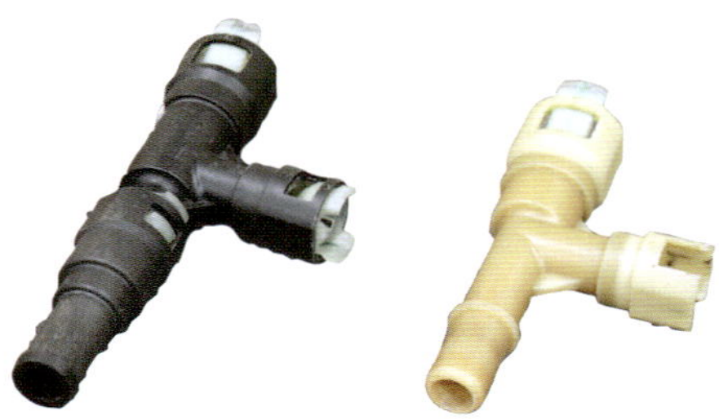

Plastic quick-connect coupling joints are used on many cooling systems to connect hoses and pipes together. These types of coupling joints require service when the plastic gets brittle with age.

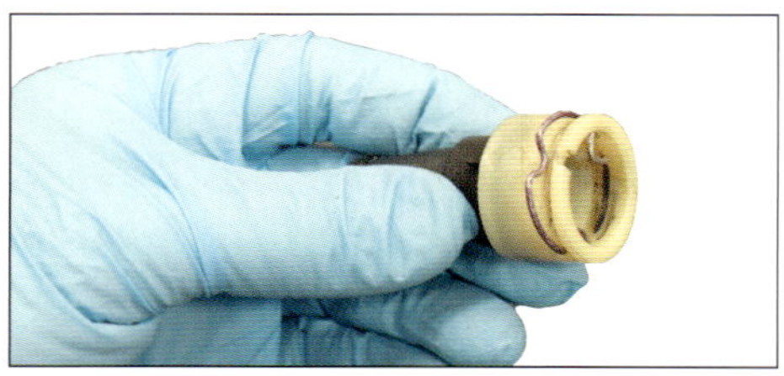

Some plastic quick-connect fittings use a small snap ring to hold the fitting together. All of these plastic coolant fittings have a shorter life span due to the deterioration of the plastic over time.

This coolant hose is fitted with a plastic quick-connect fitting that is factory crimped onto the hose. This hose assembly will need to be replaced with a similar style unit that has a quick-connect feature.

This heater core is made from copper and wrapped with an insulating foam to ensure that the duct box air must pass over the core so it can be heated up.

Heating System Operation

The cabin heating system uses heated coolant from the engine to produce warm air for the passenger compartment. This simple system has been used on cars and trucks for many years and continues to be a reliable way to warm the cabin of late-model vehicles.

Heater Core

The heater core is a small heat exchanger that looks similar to the radiator that is located in the front of the vehicle. The heater core is located in the duct box and it receives heated coolant from the engine. The materials used to manufacture heater cores include copper, aluminum, and plastic. Hoses and pipes are connected to the heater core to supply heated coolant to the device.

Coolant Flow Valve

Some manufacturers use a coolant flow valve that controls the flow of heated coolant into the heater core. This valve is located in series with the heater hoses or coolant pipes and is typically controlled with a cable or vacuum valve. The valve opens and closes by moving the heater control lever on the control panel. Not all cars and trucks will have one of these valves, because most systems use a door to control the temperature of the air that is distributed to the passenger compartment.

The heater core is the heat exchanger located in the duct box that provides the warm air for the passenger compartment. This heater core is made from aluminum and has plastic tanks as well as plastic pipes.

This heater core is made from aluminum with the end cap made from plastic. The pipes for this heater core are bolted on and are made from aluminum like the core.

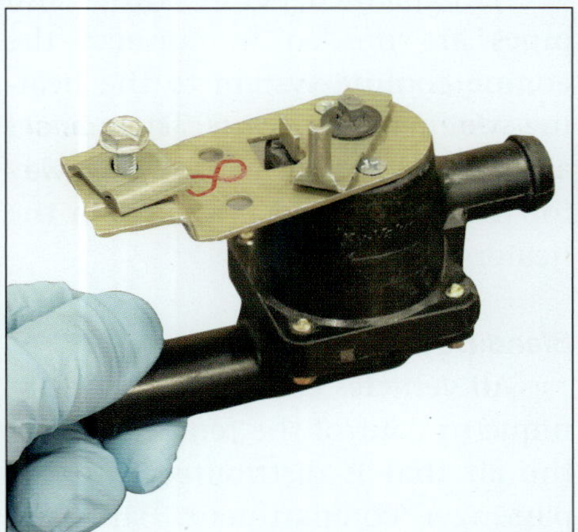

The coolant flow valve controls the flow of coolant into the heater core mechanically with a lever that is activated by a cable that connects to the temperature-control knob on the control head. This valve is made from plastic and has metallic levers that bolt to the unit.

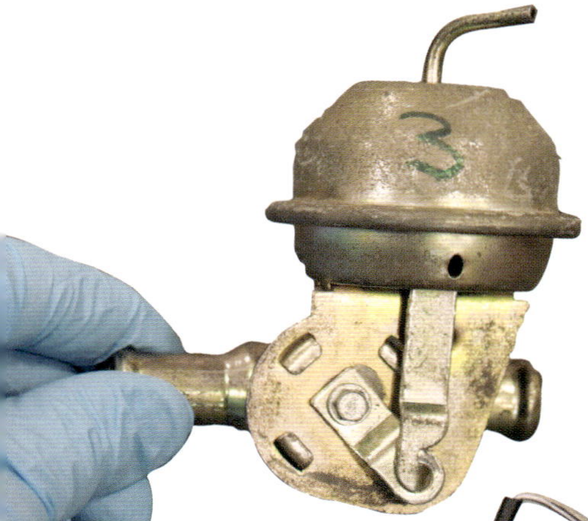

This heater control valve is controlled with a vacuum signal from the control head. The valve is open when the temperature lever is moved to the heat position and it closes when the temperature lever is moved to the cool position. The valve can be tested by using a vacuum pump connected to the vacuum port. The valve will hold a vacuum seal for at least a minute if it is good.

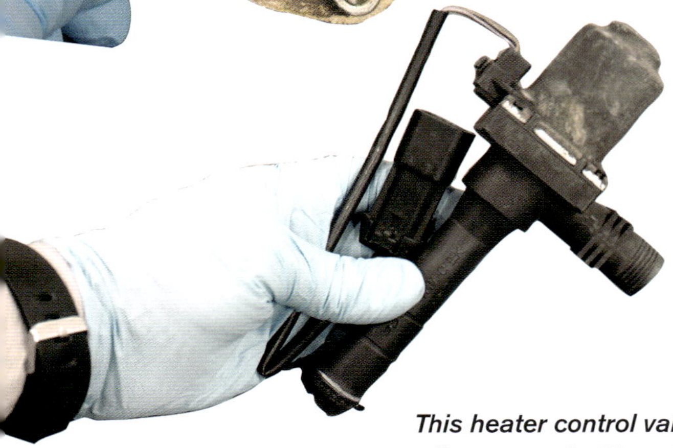

This heater control valve is electrically actuated with a signal that is received from the control head. This unit uses a solenoid that opens and closes the passage as the temperature knob is moved from hot to cold.

This heater control valve is electrically actuated with a signal that is received from the control head.

Hoses and Pipes

As explained before, hoses and pipes are needed to connect the engine cooling system to the heating system components. These hoses and pipes simply provide a pathway for the heated coolant to reach the heater core.

Blend Door

All vehicles use a blend air technique to control the temperature of the air that is distributed into the passenger compartment. This system was described in more detail in chapter 2. The main device that controls the temperature of the air is the temperature door, which is also known as the blend door. The blend door acts to control the temperature of the air by controlling the flow of the air through or around the heater core.

When the blend door is in the full-heat position, all of the duct box air passes through the heater core, which heats the air to maximum temperature. When the blend door is in the full-cool position, all of the duct box air bypasses the heater core, which prevents the air from being heated by the heater core. If the blend door is at any point between full hot and full cool, the air is blended because some to the air will pass over the heater core and some of the air will bypass the heater core.

Diagnosis

The process of troubleshooting a low heat output problem should be performed in a logical sequence. A properly functioning heater system should produce air that is 140 to 150°F. The following section provides a step-by-step sequence to use when

The heater temperature can be tested by allowing the engine to reach normal operating temperature and setting the temperature control to full heat and then inserting a temperature-sensing device into the duct. A normally functioning heating system should produce 140 to 150°F air.

diagnosing a heater that is not working well enough.

Check the Coolant Level

After verifying that the heater is not performing well enough, the engine coolant level needs to be checked for the proper level. The coolant should be at the full mark on the reservoir tank as well as in the radiator. Warning: Never remove the radiator cap or a pressurized coolant reservoir cap while the engine is hot to avoid having hot and pressurized coolant released onto your skin, which will cause injuries and burns. If the cooling system is found to be low, then the vehicle should be inspected for leaks.

The coolant level is full on this radiator. This system uses extended life coolant that is red in color. The coolant reservoir should also be checked and filled to the full cold level.

This heater core is badly deteriorated and caused a leak in the duct box. The driver of the vehicle noticed that the windshield was fogging up and coolant was leaking from the duct box drain tube.

This heater core developed a slow coolant leak that caused a light fog on the windshield when the heat was turned on. A pressure test was performed on the cooling system and caused coolant to drain from the duct box drain tube.

Checking the Cooling System for Leaks

1 Look for signs of coolant on the various parts of the engine and cooling system. The coolant will be affected by gravity, create a downward trail, and then drip onto the ground. Be sure to find the exact location where the coolant is exiting the engine or cooling system component.

2 A pressure test is sometimes necessary to aid in locating leaks in the cooling system. This device uses a pump to add pressure to the system, which will often make the leak easier to see. Be sure to only add pressure that does not exceed the radiator cap pressure rating, which is usually around 15 psi.

3 On leaks that are difficult to locate, coolant dye can be added to the cooling system to aid in locating the source of the coolant leak. After installing the dye to the system, the engine should be operated for several minutes to circulate the dye. A black light is used to increase the visibility of the dye.

4 A block tester tool can be used if an internal coolant leak is suspected. This tool uses a chemical that changes colors if it is exposed to combustion gases. This tool provides a positive way to test for blown head gaskets or cracked cylinder heads.

Pressure Testing the Cooling System

1 ***The radiator cap must be removed after the cooling system has cooled off.***

2 ***The correct size coolant adapter is chosen and then installed onto the radiator neck.***

3 ***The pressure tester is installed onto the adapter with the release valve in the hold position. The connection should be tightened securely to prevent the pressure from leaking off when the test is being performed.***

Pressure Testing the Cooling System *(Continued)*

4 *After the pressure tester is installed onto the radiator, the test pressure must be chosen. It should not exceed the pressure rating on the radiator cap, which is typically around 14 to 16 psi.*

5 *Here, 15 psi of pressure has been applied to the pressure tester using a hand-style pump. This pressure should be held on the system for several minutes to see if it leaks off. The cooling system should be checked for leaks while the pressure is applied with the pressure tester.*

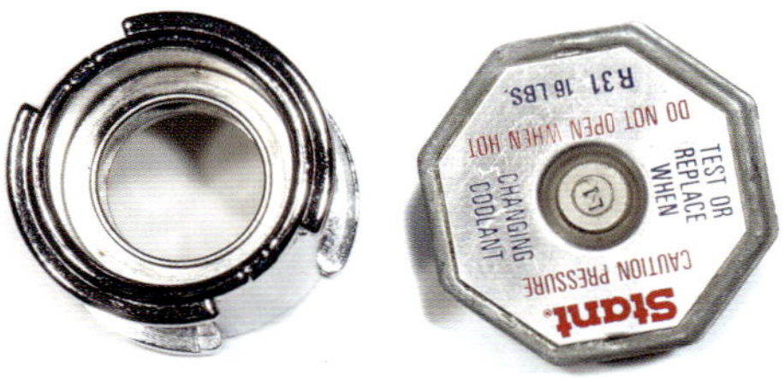

6 *Cooling system pressure testers also have a cap adapter that allows the cap to be tested with the pressure tester.*

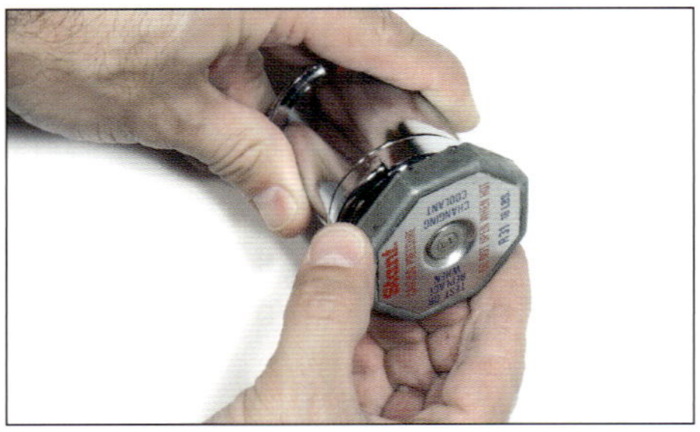

7 *The radiator cap is installed onto the cap adapter to prepare for using the cooling system pressure tester to see if the cap will hold the correct pressure.*

8 *The cooling system pressure tester is installed onto the cap adapter, which will allow the cap to be tested.*

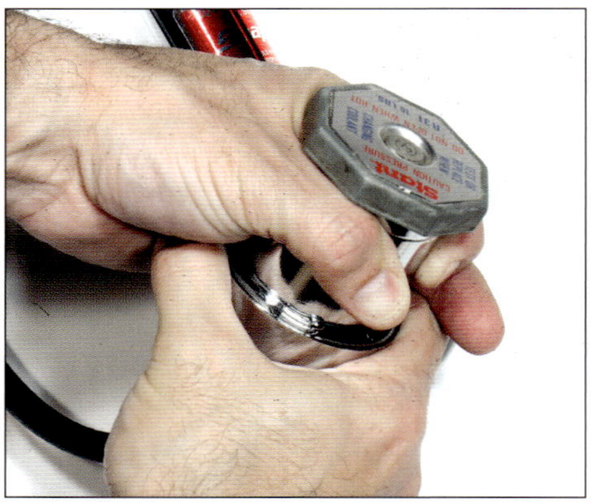

9 *The tightness of the cap as well as the pressure tester should be checked prior to adding pressure to the cap.*

10 *The pump on the cooling system tester is activated to apply the specified pressure to the cap. The cap should hold the rated pressure in order to pass the test.*

A black light and special yellow glasses are needed to assist in finding leaks using coolant dye. The glasses allow the dye to be much more visible during the leak test.

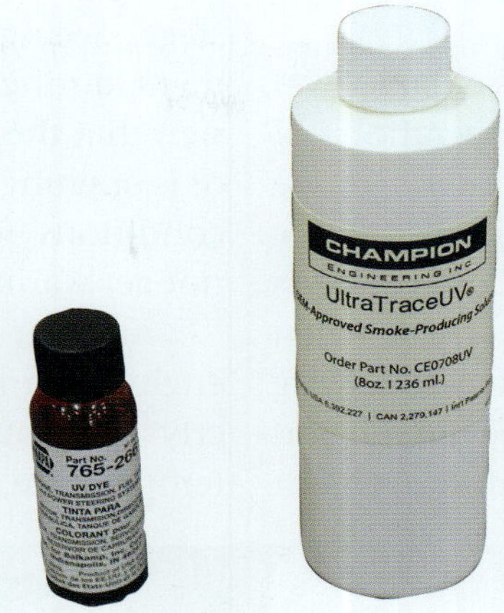

Adding a special dye to the cooling system is a wise practice when the leak is difficult to locate. The engine should be operated for a few minutes in order to thoroughly mix the dye with the coolant.

A combustion leak tester kit is useful when a blown head gasket or cracked cylinder head is suspected. This kit uses a chemical that changes colors if it is exposed to combustion gasses.

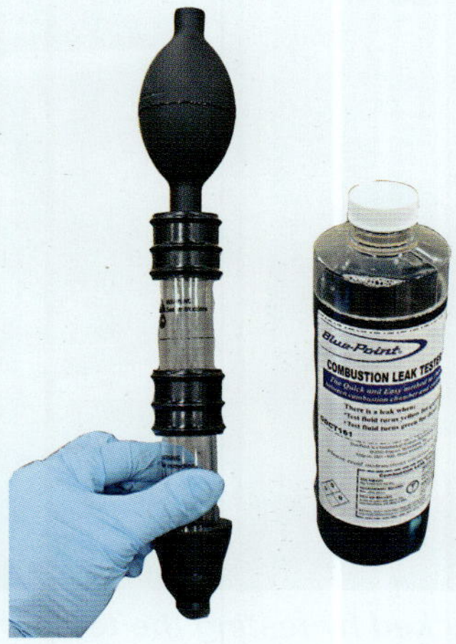

The vessel on the left is filled with the blue-color test fluid and is then installed onto the radiator neck with the engine running. If the engine has combustion gasses in the coolant, the fluid will change colors.

The engine temperature can be monitored using the temperature gauge in the instrument cluster. The temperature should rise to about 180 to 200°F within 10 minutes of engine operation.

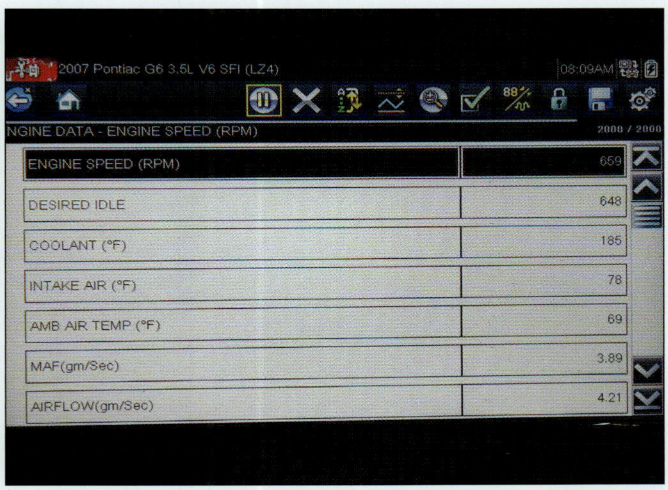

A scan tool can be used to monitor the engine temperature. A thermostat that is operating correctly will allow the engine to reach 180 to 200°F within 10 minutes of operation.

Verify Engine Reaches Normal Operating Temperature

After checking the coolant level on the engine, the operation of the engine thermostat needs to be checked. One method to test and see if the thermostat is sticking open is to monitor coolant movement when the engine is cold. After removing the radiator cap, start the engine and watch for rapid coolant movement while the engine is in the warming-up stage. Seeing a lot of coolant movement during the warm-up stage is a sign that the thermostat is stuck open or is opening too soon. Either of these conditions will cause the heater to not get warm quickly enough.

Another way to determine if the engine thermostat is operating properly is to monitor engine operating temperature to see if the engine is able to reach normal operating temperature within a short time period. This process can be performed by watching the temperature gauge or by using a scan tool to monitor the engine temperature. Either method should produce reliable results.

A normally operating thermostat will allow the engine to reach the normal range of operation within 7 to 10 minutes of fast idle conditions. A thermostat that is stuck open will cause the warm-up time to take much longer than the normal time. A stuck-open thermostat will cause the operating temperature to run much cooler than normal when the vehicle is being driven on the highway too. Thermostats can stick closed, and when they do, the engine will quickly overheat.

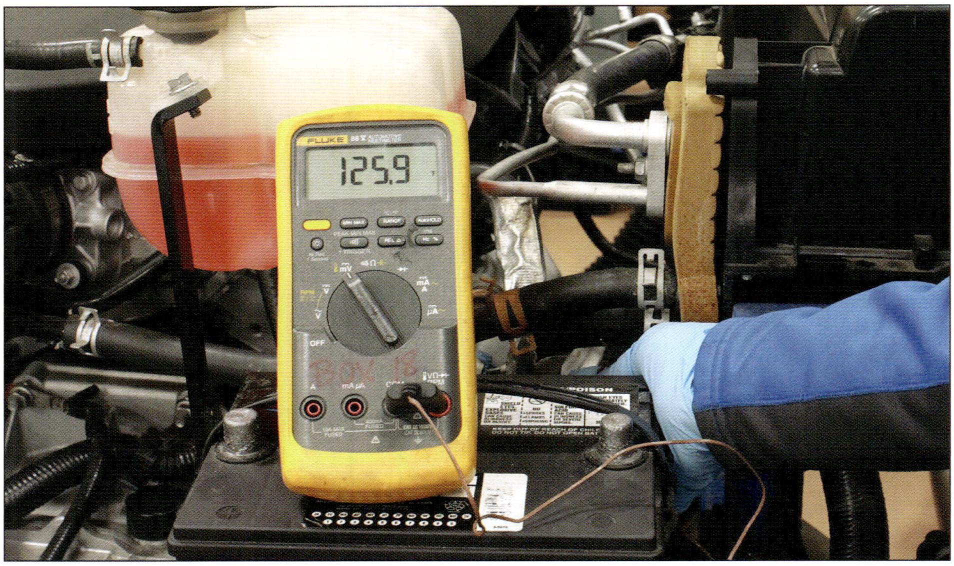

The heater core can be checked by testing the temperature of the heater hoses at the entry point and at the exit point. The temperature of this inlet heater hose is 125.9°F.

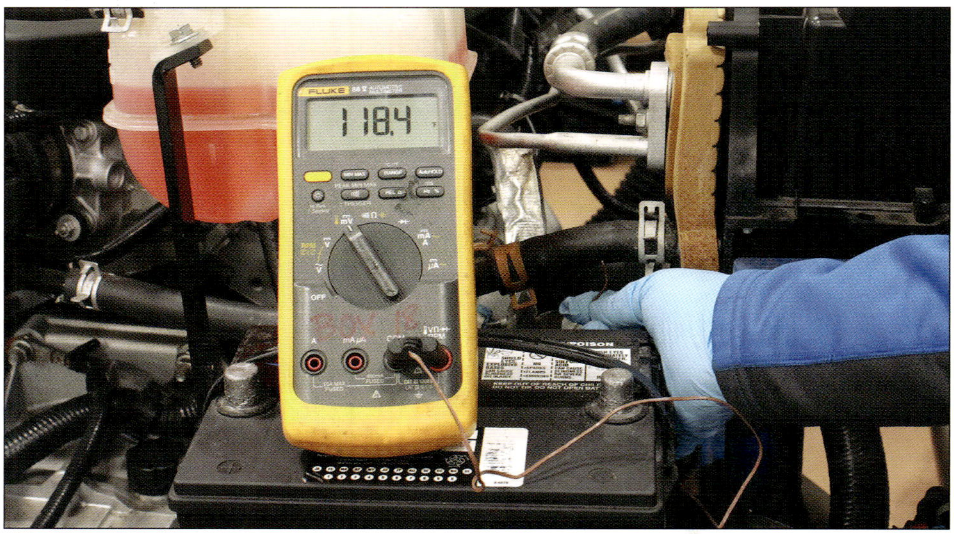

The temperature of this outlet heater hose is 118.4°F.

Verify Coolant Flow through the Heater Core

After verifying the engine is running at normal operating temperature, the coolant flow through the system should be checked. The engine should be started, the heat should be turned to full heat, and the blower should be turned to high. If the system uses a coolant flow valve, then the temperature should be measured on both sides to see if there is any drop in temperature from one side to the other. It should be the same temperature on both sides of the coolant flow valve.

With the vehicle still configured the same way, measure the temperature of the heater hose or pipes at both heater core connections. The temperature drop across the heater core should be 10 degrees or less. If a temperature drop of more than 10 degrees is found, then the heater core is restricted and should be flushed or replaced.

Verify Blend Door Operation

Another important step in diagnosing the heating system is to make sure that the blend door is functioning properly. The blend door is the part in the duct box system that controls airflow through or around the heater core. The operation of the door can be checked by moving the temperature control from full-cool mode to full-heat mode while monitoring to see if the temperature changes to the desired selections.

Systems that use a cable to move the temperature door will make a distinctive sound as the temperature selector reaches the full-heat and full-cool settings. Many systems use electric actuators that do not make an audible sound to indicate that the door is reaching the correct positions. These systems will require a calibration to be performed if possible.

The calibration procedure can be performed on most systems by pressing a sequence of buttons on the control head that forces the actuator to move to the limits of travel. The doors can be calibrated with a scan tool as well. This action will sometimes cause the system to function correctly after being performed. It may be necessary to remove the actuator and move the blend door by hand to make sure the door has full range of motion.

The temperature control electric actuator is being removed to inspect the temperature door during diagnosis. This actuator is held in place with three small fasteners.

Removing the temperature control electric actuator will allow the temperature door to be inspected as well as the door to be physically actuated by hand.

The temperature door can be actuated using pliers to physically move the door.

Repair Procedures

It should be noted that all safety precautions should be followed when performing service and repair as well as procedures for safe and legal disposal of the fluids and components removed during these processes.

Draining Engine Coolant

Follow these steps when it is necessary to drain the coolant from a vehicle for any reason.

1. Place a drain pan under the radiator near the location of the drain valve. It may be necessary to use two drain pans on some vehicles.
2. Remove the radiator cap.
3. Move the drain valve to the release position to allow the coolant to drain into the catch pan. Monitor the flow of coolant until all of the coolant has drained into the pan. Close the valve when this process is complete.

Refilling the Engine Cooling System

At this point, repairs can be made on the vehicle cooling system. Once it is time to install coolant back into the vehicle, the following steps should be followed.

1. Make sure that the coolant drain valve is fully closed to prevent leakage when adding coolant back into the vehicle.
2. Inspect the vehicle to see if there is a bleed valve present. Open the air bleed valve using the necessary tools.
3. Install premixed coolant into the coolant reservoir or radiator, being careful not to spill any fluid during the process. Slowly add coolant until the system is full.
4. Start the vehicle and let the engine warm up while watching the coolant level. Once the thermostat opens up, coolant should be added until the level is at the full cold mark.
5. Close the air bleed valve once coolant begins to pass through the valve.
6. Once the vehicle is filled with coolant, it should be cleaned of excess coolant and then taken on a road test. The vehicle should be allowed to cool down and then the coolant level should be checked again to ensure that it is full.

The radiator drain valve is located at the bottom of the tank on the driver's side of the vehicle. This valve is plastic and is opened by rotating the handle counterclockwise. The opening in the lower radiator support provides a path for the coolant to drain into a drain pan.

This radiator drain valve is a plastic hex-shaped device that screws into the bottom of the radiator tank. A socket and ratchet can be used to loosen this valve.

This radiator has a plastic pipe pointing downward to assist in draining the coolant into a drain pan.

Many engines have a cooling system air bleed device that can be opened during the cooling system refill procedure. It helps to bleed the air pockets out of the system.

The bleed valve can be opened by using two wrenches and turning the top of the bleed valve counterclockwise. The valve should be closed after coolant begins to flow from the valve during the refill and engine warm-up process.

Hoses and Clamps

The cooling system hoses and clamps perform an important function for the vehicle and require maintenance and service from time to time. The correct replacement parts should be used during the process of installing new hoses on the vehicle. All clamps should be securely installed to ensure that the system will not leak when it is put back into operation.

After removing the old radiator hose, the upper radiator hose is installed by sliding it onto the radiator neck. A small amount of lubricant can be smeared on the inside of the hose to assist with installation.

Firm pressure should be used to slide the hose into the correct position on the radiator.

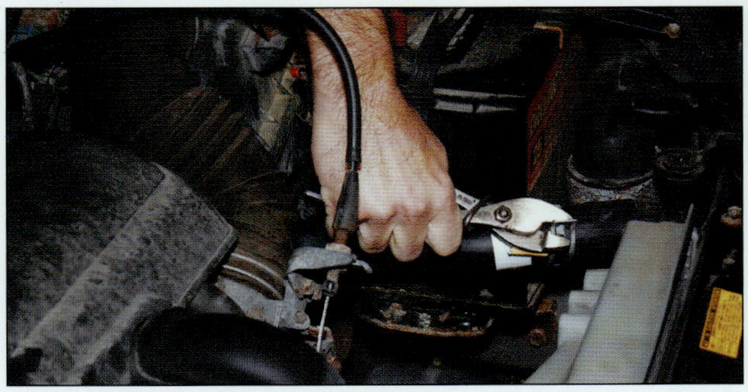

Pliers are used to install the constant tension hose clamp into place to ensure a tight seal between the hose and the radiator neck.

A close inspection should be performed to make sure that the hose clamp is installed correctly to prevent the chance of a coolant leak at that location.

Thermostat

The engine thermostat is a component that requires replacement as part of routine maintenance procedures. Follow the steps below when replacing the thermostat.

The thermostat on this engine is located on top of the intake manifold near the front of the engine. The upper radiator hose connects to the thermostat housing.

Replacing the Thermostat

1 Drain the engine coolant into a drain pan.

2 Remove the necessary hose connections from the thermostat housing.

After draining the coolant into a drain pan, the upper radiator hose constant tension clamp can be moved back for the removal of the hose. A pair of slip-joint pliers work well when removing the hose clamp.

The pick is being used to help break the hose loose from the thermostat housing. Care should be used to make sure the hose is not punctured during this process if it will be reused. If the hose is going to be replaced, then the hose can be cut with a razor or a knife to assist in the removal process.

A small pick with a 90-degree bend is effective to aid in breaking the hose loose from its mounting location.

3 Remove the fasteners for the thermostat housing and then remove the housing from the mounting location.

After removing the hose from the thermostat housing, it should be moved out of the way to allow access for fastener removal.

The fasteners for the thermostat housing can be removed once the upper radiator hose is removed and the connector is removed from the coolant sensor.

A ratchet, an extension, and a 12-mm flexible socket is used to remove the fasteners for the thermostat housing. The flexible socket allows for much greater access in locations that have limited room.

4 Remove the thermostat and compare the original unit to the new unit to make sure the new item will fit the engine.

After the fasteners for the thermostat housing are removed, the housing can be lifted up from the mounting location. The sealing surfaces will need to be thoroughly cleaned before installing a new gasket during the installation process.

The old thermostat can be lifted from the mounting area by hand. The correct thermostat is placed in the same location facing the same direction as the old thermostat.

5 Install the new thermostat along with a new gasket for the housing.

After installing the new thermostat, the thermostat housing is installed using a new gasket. The fasteners for the thermostat housing should be torqued to the correct tightness using a torque wrench. The radiator hose can be installed firmly into place and then the hose clamp can be reinstalled.

6 Install the fasteners for the thermostat housing and tighten them to the correct torque.

7 Install the hoses back into place on the thermostat housing.

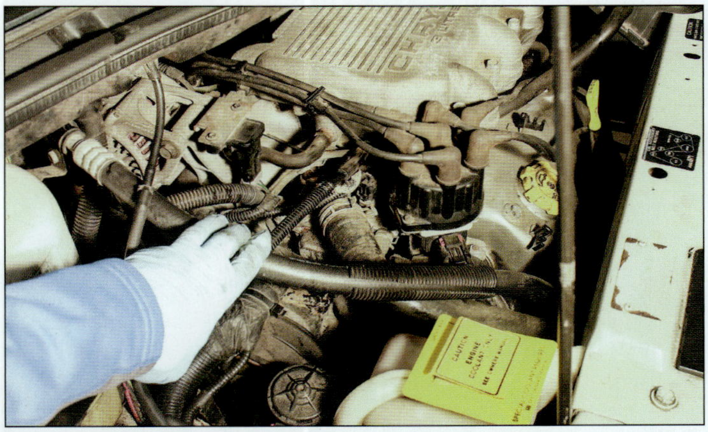

A close inspection should be performed to make sure that all items are reconnected and firmly in the correct place before refilling the cooling system with coolant.

8 After closing the radiator drain valve, refill the cooling system with the correct type of coolant.

Heater Core Flush

A heater core that has become restricted will cause poor heater performance. This condition is diagnosed by testing the temperature drop on the heater hoses with the system set to full heat and the blower turned to high. This condition can sometimes be repaired by flushing the heater core. Follow the steps below to flush the heater core.

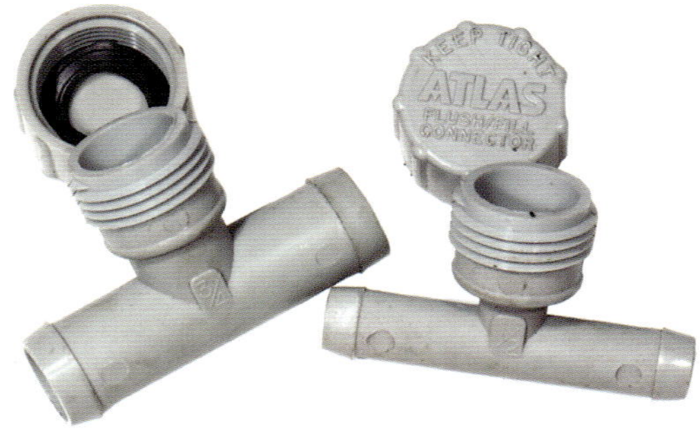

These heater hose adapters can be installed on the heater hoses to allow a water hose to be connected to the heater hose. One end will need to be blocked off to cause the water flow to go into the heater core. The flushing process needs to be done in the reverse direction of the normal flow to allow for any foreign material to be removed from the core during the process.

Flushing the Heater Core

1. Remove the inlet and outlet heater hoses at a convenient location that will allow the flush process to take place.
2. Connect a water hose to the outlet heater hose in order to flush the core in the opposite direction of normal flow.
3. Use a drain pan to catch the coolant and water that was forced through the heater core during the flush process.
4. Run water through the heater core for several minutes.
5. Reconnect all hoses in a secure manner to prevent any leaks in the system.
6. Top off the coolant to ensure the cooling system is at the correct level.
7. Start the engine, set the controls to full heat with the blower on high, and test the heater performance.

The heater hoses should be removed to allow for the adapter to be installed onto the exit hose. The inlet hose should be directed to a drain pan to catch the coolant and water that is used during the flush process.

This flush kit has several adapters that will allow for various sizes of hoses. The heater core needs to be flushed in the reverse direction of normal flow.

Heater Core Replacement

Replacing the heater core may become necessary if it is leaking or if it is badly restricted beyond the chance of being able to flush it to get it corrected. The process of replacing the heater core is very similar to the process of replacing the evaporator core, which is covered in chapter 6.

The only difference is that the heater core is replaced instead of the evaporator core. Both of these procedures require large amounts of skill and tools to complete. See the section in chapter 6 that covers evaporator core replacement for details on how to get the duct box out of the vehicle and opened up to service the items inside.

After removing the duct box from the vehicle, the top of the box is removed, which allows the heater core to be removed from the duct box.

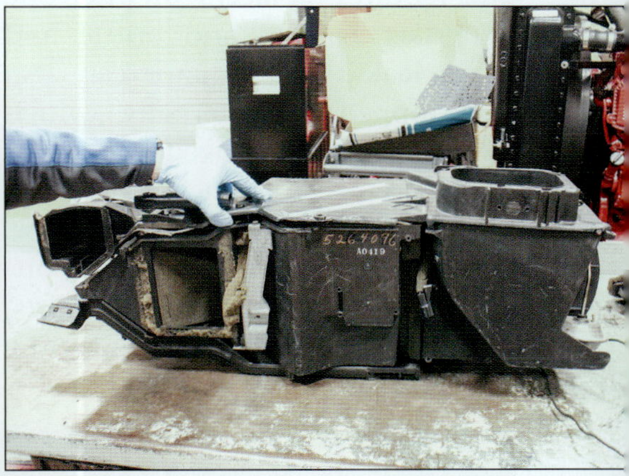

After installing the new heater core, the top of the duct box is reinstalled. Care should be taken to make sure all of the mode doors and the temperature door are aligned in the normal area of operation prior to tightening the fasteners for the top.

This heater core can be removed by releasing a couple of plastic retaining clips in the duct box top. The whole lid does not need to be removed to service the heater core.

The heater core has been removed from the duct box. The new heater core should be closely inspected to make sure it will fit properly into the duct box.

Coolant Flow Valve Replacement

The coolant flow valve can be replaced if it is inoperative or leaking. This valve is easily replaced by simply removing the hose clamps and hoses from the old valve and then reinstalling the hoses and clamps to the new valve.

Replacing the Radiator

The radiator is the device that releases the heat from the hot coolant to the surrounding air. The radiator requires replacement when the materials get old and brittle and cause leaks. The radiator can also get stopped up internally, which requires it to be removed for a repair or be replaced. The process for replacing the radiator is listed below.

1. Drain the coolant into a suitable catch pan.
2. Remove the fan shroud and fan assembly to provide the room necessary to remove the radiator.
3. Remove the transmission cooler lines from the radiator tank.
4. Remove the radiator hose clamps and hoses from the unit.
5. Remove the radiator mounting fasteners.
6. Remove the radiator from the front of the vehicle.
7. Install the new radiator into the mounting area and install the fasteners.
8. Install the radiator hoses and clamps.
9. Install the transmission cooler lines into the radiator tank, being careful to perfectly align the threads (this will prevent cross threading the lines).
10. Install the fan and shroud.
11. Refill the cooling system with the correct type and mixture of new coolant.

Replacing the Water Pump

The water pump is an important part of the engine cooling system that requires service if it develops a leak or if the bearing fails. Depending on the engine design, replacing the water pump can be a process that can be completed in just a couple of hours or a process that could take six or more hours.

Water pumps that are driven by the accessory belt typically require less labor time than water pumps that are driven by the engine timing belt or timing chain. The process of replacing a water pump that is driven by the accessory belt is listed below.

1. Drain the coolant into a suitable catch pan.
2. Remove the fan shroud.

The fan shroud needs to be removed to gain access to the drive belt, fan clutch, and water pump on this Chevrolet truck.

3. Remove the fan clutch using the correct special wrench.

The fan clutch assembly is removed by using the correct wrench and hitting it with a metal bar to assist in breaking the unit loose. This should be done prior to removing the drive belt.

The fan clutch assembly is lifted from the mounting location and should be stored in a location that is out of the way.

4. Remove the engine drive belt.
5. Remove the necessary radiator and heater hoses.

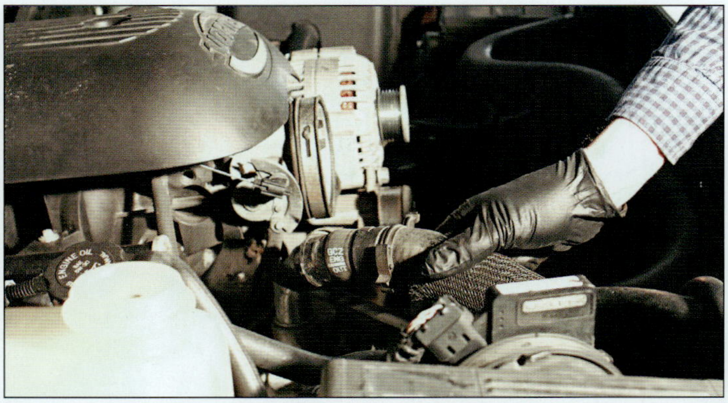

The upper and lower radiator hose along with the heater hoses must be removed prior to removing the bolts for the water pump. The engine drive belt must be removed using the appropriate belt removal tool or an extended-length wrench.

6 Remove the necessary idlers and pulleys to allow access to the water pump fasteners.

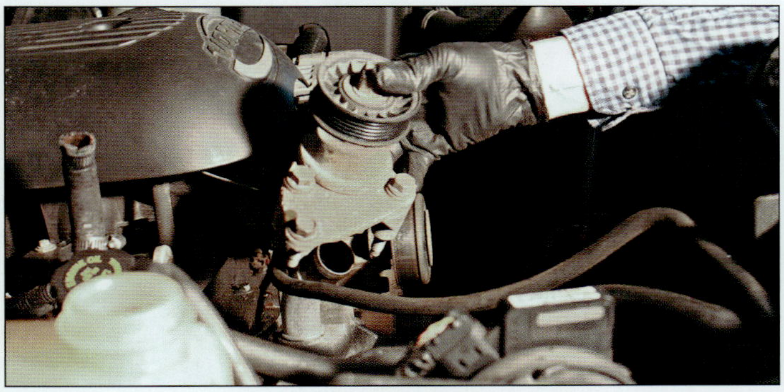

The idler pulley is removed and placed in a location that is out of the way.

7 Remove the water pump fasteners and then pry the water pump away from the front of the engine.

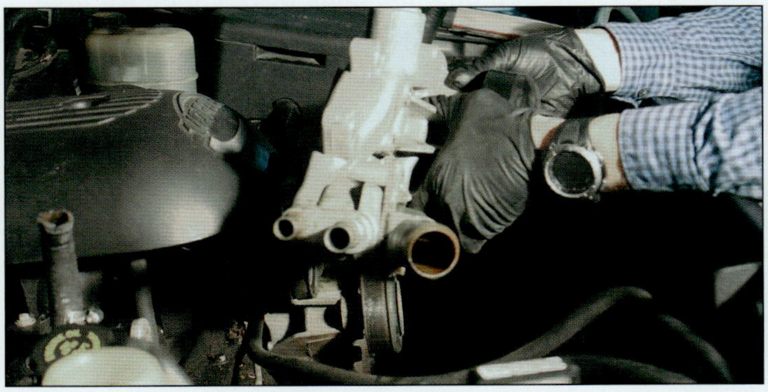

After removing the bolts for the water pump, it can be lifted from the mounting location.

8 Clean the gasket and sealing area to prepare for installing the new water pump.

The mounting surfaces for the water pump must be scraped and cleaned after the water pump has been removed. A scraper and a wire brush work well to clean these areas.

9 Install the new water pump along with a new gasket by installing the fasteners.

The thermostat and housing must be transferred to the new water pump housing. This model requires a new O-ring to provide the proper seal for this housing. Many thermostat housings use a gasket instead of an O-ring.

The new gaskets must be sprayed with gasket adhesive and then installed onto the mounting surfaces of the water pump.

10 Tighten the water pump fasteners to the correct torque.

11 Install the idler and fan clutch and tighten to the correct torque.

12 Install the drive belt, making sure that it is routed correctly and all of the belt grooves line up.

13 Refill the cooling system and install the cooling system cap.

Gasket adhesive is a great product to use when assembling various parts of the engine that have felt gaskets that need to be held in place during installation of the part.

Thread sealer with Teflon is recommended to use on the bolts of the water pump to prevent the coolant from wicking up the threads and causing a pesky coolant leak.

A coat of thread sealer should be applied to the water pump bolts prior to installing the water pump back onto the engine.

Once all of the components have been installed, a close inspection should be performed to make sure that everything is in place. The cooling system should be refilled with the correct amount of coolant and then the engine should be warmed up. It is recommended to take the vehicle on a test drive and then recheck for leaks. After the engine cools back down, the coolant level should be rechecked and topped off to ensure that the system is full.

Testing the Coolant

The coolant is a vital part of the cooling system and it needs to be inspected and tested during routine maintenance procedures and inspections. The items that need to be checked and tested with the coolant include the freeze protection and the acidity level.

Testing the Freeze Protection: The freeze protection of the engine coolant can be tested in multiple ways. A hydrometer can be used to test the freeze protection. This tool is simply dipped into the coolant reservoir or radiator and suction pulls a small amount of coolant into the tool. The coolant is basically weighed, and the hydrometer provides the level of freeze protection based on the amount of coolant that is mixed with the water.

A refractometer can also be used to test the freeze protection. This tool is used by placing one drop of the coolant onto the test surface and then closing the lid. The refractometer is more accurate than the hydrometer, but both tools are using the weight of the coolant to provide a test result.

Chemical strips are also available to test freeze protection on engine coolant. These strips are just dipped into the coolant and then interpreted by comparing the color with scale on the bottle.

Testing for Acidity of the Coolant: Chemical strips can also be used for testing the acidity level of the coolant. Another method of measuring the acidity level is using a voltmeter. The meter should be set to the DC volts setting on the dial with the ground lead connected to the battery ground position and the red lead dipped into the engine coolant. A reading of 0.2 volts or more indicates an acidity problem and the coolant should be replaced with the correct mixture of new coolant.

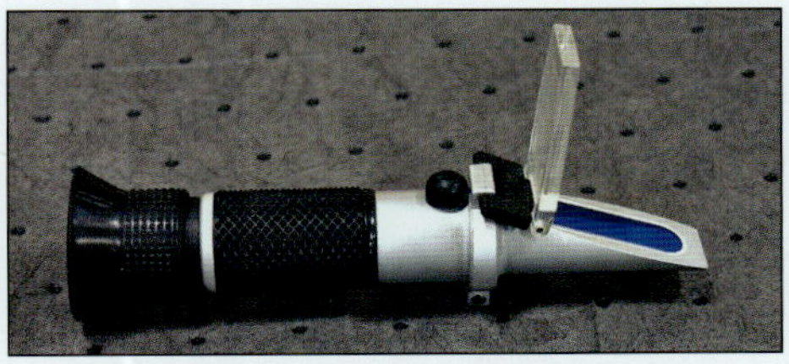

A small drop of coolant is placed onto the surface and then the lid is closed. The tool is then held upright in a well-lit area and the user looks into the view hole to find out the freeze protection level.

A hydrometer can be used to test the freeze point of the coolant. This model has a suction bulb that is used to pull coolant into the tester.

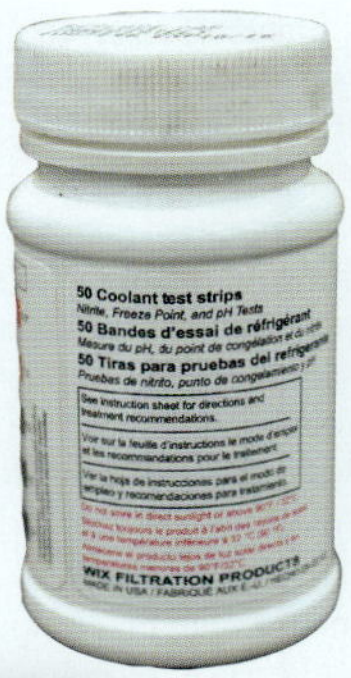

Coolant test strips provide reliable feedback on freeze point, nitrite level, and pH level.

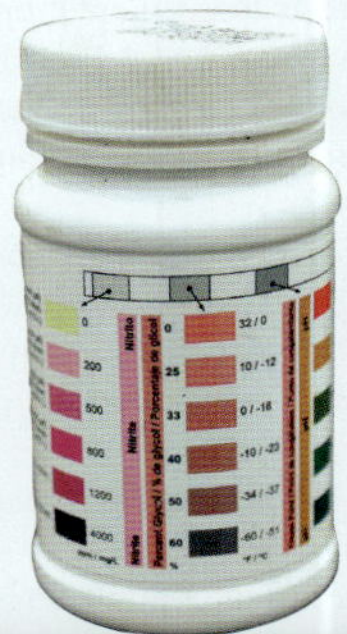

The coolant test strip is dipped into the coolant and then it is set beside the scale on the side of the container to interpret the results for each test.

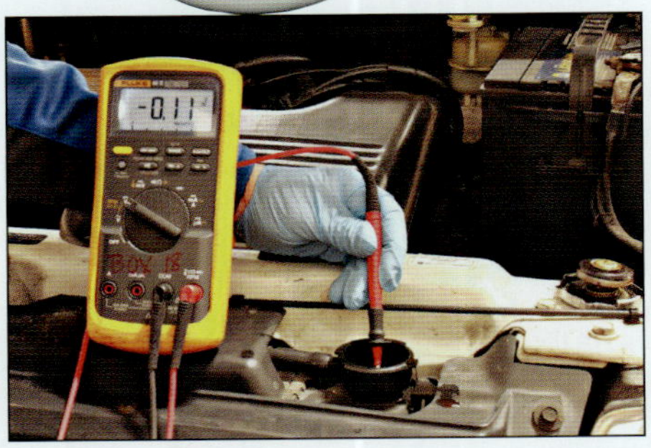

The coolant voltage is tested by connecting the ground lead of the meter to a good ground and then placing the red lead tip into the coolant. The meter should be set to DC volts or DC millivolts. A reading of more than 0.2 volts DC or 200 millivolts DC is considered excessive and would be cause for replacing the coolant with the correct blend and mixture level. This test can also be run with the engine running with all of the electrical loads turned on. A high reading under these conditions indicates that a faulty ground is present for one of the accessories.

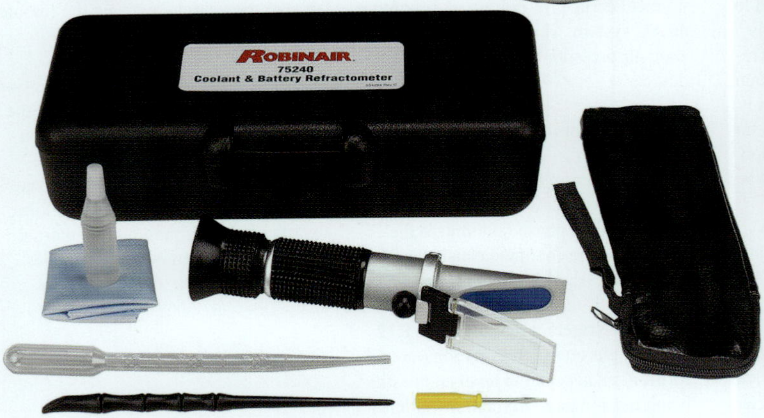

A coolant and battery refractometer can be used to test the freeze protection of the coolant. This very accurate tool provides reliable results and is recommended by many manufacturers.

SOURCE GUIDE

AESwave
5465 East Hedges Ave.
Fresno, CA 93727-2279
877-351-9573
aeswave.com

Atech Automotive Training
12290 Chandler Dr.
Walton, KY 41094
888-738-9924
atechtraining.com

Blue Point Tools
snapon-bluepoint.com

Consulab Training Aids
800-567-0791
consulab.com

Dayco Belts
1650 Research Dr., Ste. 200
Troy, MI 48083
800-848-7902
daycoproducts.com

EZ Red Hydrometer
8 Leonard Way
Deposit, NY 13754
800-522-7947
ezred.com

FJC Flush
101 Commercial Dr.
Mooresville, NC 28115
704-664-3587
fjcinc.com

Fluke
fluke.com

Gates
gates.com

Jumperkits
114 Green Oak Park
Rotonda West, FL 33947
231-645-2748
jumperkits.com

MAC Tool Company
505 N. Cleveland Ave.
Westerville, OH 43082
800-MAC-TOOLS (622-8665)
mactools.com

Mity Vac
5148 N. Hanley Rd.
St. Louis, MO 63134
314-679-4200
skf.com

Neutronics
456 Creamery Way
Exton, PA 19341
610-524-8800
neutronicsinc.com

Opteon YF
P.O. Box 2047
Wilmington, DE 19899
866-205-1664
chemours.com

Power Probe
890 Mariner St.
Brea, CA 92821
888-201-9831
powerprobe.com

Robinair
28635 Mound Rd.
Warren, MI 48092
800-533-6127
robinair.com

Schrader International
schraderinternational.com

GLOSSARY

Ammeter: A tool that is used to measure the electrical current in a circuit.

ATC: Stands for automatic temperature control. These systems operate in automatic mode by letting the operator set the desired temperature in the cab, and then the sensors, computers, and actuators operate to deliver the correct results.

BTU: Stands for British thermal unit. The BTU is the amount of heat it takes to change 1 pound of water 1 degree Fahrenheit.

Calorie: The amount of heat it takes to change 1 gram of water 1 degree Celsius.

CCOT: Stands for cycling clutch orifice tube design. CCOT systems use pressure switches or temperature switches to monitor the conditions of the AC system, which then causes the AC compressor to be turned off to prevent evaporator freeze up.

CFC: Stands for chlorofluorocarbon (CFC). A gas that causes deterioration of the atmospheric layer called the ozone.

Conduction: The transfer of heat directly from molecule to molecule.

Convection: The transfer of heat by using a substance, such as air, water, coolant, or refrigerant.

DMM: Stands for digital multimeter. Tests the voltage drop across a temperature sensor. A DMM can be connected to the electrical connector of the blower motor by back-probing the terminals.

Dual zone climate control systems: Allow the driver and the passenger to have different air temperatures delivered to each side of the car.

HVAC: Stands for heating, ventilation, and air-conditioning system. It is a series of components that all work together to help control the temperature and humidity of the cabin in a vehicle.

Hydrometer: A tool that can be used to test the freeze protection. It is simply dipped into the coolant reservoir or radiator and suction pulls a small amount of coolant into the tool. The coolant is basically weighed, and the hydrometer provides the level of freeze protection based on the amount of coolant that is mixed with the water.

O-rings: Gaskets that are often used to seal the various components of the AC system together.

Ohmmeter: A tool that is used to measure electrical resistance in a component or circuit. Common uses for ohmmeters include testing sensors, coils, switches, and wires.

Orifice tube: A metering device that is located inside the liquid line and can be found at some point between the condenser exit and the evaporator core inlet.

PAG: Stands for polyalkylene glycol. This synthetic hygroscopic oil was specifically designed for compressors. It comes in several viscosity levels and extreme attention should be used when installing lubricant into a system. PAG oil purchased in small quantities and resealed when not in use. PAG oil that has been open for longer than a few days should be discarded due to moisture absorption.

Pneumatic vacuum pump: A very economical choice for pulling a vacuum on an AC system. This type of pump uses shop air pressure to create a vacuum device.

PSI: Stands for pounds per square inch.

R12: Refrigerant that was first used in mobile AC systems in the early 1930s. It began being phased out due to the chlorine in the chemical causing ozone depletion in Earth's atmosphere.

R134a: Refrigerant that followed R12 beginning around 1993. R134a performs at an acceptable level and is still being used in new production vehicles at the time of this writing.

R1234yf: Refrigerant that new model vehicles have begun using. Beginning with model year 2021, all new cars and trucks will have the new refrigerant installed in the AC system.

Radiation: The transfer of heat through rays without heating the air as it passes through.

Refractometer: A tool that can be used to test the freeze protection. It is used by placing one drop of coolant onto the test surface and then closing the lid. The refractometer is more accurate than the hydrometer, but both tools are using the weight of the coolant to provide a test result.

Remote start systems: Allow the user to start the vehicle by using the remote transmitter.

TXV: Stands for the thermal expansion valve. This metering device varies the flow rate through the valve based on operating conditions. This variable operation occurs by the valve sensing the temperature of the exit line of the evaporator and changing the internal opening as the temperature changes.